INTELLIGENCE
MATTERS

Senator Bob Graham

WITH JEFF NUSSBAUM

RANDOM HOUSE

NEW YORK

INTELLIGENCE

MATTERS

★

The CIA, the FBI, Saudi Arabia,

and the Failure of America's

War on Terror

RANDOM HOUSE and colophon are registered
trademarks of Random House, Inc.

Library of Congress Cataloging-in-Publication Data is available.

ISBN: 1-4000-6352-3

Printed in the United States of America on acid-free paper

Random House website address: www.atrandom.com

2 4 6 8 9 7 5 3 1

FIRST EDITION

Book design by Dana Leigh Blanchette

For my wife, Adele, and our daughters, Gwen, Cissy, Suzanne, and Kendall—my constant and continuing sources of inspiration

and for my father, Ernest, and my brothers, Bill and Phil, for helping instill my values

CONTENTS

INTRODUCTION

The Realities of Today

When I entered the conference room on the fourth floor of the U.S. Capitol, the other meeting participants were already there—General Mahmood Ahmed, the director of the Pakistani intelligence service (ISI); Representative Porter Goss, a former CIA agent and the chairman of the House Intelligence Committee; Senator Jon Kyl, a member of the Senate Intelligence Committee; as well as a number of staff members.

The breakfast was in reciprocation for General Ahmed's hospitality during our trip to Pakistan two weeks earlier, although the scrambled eggs and sausages we had to offer didn't compare with the exotic menu at the nighttime tribal feast that General Ahmed had hosted on the spacious rear lawn of ISI headquarters in Islamabad.

General Ahmed was a Civil War enthusiast and was studying the Civil War pictures on the walls. Knowing this, Porter Goss had bought him a one-volume history of the Civil War as a gift.

As we were sitting down, I glanced at my watch and checked the time—8:00 A.M.—against my printed schedule for the day: September 11, 2001.

The first half-hour of our conversation was on the subject of Pakistan's tense nuclear standoff with India. We then turned to the intelligence that the ISI had developed on the Taliban, the Afghan government, and al-Qaeda, Osama bin Laden's terrorist organization.

General Ahmed was a career military officer. In Pakistan, he wore a brown-olive uniform, but this morning he was dressed in a blue English suit. Since he was the man in charge of the ISI, keeping up Pakistan's relations with the Taliban was his jurisdiction. This was a delicate dance for Pakistan. Bordered on one side by India, an avowed enemy, Pakistan saw Afghanistan as strategic depth should India ever attack. Thus, Pakistan invested a great deal of time and energy in keeping Afghanistan's government, such as it was, friendly, and Ahmed was often the point of contact. Where his loyalties actually lay was an open question. In our visit with him in Pakistan, he seemed personally torn, favorably inclined toward America but aware of the necessities of his job. It seemed as if he wanted to help us more and to tell us more than he actually did. Or perhaps that was just a show put on for our benefit; there was no way to know. One thing was certain, though: of all the people we could talk to, he was the one who best knew the Taliban and al-Qaeda, and that is what we began asking him about. For a man of his commanding presence, with the arms and chest of a weight lifter, he spoke softly and precisely, with a British accent:

"Most people live in three stages of life—the accumulated experiences of the past, the realities of today, the dreams of tomorrow."

He was interrupted by a young aide to Congressman Goss, who slid into the room and delivered a yellow note card to Tim Sample, the staff director of the House Intelligence Committee, who read it and passed it on to Congressman Goss.

The congressman read the single sentence and turned to his guests: "An airplane has hit the World Trade Center's North Tower."

I was perplexed but not stunned. There has been a history of airplanes crashing into tall buildings, and that knowledge kept me from feeling a sense of alarm. Congressman Goss requested more details, and then urged General Ahmed to continue.

"Most people are aware of their past and fantasize about the future.

But their primary focus is on the present—getting along day by day. The Taliban and al-Qaeda are different. For them, only the future of paradise after death matters. Any activities of the present are trivial interludes until the ultimate is achieved.

"The discipline, the norms of behavior which influence today, are irrelevant for those who dismiss the worthiness of today."

The same young staffer entered with a second yellow note. It made its way to Congressman Goss, who read it. This time Goss passed the note to Ahmed. As Ahmed was reading it, Goss said, "Another plane has struck the South Tower."

The color drained from General Ahmed's face. Seeing Ahmed's immediate reaction, I recalled a moment from the trip I had taken two weeks earlier, when I stood above the Khyber Pass and looked into Afghanistan. Could this primitive country be attacking the United States of America?

Though we hadn't finished our meeting yet, the breakfast disbanded. Senator Kyl escorted General Ahmed down to his waiting car. Porter, who had been informed by a staffer that there might be more planes in the air, headed directly for the office of the House Speaker, Dennis Hastert. Leaving the room, I noticed that our gift for General Ahmed had been left behind. I ran down three flights of stairs to my hideaway office on the first floor of the Capitol. On most days, I will meet there with key members of my staff to start the day with a review of my schedule and the priority items I have listed in my spiral notebook to accomplish that day. On that Tuesday morning, we were captivated by the images on the television screen: smoke pouring from the crippled Twin Towers. Nearly as soon as we sat down, Capitol Police officers began running down the halls, banging on doors, and shouting for everyone to leave the complex.

After a chaotic race through the tunnels underneath the Capitol Building, we emerged out onto the Capitol's East Lawn. Out into a changed America.

★

The attacks of September 11 did more than take 3,000 innocent American lives; they laid bare the holes in America's intelligence system and forced us to ask tough questions about how these agencies, their leaders, and we as elected officials failed to fulfill one of the most fundamental obligations of government—to provide for the common defense of the American people.

The next two years of my life came to be dominated by September 11. In that time, I would organize and cochair an unprecedented joint House-Senate investigation of the intelligence failures that allowed the attacks to take place. Ultimately, I would reach the conclusion that September 11 was the culmination of a long trail of American intelligence failures both at home and abroad—an almost bewildering array of mistakes, missteps, and missed opportunities caused by warring governmental cultures, bureaucratic incompetence and neglect, lack of imagination, and perhaps, most tragic of all, a failure of leadership at the highest levels of government.

In the following pages, I intend to offer an inside view of the investigation of the events that led up to September 11, 2001, including new information on the role of foreign governments in aiding the terrorists within the United States and the extent of the failures among and between American and international intelligence agencies.

I also intend to outline the disgraceful manner in which the administration of President George W. Bush has repeatedly hindered the full investigation of September 11, and then turned its attention and resources to Iraq—an act that has served to make Americans less secure than they were before that fateful Tuesday morning in September 2001.

★

While America has understood the utility of intelligence since Paul Revere's midnight ride from Boston to Lexington warning that the British were coming, we have never embraced it. Intelligence gathering was distasteful to a nation that had fought a seven-year war for independence to secure liberty from the very things that were the stock-in-trade of King George III's intelligence gathering: the late-night knock on the door to separate a husband, father, or son from a frightened family; the use of torture to discover the rebellious plans of patriots; the clandestine search of private effects without notice or permission. That the United States was the last advanced nation to establish a permanent civilian intelligence agency is evidence of the depth of this aversion.

However, as more came to be known about the attacks of September 11, a new consensus began to emerge. As much as our intelligence community may have failed us, Americans, pragmatic people that we are, recognized that September 11 was not the first attack on America by a new and shadowy foe, nor did that foe intend it to be the last. We realized that in this new world, where an attack can come not only from the army of an enemy, but also in the form of a boat, a backpack, or a vial, intelligence becomes a crucial shield, an ever more integral part of our national and personal security.

In this new century, effective intelligence will be more important than ever before for six reasons.

First, our adversary is different from any we have engaged in the past. It is not a nation but a tribe of tribes united by an ideology. The terrorists are not constrained by the global standards and values of the West; to them, death and an afterlife in paradise are the highest goals of life. Theirs is not a society with which we share mutually understood cultures and languages; rather, it is remote, mysterious, and insular. To know this enemy is essential to defeating this enemy, and Americans will depend on effective intelligence to gain that knowledge.

Second, we learned on September 11 that the Atlantic and the Pacific are not the shields they have been in the past. Our new enemy was capable of insinuating nineteen or more of its trained killers into our nation, where they were able to refine, rehearse, and execute the most deadly attack on the continental United States in our history. America will look to alert intelligence to do what two oceans no longer can: protect us at home.

Third, America can no longer be driven to act only after we have been acted upon. The consequences of waiting for threats to gather is too risky—imagine the consequences if terrorists managed to get their hands on a nuclear weapon. But to be anticipatory and preemptive requires the highest quality of intelligence, or we risk something else—the lives of soldiers and civilians, and our international credibility. If we are to adhere to a doctrine of preemption, we have to be certain of what we are preempting. We can't afford to be deceived, manipulated, or blinded by ideology—as we have been in Iraq—or to waste time and resources fighting threats that aren't real.

Fourth, sound intelligence will enhance our long-term security. America's political, economic, and security interests now span the globe.

A vigilant intelligence community will alert us to emerging threats against our interests beyond the homeland. Terrorists gaining possession of nuclear weapons has been described as "the problem from hell." Some have also said it is an inevitability. Retired four-star general Eugene Habiger, who has overseen nuclear weapons programs at the Departments of Defense and Energy, has stated, "It is not a matter of if; it's a matter of when." The very best intelligence is an absolutely crucial capability if we are to make what is thought to be inevitable preventable. Through both strategic intelligence, that intellegence which tells us about the longer-term posture and intentions of others, and actionable intelligence, which alerts us to specific imminent acts, we will be better able to confront terrorist threats abroad before those threats materialize at home.

Fifth, effective intelligence is important to maintaining our international relationships. Success in the twenty-first century will require alliances with nations that share our vision, if not our views on all subjects. Credible information upon which wise judgments can be founded must be a bedrock of those relationships.

Sixth and finally, with better intelligence, our nation and its leaders will be more able to focus on the challenges of the future rather than the failures of the past. The pace of technological change will only continue to accelerate, and the rising tide of globalization will lead to a new and complex web of relationships between state and nonstate actors. Better intelligence will help us keep up with the pace of change as we continue to identify new challenges.

For all these reasons, in the twenty-first century intelligence will have a role in almost every way we seek to provide greater security at home and advance our interests abroad.

★

This book is divided into two parts.

The first part is focused on events taking place before the attacks of September 11, 2001. I follow the trail of two of the September 11 hijackers—Nawaf al-Hazmi and Khalid al-Mihdhar. These two individuals differed from the other September 11 hijackers in that they entered the United States earlier, had more terrorism training, and interacted far more with members of the Arab community in America, including a number of people who, I believe, were either agents of a foreign government or ordered by representatives of a foreign government to give the two men aid and comfort. Charting their course, their lives in America, and their preparations for their final act serves to illustrate the significant failures that allowed the September 11 hijackers to put their plans into place.

While the responsibility for what happened on that day rests with the men who carried out the attack and the people who supported them, the investigation I cochaired has led me to a simple, disturbing conclusion: September 11 was an avoidable tragedy.

From at least January of 2000 until days before the tragedy, both the CIA and the FBI had information that they withheld from one another and from state and local law enforcement and that, if shared, would have cracked the terrorists' plot. In this book, I will identify twelve points at which the plot could have been discovered and potentially thwarted.

The first part of this book also includes brief histories on the development of our nation's intelligence capabilities, congressional oversight of the intelligence community, the rise of al-Qaeda, and the challenges facing the American intelligence community today.

The second part of the book takes place after September 11. It describes my efforts and those of my colleagues to fully investigate the failures that led to the attacks, the creation and proceedings of the unprecedented joint House-Senate inquiry into the attacks, the resistance we faced from the Bush administration, and ultimately the folly of allowing the war on terrorism to be left incomplete—and a battered al-Qaeda left able to regroup and recruit—by a mistaken and misrepresented focus on Iraq. I will produce evidence that the decision to go to war in Iraq was not made in March 2003, as the Bush administration has claimed, but a full thirteen months earlier, drawing resources from a mission in Afghanistan that was not yet finished and frustrating U.S. commanders who were close to winning a decisive victory against al-Qaeda. I will also lay out evidence supporting what I believe to be a cover-up orchestrated by the White House to protect not only the agencies that had failed but also America's relationship with the Kingdom of Saudi Arabia.

In sum, I will argue that the Bush administration's action and inaction—in protecting a foreign government which played a central role in the loss of nearly 3,000 lives; in failing to alert government agencies of known tactics of terrorists; in diverting the nation from the real war on terrorism in Afghanistan to a falsely justified war in Iraq; and in politicizing and falsifying intelligence in order to build support for that war, and then in covering up these and other actions—constitute an indictment of President Bush's leadership so serious that it warrants his removal from office.

Finally, this book will include a series of recommendations, drawn largely from the conclusions reached by the Joint Inquiry into Intelligence Community Activities before and after the Terrorist Attacks of September 11, 2001 (hereinafter referred to as the Joint Inquiry), about how to improve our intelligence capabilities in the future and thereby reduce the likelihood of America falling victim to another such attack.

Throughout the book, events have been reconstructed from my memory and notes made at the time. I have a much-remarked-upon habit of keeping notebooks—small spiral-bound flip-top notebooks in which I record the events and interactions I experience over the course of a day. The practice goes back to my father, who would put me and our Dalmatian, Major, in the passenger seat of his World War II–vintage Jeep and drive around our dairy farm, notebook in hand, writing down the tasks that needed to be completed. When I entered public life, I found myself meeting daily with dozens of people who wanted to relay a piece of information or make a request or ask for some action, and I needed a way to capture all that so that I wouldn't forget. I began taking notes of these exchanges. Thus, my notebooks serve not only as a record but also a way for me to perform a self-imposed check on my follow-up. For that reason, my notebooks are logs rather than diaries. To date, I have filled more than 2,100 of them, and though some people can't seem to understand the practice, it has proved invaluable in allowing me to reconstruct the events of this turbulent time. Where my memories and notes are supplemented with outside material and interviews, I have cited my source in the endnotes.

This book is by no means a complete and definitive history of the attacks of September 11. That is a task best left to historians, who will benefit from the perspective only time can bring and from a far larger body of information than we have at our disposal today. Rather, this is one thread of that history; when followed, it traces the state of U.S. intelligence today and leads to my recommendations for necessary reforms.

★

When the House and Senate Intelligence Committees began the Joint Inquiry into the attacks of September 11, the first witness we called in public session was Kristen Breitweiser. Kristen had lost her husband, Ronald, in the World Trade Center, and was serving as a cochairperson of a group called September 11 Advocates, which represented families of the victims.

She repeated her husband's last words to her and described her daughter placing flowers on an empty grave. On her right hand, she was wearing her husband's wedding band, charred, scratched, but intact— recovered from Ground Zero with a part of his left arm.

Her testimony furthered the sense of seriousness and purpose under which our investigation operated from day one. Her closing words presented a call to action that I have tried my best to heed:

> All we have are tears and a resolve to find the answers because we continue to look into the eyes of our young children who ask us why. We have an obligation as parents and as a nation to provide these innocent children with answers as to why their mother or father never returned home from work that day.
>
> We need people to be held accountable for their failures. We need leaders with the courage to take responsibility for what went wrong. Mistakes were made and too many lives were lost. We must investigate these errors so that they will never happen again. It is our responsibility as a nation to turn the dark events of September 11 into something from which we can all learn and grow, so that we, as a nation, can look forward to a safe future.

It is my intention that this book sound the call to action and provide an understanding of why and by what means that action should be undertaken. I hope that my experience and the lessons I drew from it will convince you that, indeed, intelligence matters.

11 SEPTEMBER 2001 HIJACKER

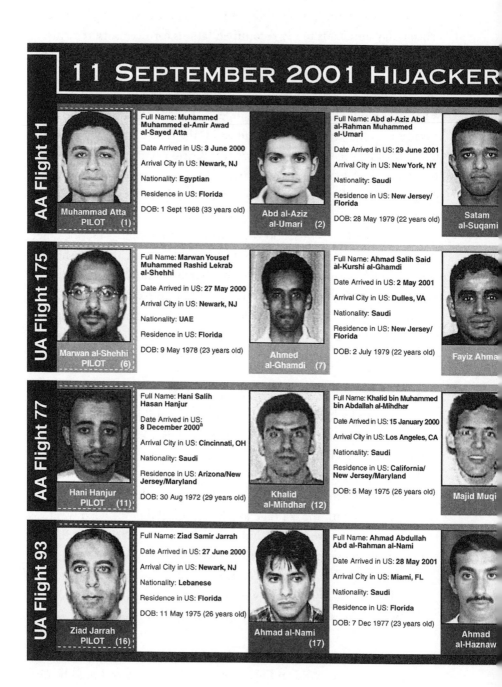

AA Flight 11

Muhammad Atta
PILOT (1)

Full Name: **Muhammed Muhammed el-Amir Awad al-Sayed Atta**

Date Arrived in US: **3 June 2000**

Arrival City in US: **Newark, NJ**

Nationality: **Egyptian**

Residence in US: **Florida**

DOB: **1 Sept 1968 (33 years old)**

Abd al-Aziz al-Umari (2)

Full Name: **Abd al-Aziz Abd al-Rahman Muhammed al-Umari**

Date Arrived in US: **29 June 2001**

Arrival City in US: **New York, NY**

Nationality: **Saudi**

Residence in US: **New Jersey/ Florida**

DOB: **28 May 1979 (22 years old)**

Satam al-Suqami

UA Flight 175

Marwan al-Shehhi
PILOT (6)

Full Name: **Marwan Yousef Muhammed Rashid Lekrab al-Shehhi**

Date Arrived in US: **27 May 2000**

Arrival City in US: **Newark, NJ**

Nationality: **UAE**

Residence in US: **Florida**

DOB: **9 May 1978 (23 years old)**

Ahmed al-Ghamdi (7)

Full Name: **Ahmad Salih Said al-Kurshi al-Ghamdi**

Date Arrived in US: **2 May 2001**

Arrival City in US: **Dulles, VA**

Nationality: **Saudi**

Residence in US: **New Jersey/ Florida**

DOB: **2 July 1979 (22 years old)**

Fayiz Ahma

AA Flight 77

Hani Hanjur
PILOT (11)

Full Name: **Hani Salih Hasan Hanjur**

Date Arrived in US: **8 December 2000[a]**

Arrival City in US: **Cincinnati, OH**

Nationality: **Saudi**

Residence in US: **Arizona/New Jersey/Maryland**

DOB: **30 Aug 1972 (29 years old)**

Khalid al-Mihdhar (12)

Full Name: **Khalid bin Muhammed bin Abdallah al-Mihdhar**

Date Arrived in US: **15 January 2000**

Arrival City in US: **Los Angeles, CA**

Nationality: **Saudi**

Residence in US: **California/ New Jersey/Maryland**

DOB: **5 May 1975 (26 years old)**

Majid Muqi

UA Flight 93

Ziad Jarrah
PILOT (16)

Full Name: **Ziad Samir Jarrah**

Date Arrived in US: **27 June 2000**

Arrival City in US: **Newark, NJ**

Nationality: **Lebanese**

Residence in US: **Florida**

DOB: **11 May 1975 (26 years old)**

Ahmad al-Nami (17)

Full Name: **Ahmad Abdullah Abd al-Rahman al-Nami**

Date Arrived in US: **28 May 2001**

Arrival City in US: **Miami, FL**

Nationality: **Saudi**

Residence in US: **Florida**

DOB: **7 Dec 1977 (23 years old)**

Ahmad al-Haznaw

ame: Ustam bin
nmad Abd al-Rahman
ami

rrived in US: **23 April 2001**

City in US: **Orlando, FL**

ality: **Saudi**

nce in US: **Florida**

28 June 1976 (25 years old)

**Wail al-Shehri
(4)**

Full Name: **Wail Muhammad
Abdallah al-Shehri**

Date Arrived in US: **8 June 2001**

Arrival City in US: **Miami, FL**

Nationality: **Saudi**

Residence in US: **Florida**

DOB: 31 July 1973 (28 years old)

Full Name: **Walid Muhammad
Abdallah al-Shehri**

Date Arrived in US: **23 April 2001**

Arrival City in US: **Orlando, FL**

Nationality: **Saudi**

Residence in US: **Florida**

DOB: 20 Dec 1978 (22 years old)

**Walid al-Shehri
(5)**

---

ame: Fayez Rashid
d Banihammad

rrived in US: **27 June 2001**

City in US: **Orlando, FL**

ality: **UAE**

nce in US: **Florida**

9 Mar 1977 (24 years old)

**Hamza
al-Ghamdi (9)**

Full Name: **Hamza Salih Ahmad
al-Hamid al-Ghamdi**

Date Arrived in US: **28 May 2001**

Arrival City in US: **Miami, FL**

Nationality: **Saudi**

Residence in US: **Florida**

DOB: 18 Nov 1980 (20 years old)

Full Name: **Mahanid Muhammad
Fayiz al-Shehri**

Date Arrived in US: **28 May 2001**

Arrival City in US: **Miami, FL**

Nationality: **Saudi**

Residence in US: **Florida**

DOB: 7 May 1979 (22 years old)

**Mohand
al-Shehri (10)**

---

me: Majid Muqid
n bin Ghanim

rrived in US: **2 May 2001**

City in US: **Dulles, VA**

ality: **Saudi**

nce in US: **New Jersey/
nd**

8 June 1977 (24 years old)

**Nawaf al-Hazmi
(14)**

Full Name: **Nawaf bin
Muhammad Salim al-Hazmi**

Date Arrived in US: **15 January 2000**

Arrival City in US: **Los Angeles, CA**

Nationality: **Saudi**

Residence in US: **California/
Arizona/New Jersey/Maryland**

DOB: 9 Aug 1976 (25 years old)

Full Name: **Salim Muhammad
Salim al-Hazmi**

Date Arrived in US: **29 June 2001**

Arrival City in US: **New York, NY**

Nationality: **Saudi**

Residence in US: **New Jersey/
Maryland**

DOB: 2 Feb 1981 (20 years old)

**Salim al-Hazmi
(15)**

---

me: Ahmad Ibrahim
Jaznawi

rrived in US: **8 June 2001**

City in US: **Miami, FL**

ality: **Saudi**

nce in US: **Florida**

1 Oct 1980 (20 years old)

**Said al-Ghamdi
(19)**

Full Name: **Said Abdalah Ali
Sulayman al-Ghamdi**

Date Arrived in US: **27 June 2001**

Arrival City in US: **Orlando, FL**

Nationality: **Saudi**

Residence in US: **Florida**

DOB: 21 Nov 1979 (21 years old)

Entered US alone.

[a] Date represents entry we believe is related to
11 September attacks, but Hanjur, unlike the
other suspected hijackers, had traveled in and
out of the US since 1991.

Part I

BEFORE

1

A Meeting in Malaysia

The First Failures

Kuala Lumpur, Malaysia
January 5, 2000

Cameras clicked from a distance as nearly a dozen men gathered at the suburban condominium overlooking a Jack Nicklaus–designed golf course on the southern outskirts of Kuala Lumpur, Malaysia.

Anyone who had happened upon the group would probably have found them eminently forgettable, a group of clean-cut Arab men in a diverse international city of one and a half million.

The meeting could have been a reunion of vacationing friends, or a gathering of graduate students. It wasn't. It was a summit of terrorists.

Two of the Saudi participants arriving at the placidly named Hazel Evergreen resort community were Nawaf al-Hazmi and Khalid al-Mihdhar, who had already been identified by United States intelligence as terrorist operatives. They had been involved in planning and providing logistical support for the near-simultaneous bombings of the United States embassies in Kenya and Tanzania that had killed 224 people and left more than 5,000 injured. Both would later hijack American Airlines flight number 77, and were restraining passengers as the Boeing 757 rammed into the Pentagon.

For American intelligence, the trail to the meeting in Malaysia began on the morning of August 7, 1998, in the rubble and confusion outside our embassy in Nairobi, Kenya.

That morning, the ordinary bustle of Nairobi's Haile Selassie Avenue was shattered as a Toyota cargo truck exploded next to the five-story U.S. embassy. Within seconds, black smoke filled the sky and the road's tar paving ignited, setting fire to parked cars and passing buses. The blast shattered every window within a quarter-mile radius, blew the bombproof doors off the embassy, sucked out ceilings and furniture and people, and collapsed the four-story office building next door.

Less than five minutes earlier and nearly 450 miles away in Tanzania, a vehicle had driven onto the grounds of the U.S. embassy in Dar es Salaam and exploded, wrecking the entrance, blowing off parts of the building's right side, and setting cars ablaze.

One of those involved in the Nairobi bombing was a Yemeni named Mohamed Rashed Daoud al-Owhali. His job was a minor one. As the truck packed with explosives headed for the embassy, al-Owhali was to throw four flash grenades at the front door—bringing curious people toward the windows in order to make the truck's explosion all the more deadly.

Al-Owhali had expected to die in the blast. The truck bomb was supposed to detonate seconds after his task was finished, making him a martyr and assuring him a place in paradise. Instead, two things happened that kept al-Owhali alive. First, the truck's driver decided, before detonating the bomb, to fire a number of bullets at the embassy. Second, after throwing his flash grenades, al-Owhali ran. The seconds the driver spent picking up his gun allowed al-Owhali to get around the corner of the building, which, in standing up to the blast, also saved his life. When the bomb was detonated, al-Owhali was thrown from his feet; his arm and forehead were cut. A stranger put him into a car and took him to the hospital, where he was stitched up. He hid his gun in the bathroom of the hospital, then got into a cab and headed for an apartment where he expected to wait until he could arrange to be smuggled out of the country. When authorities began asking about an injured Arab, the taxi driver remembered both the passenger and the address.

Within two days of the bombing, al-Owhali was in custody, and—stunned and remorseful over the carnage he had helped bring about—willing to talk about the attack that was supposed to have taken his life. His confession included the location of an al-Qaeda safe house in Yemen, and, importantly, its telephone number.[1]

The number allowed the National Security Agency (NSA), the American intelligence agency responsible for electronic eavesdropping, to do what it does best: collect signals intelligence. Using an array of satellites and other signals technologies, the United States began listening to the conversations emanating from the safe house. It quickly became clear that the place was more than a safe house: it was an al-Qaeda logistics center. Information flowed in from operatives around the world, where it was then relayed to Osama bin Laden at his Afghanistan hideout.

As far as intelligence work goes, finding this switchboard was the equivalent of striking gold.

In the last weeks of 1999, as the United States became increasingly fearful of terrorist attacks around the turn of the millennium, the level of monitoring was ratcheted up.

In December, an intercepted communiqué alerted the United States to a summit of al-Qaeda operatives scheduled for Kuala Lumpur in January 2000. The United States wanted to keep tabs on the meeting, and, in particular, to get some ears inside it.

The summit was to be held at the weekend retreat of Yazid Sufaat, a 37-year-old Malaysian citizen trained in microbiology. Sufaat was an example of what the Malaysian government under Prime Minister Mahathir Mohamad sought to encourage—a progressive Muslim professional. He was also a case study in the making of a terrorist sympathizer.

The son of a rubber tapper, Sufaat had won a scholarship to study at the government's prestigious Royal Military College. From there he won another scholarship to continue his studies, this time at California State University in Sacramento—one of several thousand Malaysian students sent abroad annually to study. Upon returning home, Sufaat founded a profitable laboratory analysis company, built on government contracts and the Malaysian government's preferential treatment of Muslim-owned businesses. During that time, he was successful in his business enterprise and not a particularly devout Muslim, occasionally enjoying a beer. And then, in 1993, he began to change. At the insistence of his wife, he began going to a mosque, an activity that furthered his interest in his Muslim roots and left him increasingly disillusioned with Malaysia's secular government. He began spending more and more time with militant Islamic teachers, who told him that Muslims should take up arms and defend their brothers in Indonesia's Maluku islands, where Christians and Muslims had been involved in bloody clashes. By all accounts, he was an eager recipient of such teachings.[2]

Seeing this enthusiasm, one of his teachers, who police now believe is al-Qaeda's Southeast Asian operations chief, began tapping him for small assignments.

In January 2000, his assignment was to make his condominium available for a meeting that the United States now knew was about to take place.

And so, as the terrorists gathered in Sufaat's neighborhood, the Special Branch, Malaysia's security service, was there, watching them sightsee and check Arabic web sites from cybercafés.

And as Nawaf al-Hazmi and Khalid al-Mihdhar stepped into the apartment where they would begin to plan an attack that would change the world forever, a camera shutter clicked.

★

Shortly after the meeting, Special Branch transmitted the photos they had taken to CIA headquarters in Langley, Virginia.

At CIA headquarters, two of the meeting participants photographed were identified as Nawaf al-Hazmi and Khalid al-Mihdhar. This was not the first the CIA had heard of these two men.

Since early 1999, the NSA had information associating al-Hazmi with al-Qaeda. But the NSA considered the relationship to be "unexceptional" and did not disseminate information on al-Hazmi to other intelligence agencies.

In April 1999, the State Department recorded that Nawaf al-Hazmi and his brother Salim al-Hazmi (who had also attended the meeting in

Malaysia) had been issued U.S. visas at our consulate in Jeddah, Saudi Arabia.

While he was en route to Kuala Lumpur in the first days of January 2000, the CIA was able to obtain a photograph of Khalid al-Mihdhar's Saudi passport. This provided the CIA al-Mihdhar's full name, passport number, date of birth (May 5, 1975) and the multiple-entry visa issued by the Jeddah consulate in April 1999.[3]

Although both al-Mihdhar and al-Hazmi were young (al-Mihdhar was 25 when he entered the United States, al-Hazmi 24), they had already developed impressive terror résumés.

Both Saudi citizens, the two grew up together in Mecca in merchant families. In the mid-1990s, as teenagers, they traveled together to Bosnia, presumably to fight alongside the Muslims there. After that, their involvement with al-Qaeda strengthened, and sometime before 1998, al-Hazmi traveled to Afghanistan and swore loyalty to Osama bin Laden and to his jihad agenda, an act known as *bayat*. Later, al-Mihdhar would do the same. In Afghanistan, during the latter half of 1999, the two would receive special training alongside a number of other terrorists, including one who later died in a suicide attack on the American destroyer U.S.S. *Cole* at the port of Aden in Yemen.

George Tenet, then the Director of Central Intelligence, would later testify to the Joint Inquiry, "We had at that point [January 2000] the level of detail needed to watch list [al-Mihdhar]—that is to nominate him to [the] State Department for refusal of entry into the US or to deny him another visa. Our officers . . . did not do so."

This was the first failure that contributed to the tragedy of September 11, 2001.

The "watch list" is increasingly significant in protecting America in an age of terror, when an individual entering our country can be as dangerous as a missile being launched at it. A watch list is a list of people who are of interest to law enforcement, visa issuance, or border inspection agencies. The agencies of the federal government keep a number of different watch lists. The principal and largest database is the State Department's TIPOFF system. Created in 1987, it originally consisted of three-by-five-inch index cards in a shoebox. Today, TIPOFF staff use specialized search engines to systematically comb through all-source data, ranging from highly classified Central Intelligence reports to intelligence products based on public information, to identify known and suspected terrorists. These classified records are then scrubbed to protect intelligence sources and methods; biographic identifiers such as aliases, physical characteristics, and photos are then declassified and exported into lookout systems. For example, employees at our embassies and consulates who handle visa applications can look up records electronically and deny visas to terrorists, their supporters, and those suspected of being either. This is vitally important in an age when a victory against terror can be as simple as a red "denied" stamp on a visa application.

Other agencies keep watch lists as well, including U.S. Customs and Border Protection and U.S. Citizenship and Immigration Services (formerly the Immigration and Naturalization Service), which are now part of the Department of Homeland Security.

America's watch-list system was not (and has not yet been) fully integrated into a single stand-alone terrorist screening database available not only to government officials overseas but also to state and local law enforcement in the United States. That is one problem that must be fixed. The second problem was one of attitude. As one intelligence official told me, watch-listing was not viewed as integral to intelligence work; rather it was considered a "chore off to the side."

In practice, watch-list suggestions often appeared at the very end of CIA communications and were often overlooked. In many cases, like the case of al-Mihdhar and al-Hazmi, the names didn't make it onto a list to begin with.

Had the CIA placed al-Mihdhar on the watch list in January 2000, he and possibly his companion al-Hazmi would have been denied entry into the United States and detained for interrogation.

That the meeting participants in Kuala Lumpur were photographed and that we were able to obtain a photo of al-Mihdhar's passport are a testament to how the skillful gathering of intelligence could open a window into the shadowy world of al-Qaeda; these successes also demonstrated how easily the thread of intelligence can be dropped, and how the smallest mistakes can lead to the largest failures.

For example, for reasons of priority and personnel, and possibly other reasons not publicly disclosed, the CIA turned to Special Branch to survey the condominium and the meeting participants.[4]

To entrust the monitoring of the meeting to the Malaysians was an error. The agents of Special Branch were unable to place a listening device inside the condominium, a failure they attributed to the constant coming and going of the meeting participants.

As a consequence, the intelligence community was unable to listen in on the conversations that took place inside. Intelligence analysts now believe that the strategic planning for the October 2000 attack on the U.S.S. *Cole* was definitely discussed, and that the multiple hijackings and murders of September 11, 2001, may have been. Had this information been obtained, it is possible—even likely—that both attacks could have been averted.

This was the second failure that contributed to the tragedy of September 11, 2001.

That mistake in Malaysia was compounded by another in the United States. Upon receiving the photographs of al-Hazmi and al-Mihdhar, the CIA did nothing. It failed to notify the State Department, the agency that, at the time, maintained our largest watch list of suspect persons. The then Immigration and Naturalization Service was not notified and was therefore unable to deny entry at the border. The CIA also may have failed to notify the Federal Bureau of Investigation, which, had it known of the significance and the likely imminent presence inside the United States of these al-Qaeda operatives, would have placed them under surveillance.*

A third opportunity to discover the September 11, 2001, plot was missed.

Had U.S. or Malaysian intelligence services continued to monitor the Kuala Lumpur condominium, in October 2000 they would have seen another visitor: Zacarias Moussaoui, whose connection to the plot remains unclear but who has been charged in the United States on four counts related to the September 11 attacks: conspiracy to commit acts of terrorism, conspiracy to commit aircraft piracy, conspiracy to destroy aircraft, and conspiracy to use weapons of mass destruction.[5]

Not only did Yazid Sufaat, the condominium's owner, allow Mous-

---

* The CIA maintains that it actually did notify the FBI; the FBI says it never received this information from the CIA. During the course of the Joint Inquiry, we were unable to determine where this information fell through the cracks, but given the antiquated nature of the FBI's systems, I suspect that the fault may be with the FBI.

saoui to stay there, he also eased Moussaoui's entry into the United States by providing a phony letter of employment listing Moussaoui as the overseas sales representative of his company, InfocusTech.

On January 8, 2000, al-Hazmi and al-Mihdhar flew together to Bangkok, Thailand, and a week later to Los Angeles. An unknowing immigration agent uneventfully ushered them into the United States.

Two of the eventual nineteen hijackers had entered the country.

2

Arrival in America

A Brief History of U.S. Intelligence

To all outward appearances, 44-year-old Omar al-Bayoumi was employed marginally, if at all. On a rental application for his apartment in the suburbs east of San Diego, he listed his job as a student and his income as $2,800 a month, which he claimed was a stipend from a family in India. He kept an office at the Al-Madina Al-Munawara mosque in the town of El Cajon, where he acted as the unpaid building manager. He was known throughout the local Muslim community as a devout man with a large circle of friends.

Al-Bayoumi was neither Indian nor a student, however. He was a Saudi national, serving his nation as a spy.* Al-Bayoumi's responsibility

---

* The FBI has recently concluded that al-Bayoumi was not a Saudi intelligence officer, a claim that I believe is being made to save the FBI from the embarrassment of having to admit that it failed to monitor a known Saudi spy within the United States, as well as to protect the Kingdom of Saudi Arabia from the strain on relations that such a disclosure would inevitably cause. This is discussed in greater depth in this book's conclusion.

was to keep an eye on Saudis in San Diego, particularly college students who might be engaged in activities threatening to the Saudi Kingdom.

Since 1996, al-Bayoumi had lived in the San Diego suburb of Clairemont with his wife, Mamal, and four children. According to one associate, al-Bayoumi "knew everyone. He interacted with all the mosques. He was widely accepted in the local community, and if he vouched for some people, they would be accepted."

Two of the people he would soon vouch for were the future hijackers Nawaf al-Hazmi and Khalid al-Mihdhar.

During the last week of January 2000, al-Bayoumi and an unidentified companion got into al-Bayoumi's late-model Mercedes and made the roughly two-hour drive from San Diego to Los Angeles. Before departing, al-Bayoumi had told at least one other person that he was going to Los Angeles to pick up visitors.

Upon arriving in Los Angeles, al-Bayoumi made two stops. The first was the Saudi consulate. There, he met privately for an hour with an official from the consulate's section on Islamic and cultural affairs, Fahad al-Thumairy.[1] Al-Thumairy, 29 at the time, had held a diplomatic position at the consulate since his assignment to Los Angeles in 1996. He also served as a prayer leader at the King Fahd Mosque in Culver City, a mosque that was constructed with financial support from the Saudi government and had grown to be one of southern California's largest houses of worship. With a number of suspected terrorist ties, he was no friend of the United States. In fact, in May 2003, the United States would revoke al-Thumairy's diplomatic visa, ban him from the United States, and put him on a plane back to Riyadh. In January 2000, however, al-Thumairy was comfortably in the United States. What he discussed with al-Bayoumi on that day is still unknown.

Following the meeting, al-Bayoumi rejoined his unknown companion and they made their second stop—a Middle Eastern restaurant several miles from the Los Angeles airport.

Al-Bayoumi would later claim that he heard Arabic being spoken at an adjacent table and in his typical hospitable manner invited the two young men to join him. They introduced themselves as Nawaf al-Hazmi and Khalid al-Mihdhar.

Al-Bayoumi claimed that during the luncheon conversation, al-

Hazmi indicated that he and al-Mihdhar did not feel comfortable in Los Angeles. The city was too big, too intimidating, and they had been unable to integrate themselves into the Saudi community.

Al-Bayoumi expressed his disappointment at their unsatisfactory experience and offered to be of assistance should they decide to move to San Diego.[2]

That a suspected Saudi spy would drive 125 miles to a meeting at the Saudi consulate in Los Angeles, where he would meet with a consular officer with suspected terrorist ties, and then drive another 7 miles to the one Middle Eastern restaurant—out of the more than 134 Middle Eastern restaurants in Los Angeles—where he would happen to sit next to two future terrorists, to whom he would happen to offer friendship and support, cannot credibly be described as a coincidence. In any case, al-Hazmi and al-Mihdhar now had an offer of support.

★

From the earliest days of the Republic, accurate, clandestine intelligence information has been understood as a necessity. Our founders realized that effective gathering of intelligence would provide us with advantages both military and diplomatic.

George Washington said during the Revolution that the "necessity of procuring good intelligence is apparent and need not be further urged," instructing his generals to "leave no stone unturned nor do not stick to expense" in gathering intelligence.[3] In 1776, the Continental Congress established America's first intelligence service, the Committee of Secret Correspondence.

When he became President, Washington requested in his first State of the Union message that Congress establish a "secret service fund" for clandestine activities.

Congress did, and within two years the fund represented over 10 percent of the federal budget.

For the next century and a half—through the Civil War and two world wars—America's "intelligence community" was no more than a series of uncoordinated groups housed in a number of different government agencies and military branches, each charged with fulfilling its respective organization's intelligence and counterintelligence needs.

By the 1930s, a diagram of our "intelligence community" would show the Department of State and the branches of the military each collecting intelligence and developing its own security and counterintelligence procedures—the methods by which they'd protect their sources and keep their organizations from being penetrated by a spy or a double agent. Within that system, the Army and Navy each created its own office to decipher and read foreign communications. Again, important information would go up the chain of command, occasionally making its way to the President, but no one short of the White House tried to assemble and assess all of the vital information acquired by the U.S. government.

America's entry into World War II triggered a reassessment of our national intelligence and espionage capabilities and led to the creation of the Office of Strategic Services (OSS), the forerunner to today's CIA.

Headed by Major General William J. "Wild Bill" Donovan—a lawyer trained at Columbia University, and a World War I hero—the OSS recruited a different kind of intelligence operative. Commenting on the penchant of some investigative agencies to hire cat burglars—"second-story men"—Donovan was quoted as saying, "You can hire a second-story man and make him a better second-story man. But if you hire a lawyer or an investment banker or a professor, you'll have something else besides."[4] As a result, the OSS came to be populated with northeastern, Ivy League–educated men who were confident and intelligent. Other agencies both admired their élan and mocked them as socialites. But their demographic makeup—overwhelmingly male, white, northeastern, and educated—came to define the OSS and later the CIA. Congresswoman Jane Harman, a member of the House Intelligence Committee and one of the sharpest thinkers on American intelligence, calls this the "white male from Yale" bias. (Ironically, the current chairman of her committee is my friend Porter Goss, a former CIA agent who happens to be white, male, and a graduate of Yale.)

During the war, the OSS established liaisons with the intelligence services of several other countries and began to build its own worldwide clandestine capability. In 1942, the OSS began gathering intelligence, identifying informants, rallying political support, and laying a communications network in North Africa in order to "soften up" that region in advance of Allied operations.[5]

In an early application of economic theory to military practice, London-based OSS economists worked to develop a program of strategic aerial warfare based on precision bombing of selected industrial targets with the goal of disrupting strategic supplies. And the OSS also worked to penetrate Nazi Germany by recruiting exiled Communists and Socialist party members to identify strategic targets and to promote acts of resistance, sabotage, and subversion. Of the OSS's willingness to do business with suspect characters, Donovan commented, "I'd put Stalin on the OSS payroll if I thought it would help defeat Hitler."[6]

The aftermath of World War II gave rise to the Cold War, and with it the fear that we simply didn't know enough about the plans and capabilities of the Soviet Union, our competitor for global dominance. That concern and the lingering fear and frustration caused by the Japanese surprise attack on Pearl Harbor were the two main factors that led President Harry Truman to call for a centralized intelligence organization.

This was accomplished through the passage of the National Security Act of 1947—one of the most significant pieces of legislation in our history. This legislation established not only the Central Intelligence Agency, but also the National Security Council and the Department of Defense.

Over the next fifty years, what is known as the intelligence community would grow to include thirteen government agencies and organizations that, either in whole or in part, conduct the intelligence activities of the U.S. government. These were the Central Intelligence Agency, the Department of Energy, the Department of State, the Defense Intelligence Agency, the Federal Bureau of Investigation, the National Geospatial-Intelligence Agency, the National Reconnaissance Office, the National Security Agency, U.S. Air Force Intelligence, U.S. Army Intelligence, U.S. Coast Guard Intelligence, U.S. Navy Intelligence, and U.S. Marine Corps Intelligence.

These are the agencies charged with warning policy makers about emerging dangers; supporting diplomatic, legal, and military operations against the full array of threats we face (economic, military, political, terrorist, and the threats posed by illicit activities, such as drug trafficking); and protecting our state secrets through counterintelligence.

From its creation in 1947, the primary target of the CIA and the intelligence community that grew up around it was the Soviet Union, its allies, and its sympathizers. This near singleness of focus contributed to the structural and cultural bias of the CIA that we still see today. Early in the Cold War, the United States relied on human intelligence—spies—to collect information on the Soviets. Spying proved to be an extremely dangerous undertaking, and information collected from human intelligence was procured at great risk and great cost. The Soviets and their Eastern European Warsaw Pact partners were adept at counterespionage and were able to "roll up"—a euphemism for "capture or kill"—many of the U.S. spies who had infiltrated the Soviet sphere.

As satellite technology became more reliable and surveillance tools more sophisticated, the need for human intelligence waned. We were able to learn almost everything we needed to know about the Soviets by observing and listening from the safe distance of space. During that time, a significant percentage of the intelligence community's budget was spent on our satellite architecture. We invested heavily in large multipurpose satellites. These were expensive to build—they cost hundreds of millions of dollars per copy—and expensive to operate. But once in orbit the satellites functioned well, because much of what we wanted to know could be learned from imagery. For example, if we wanted to find out how many submarines the Soviets had, we could take pictures of their maintenance yards and their new construction facilities and get an answer likely to be as good as the answer that human intelligence would yield.*

As a result, the human intelligence capabilities of the CIA declined throughout the 1970s, and by the end of the 1980s the number of CIA agents recruited and trained to serve as case officers had fallen below the number required to replace those who resigned or retired. The agents who remained were predominately skilled in the capabilities, cultures, and languages of the Soviet Union and its Eastern European allies.

A major use of human intelligence is to recruit "assets," individuals operating within or around targets of our interest who are privy to the information we seek. The deficiency of men and women prepared to

* The Soviets were aware of this monitoring and often tried to deceive our satellites. In one instance, our satellites took pictures of a Soviet submarine yard on a particularly windy day, and analysis showed that all of the boats were bowed. The Soviets had been substituting large balloons for submarines, either so that we would think they had more subs than they did, or so that we would believe subs to be in the yards when they were actually out at sea.

either do the recruiting, or, in rarer cases, insinuate themselves directly into the opposition, has been a major liability as America strives to understand the capabilities and will of our new adversaries: international terrorists.

In many significant security characteristics, the Soviet Union was a mirror image of the United States. It was a large nation-state, and, as such, behaved in a logical, predictable manner. Using information acquired from our satellites, we were able to anticipate what the Soviets would do (for instance, test missiles) and counter their initiatives. Likewise for the Soviets against us. Our militaries, diplomats, and intelligence services were analogous and, for the most part, mutually predictable.

However, terrorists and non-nation-state actors operate differently. They do not have the infrastructure of a society to worry about. They do not have diplomatic avenues of communication. They do not have borders to protect. For these and other reasons, the Cold War methods of gathering intelligence by satellite are far less effective against them. Sending a satellite over his training camps cannot uncover the plans and intentions of Osama bin Laden. Only he and a small inner circle of henchmen know them. Only effective human intelligence will make them knowable to us and allow us to frustrate them.

That is why the intelligence community—almost completely in place by the 1950s and largely unchanged since that time—has been inadequate to confront the new threats America faces.

When an intelligence community encrusted with its own history of almost fifty years of preponderant focus on the Soviet Union is combined with the politicized use of intelligence by a Bush administration bent on regime change in Iraq, the result is disastrous. The U.S. intelligence services, amid an incomplete transition from their concentration on old threats, now made a glaringly incorrect assessment of new ones.

3

Settled in San Diego

Overseeing Intelligence

In late January 2000, less than a week after what he would later describe as his chance meeting in the Los Angeles restaurant, Omar al-Bayoumi received a telephone call from Nawaf al-Hazmi. He and Khalid al-Mihdhar had decided to accept al-Bayoumi's invitation to relocate to San Diego.

Upon their arrival in San Diego, al-Hazmi and al-Mihdhar also accepted al-Bayoumi's offer to stay at his place until they could find one of their own, and they began the search for their own apartment the next day.

Al-Hazmi was particularly anxious to find a place that was afford-able, and al-Bayoumi assured them that they would not have to scrimp, that he would supplement the funds the two hijackers were receiving from unidentified sources at "home." A week and a dozen inspections later, al-Hazmi and al-Mihdhar settled on a one-bedroom apartment in the Parkwood complex, almost directly across the street from that of al-Bayoumi. Al-Bayoumi had secured the unit for the newcomers with a six-month lease on which he paid the first two months' rent, a total of more than $1,500. There are no bank records or documents to indicate that that amount was ever repaid. Again, al-Bayoumi would later claim that he was simply being hospitable to two Muslim "brothers" he had met by chance at a Middle Eastern restaurant in Los Angeles.

In keeping with his promise to help the two newcomers get settled, sometime during the next several weeks, al-Bayoumi arranged a party at his apartment to introduce the two new arrivals to the Saudi community in San Diego. Although some in the community suspected al-Bayoumi was a spy for the Saudi government, that whispered suspicion only added to his intrigue, and his social functions were not to be missed. Al-Bayoumi's acceptance served as a social seal of approval, and by hosting a party for al-Hazmi and al-Mihdhar, he sent a message to the community that these men were to be welcomed. So, on a mild evening shortly after the end of Ramadan, two dozen men to whom al-Bayoumi had delivered invitations at mosques around the city gathered to eat a meal of whole baked lamb and welcome the two newcomers. While his friends mingled and enjoyed the evening, al-Bayoumi flitted in and out of the crowd. As was his practice at social occasions—and, it was speculated, as part of his surveillance job—al-Bayoumi videotaped his guests.

The party achieved its purpose. Al-Hazmi and al-Mihdhar formed acquaintanceships that over the following months would grow into a supportive and trusted base of Saudi friends in San Diego.

Most significantly, the two were invited to attend al-Bayoumi's Al-Medina Al-Munawara mosque, the principal mosque for the Saudi community in San Diego. It was at the mosque that al-Hazmi and al-Mihdhar met three of the people who would be most significant in their lives in the United States.

The first was Mohdar Abdullah, who would go on to help the two get driver's licenses and locate flight schools, and may actually have been the person who drove them from Los Angeles to San Diego once they informed al-Bayoumi of their decision to relocate.

The second was the mosque's imam, Anwar Aulaqi. In addition to serving as the religious leader for the two young men, Aulaqi also became a friend and confidant. Some believe that Aulaqi was the first person since the summit meeting in Malaysia with whom al-Mihdhar and al-Hazmi shared their terrorist intentions and plans. The bond was so close that when, in the summer of 2001, al-Hazmi, al-Mihdhar, and other terrorists were directed to establish a final base of operation in northern Virginia, Anwar Aulaqi followed.

The third would later be identified in *The San Diego Union-Tribune* and other press accounts as Abdussattar Shaikh—one of the most respected members of the mosque. An Indian-born Muslim, Shaikh was a retired English professor from San Diego State University who lived in the neighboring community of Lemon Grove, in a two-story house on a bluff overlooking a valley east of San Diego. Shaikh's home was a gathering place for young Middle Eastern men. They would discuss their faith and culture amid the professor's voluminous collection of books and pamphlets on Islam. The professor also had a practice of inviting young Arab men to board in his home, more frequently after his bitter 1997 divorce from his wife left him $60,000 in debt and with more room to rent.

As they were becoming closer to Professor Shaikh, al-Hazmi and al-Mihdhar were also becoming increasingly dissatisfied with the apartment al-Bayoumi had secured for them. Their dissatisfaction may have had something to do with basic hygiene. One resident of the Parkwood apartment complex described unit 127 as being squalid: "They were just sleeping on the floor . . . just blankets everywhere and pillows . . . trash everywhere, like Jack-in-the-Box cups, old bags and things like that."

When al-Mihdhar left the United States in June 2000, al-Hazmi noticed a posting on the mosque's bulletin board that Abdussattar Shaikh was offering quarters in his home for a committed young Muslim. Explaining to the landlord that he could no longer afford the rent in the current apartment, he moved out in September before the expiration of their lease, and into Professor Shaikh's home.

The reasons for al-Hazmi and al-Mihdhar's presence in the United States were unknown at the time to Professor Shaikh. Similarly, they were unaware of Shaikh's clandestine post-retirement occupation. Professor Shaikh was on the payroll of the San Diego office of the Federal Bureau of Investigation as an agency asset. His job was to monitor the Saudi community in San Diego and report to the FBI any suspicious behavior he observed.[1]

Two future terrorists, both of whom would later be placed on the government's watch list, were living under the nose of an FBI informant, and one would later actually live with him, yet the informant was never asked to draw more information from them, get closer to them, or gain their confidence. The failure to pursue this information marked the fourth and perhaps the most significant missed opportunity to break open the September 11 plot.

★

My first window into the world of intelligence opened during my time as governor of Florida, an office I held from 1978 to 1986. In Florida, the chief law enforcement official is the governor, not the attorney general. The governor has responsibility for the state attorneys, the state's Department of Law Enforcement, and the other law enforcement agencies. My friend and longtime advisor Robin Gibson jokes that all of Florida's law enforcement agencies would wind up investigating each other; the only thing that united them was their distrust for the FBI. They were dismissive of the FBI as "college boys" who showed up at crime scenes after the danger had passed, and were concerned that if they worked with the FBI, the FBI would get credit for their arrests and prosecutions.

Most of the FBI's focus in Florida was on drug trafficking and white-collar crime, specifically on the corruption scandals that have plagued Florida as it has grown and more and more money is at stake in land development debates. However, the Bureau did come to me once with information that a threat had been made on my life by a Colombian group. After informing me of this, they made sure that the window to my office was bulletproofed. I don't remember them telling me how they got the information or what became of the threat, but the experience instilled in me a respect for the importance of sound, actionable intelligence—an issue to which I would return when I began serving in the U.S. Senate.

In 1993, I was asked to be the chairman of the Democratic Senate Campaign Committee (DSCC), the political organization that is dedicated to getting Democrats elected to the Senate. The job, which consists largely of fund-raising, is both time-consuming and thankless. George Mitchell, the majority leader at the time, saw my taking the position as a favor and asked if there was any way he could repay it. I asked him to put me on the Senate Select Committee on Intelligence.

There are a number of ways in which the Intelligence Committee differs from other Senate committees. One of them is that the other committees are appointed by a steering committee made up of other senators. As a "select" committee, the Intelligence Committee is appointed directly by the leader, and its appointees don't go through a committee process. So appointing me to a prized seat on the Senate Select Committee on Intelligence was within Senator Mitchell's power. If the DSCC chairmanship was the stick, a seat on the Intelligence Committee was the carrot.

The election of 1994 would come to be called the Republican Revolution, and Democrats running for offices at all levels across the country were swamped by Republican victories. Democrats, having lost eight Senate seats, returned to the 104th Congress in the minority. I took my seat on the Intelligence Committee and waded into the often contentious work of intelligence oversight.

Until the mid-1970s, "intelligence oversight" was practically an oxymoron, because when it came to intelligence, Congress interfered as little as possible and trusted our intelligence agencies as much as possible.

That desire not to interfere was understandable. There is little incentive for someone in Congress to spend a great deal of time on an area where much of the information is sensitive or classified, so that members are forbidden to talk about the good work they are doing. Certainly there are times when I found it much more rewarding to be involved in areas where I could discuss my involvement and be recognized for results. Another disincentive to service on the Intelligence Committee is that it doesn't present significant opportunities to steer projects to your home state. This lack of "pork" makes intelligence oversight less appealing for those members of Congress who pride themselves on what they can deliver for their constituents.

The desire not to interfere was matched, on the part of the intelligence community, by a desire not to be interfered with. As former CIA director Richard Helms once said, "The nation must, to a degree, take it on faith that we . . . are honorable men devoted to her service."[2]

Under this trusting relationship, the authority of the CIA went largely unchecked until 1973, when a new CIA director, James Schlesinger, having seen the CIA implicated in aspects of the Watergate scandal, sent a memorandum to all agency employees requesting that they report to him any activities that fell "outside the CIA's charter."

Schlesinger must have been stunned to see the list of possible abuses grow to 693 items spanning the agency's entire history. This full list became known to people with access to it as "the family jewels"—and a year later one of those jewels would find its way onto public display.

On December 22, 1974, the *New York Times* reporter Seymour M. Hersh published the first of a series of articles that accused the CIA of "massive" spying not on other countries, but on American antiwar activists and dissidents. The article further disclosed that the CIA had compiled files on more than 10,000 American citizens, directly contravening the 1947 act that barred the CIA from any security or police function within the United States.[3]

The outcry was immediate and fierce. Congress, the sleeping watchdog, was roused, launching what came to be known as the Church Committee, named for Frank Church, the Idaho Democrat who chaired it. The Church Committee's sixteen-month investigation delved into not only the CIA, but also the FBI and a number of other federal agencies.

In the course of its investigation, the Church Committee found that the FBI performed illegal break-ins and wiretaps, and that the CIA had, as Hersh reported, kept dossiers on thousands of American citizens. It further found that, among other things, the CIA had illegally intercepted and opened mail between the United States and the Soviet bloc, experimented with LSD on unsuspecting Americans, and unsuccessfully attempted to kill at least five foreign leaders, including Fidel Castro. As news of these activities leaked out over the course of the investigation, President Gerald Ford reversed his initial support for the inquiry and began to urge members of the committee to keep their findings secret. Over twenty-five years later, I was to be exposed to another President who wanted to suppress a congressional investigation of an intelligence failure.

President Ford's pressure became so great that the Senate, fearful of taking a stand one way or the other, refused either to support or oppose publication of the report. Only after Senator Church threatened to resign in protest if his committee repudiated its own work were the findings made public.

In putting out its findings, the committee also put forward ninety-six proposals for reform, one of which called for the establishment of a permanent Select Committee on Intelligence, the committee that I would later come to chair.

4

Beginning Training

The Rise of al-Qaeda

When Omar al-Bayoumi promised the two future hijackers Nawaf al-Hazmi and Khalid al-Mihdhar that he would not only help get them settled in San Diego but would also be happy to help them financially, he was in a position to do so. He had served as a conduit for huge sums of money from the Saudi Kingdom into America. One FBI source identified al-Bayoumi as the man who delivered $400,000 from Saudi Arabia to a Kurdish mosque in San Diego. In addition to whatever large sums of money were flowing through him from Saudi Arabia, he had other streams of income, also from Saudi Arabia. From his ghost job with the Saudi aviation services company, Ercan, he received 11,500 Saudi riyals—approximately $2,800—per month. The second stream of income was an "allowances" fund, paid by Ercan. And the third stream of income came through transfers from the wife of Osama Bassnan, another Saudi spy who was suspected of being groomed to replace al-Bayoumi in San Diego.

The discovery of these income streams, their size, their origin, and the details of how they operated would constitute one of the most explosive and damning revelations of the investigation I would later chair. It was a discovery that would draw a direct line between the terrorists and the government of Saudi Arabia, and trigger an attempted cover-up by the Bush administration.*

The FBI had been aware of Bassnan for a while. In May 1992, the State Department provided the FBI with a box of documents recovered from an abandoned car. One of the documents, marked "Confidential," was a newsletter written in Arabic to supporters of the Eritrean Islamic Jihad Movement. Also in the box were a number of letters addressed to Bassnan that discussed plans to import used cars to the United States. In 1993, the FBI received reports that Bassnan had hosted a 1992 party in Washington, D.C., for Omar Abdul Rahman, the "Blind Sheikh" who is now imprisoned after being convicted of planning the 1993 bombing of the World Trade Center and of plotting a "day of terror" in which the tunnels leading to Manhattan would all be bombed. The FBI did not open an investigation.

Meanwhile, al-Hazmi and al-Mihdhar were becoming comfortable in San Diego. Largely through the mosque where they prayed, they developed a network of friends. When asked why they were in San Diego, they told people that they were trying to learn English and train to be commercial airline pilots. They became part of the tight-knit San Diego Muslim community, playing soccer in a neighborhood park, acquiring season passes to Sea World. Al-Bayoumi and Modhar Abdullah also helped them obtain driver's licenses, car insurance, credit cards, and even Social Security cards.

Free from the strictures of Saudi society, and counter to their religious beliefs, al-Hazmi and al-Mihdhar also "practiced the sins of the infidels."[1] Their apartment was close to two Clairemont Mesa strip clubs, and credit card records indicate that they visited both. Al-Hazmi even went so far as to ask Abdussattar Shaikh, his landlord, for help in composing a personal ad on the Internet for a Mexican bride. For a time, al-Hazmi worked for a San Diego business whose manager was the subject of an ongoing FBI counterterror investigation. The FBI's failure to ac-

* This is discussed in greater depth in chapter 15.

tively pursue this investigation, or even to broaden it to the business manager's new employee in the most cursory manner, marked the fifth opportunity at which a more thorough investigation could have penetrated the planning for the September 11 attacks.

People who knew the two plotters at the time describe them as an odd couple. Al-Hazmi was the friendly one. Outgoing and cheerful, he made friends and worked to improve his English. Al-Mihdhar was more brooding, seemingly disgusted with American culture. In one telling exchange reported in the June 2, 2002, issue of *Newsweek,* al-Mihdhar chided a Muslim acquaintance for watching "immoral" American television. "If you're so religious, why don't you have facial hair?" the friend replied. Al-Mihdhar patted him on the knee. "You'll know someday, brother," he answered.

Beyond that small hint, the two lived a life in San Diego that was equal parts boring, normal, and secretive. They hung around the house; they prayed. They didn't watch television, read books, or make phone calls from the house. Though their communications were discreet—they often stepped outside to prevent their cell phone conversations from being overheard, and they went online using computers at public libraries— al-Hazmi's address and telephone number were listed in the San Diego phone book. Acquaintances found them sometimes cordial, sometimes withdrawn, and suspected them of not being particularly smart.[2]

In May, al-Hazmi and al-Mihdhar began aviation training at Sorbi's Flying Club in San Diego. Initially, they declared that they wanted to fly Boeing jet aircraft, but the chief flight instructor, Rick Garza, told them they'd have to start on something smaller, and pointed them toward a single-engine Cessna. It was immediately apparent that the two had little aptitude for aviation. For starters, their poor English prevented them from following instructions. Beyond that, they seemed woefully unaware of even the most basic principles of aviation. When asked to draw a plane, one man got the wings backward. When one of them was trying to land a single-engine Cessna, the other became frightened and began praying loudly to Allah. Garza had no way of knowing that his two students never had any intention of learning how to land a plane.

After a half-dozen lessons, it became clear that the two would never become pilots. Rick Garza eventually gave up, describing his inept charges as "like Dumb and Dumber."[3]

★

In one of the tragic ironies of history, the enemy we know today as al-Qaeda was brought together largely by the actions of the United States. In December 1979, Soviet forces invaded Afghanistan, fearful that their puppet Communist government was falling, and that, should it fall, the United States would be able to step in and establish its own sphere of influence at the southern border of the Soviet Union.

Russia's invasion was met by the mujahedin, a group of warlords who, although divided by region, clan, and politics, formed a loose alliance to beat back the invasion. One of the mujahedin commanders was Mullah Mohammed Omar, who would later rise to lead the Taliban. The mujahedin ranged in ideology from strict Islamists like Omar to freedom fighters. The United States didn't make such distinctions, anyway. Eager to have confederates in the Cold War, we began supporting the anti-Soviet mujahedin with money, weaponry, and logistical support. This aid, which would ultimately total nearly $3 billion, was mainly coordinated through the Pakistani intelligence service, ISI.

Saudi Arabia, as an ally of the United States, joined in the effort, matching the U.S. funding dollar for dollar, and offering logistical and engineering help as well. Spoiling to support the fight, the scion of a wealthy Saudi construction family traveled all over his country, raising money for the freedom fighters. That young man was Osama bin Laden.

Osama bin Muhammad bin Awad bin Laden was born in 1955, one of more than fifty children of Muhammad bin Laden. As a young man, Osama bin Laden worked on the roads being built by his family's business. His father died in a helicopter crash when bin Laden was in his early teens, and bin Laden inherited a multimillion-dollar fortune. That death, according to some accounts, unhinged the young man, sending him veering between a hermitic life of books and faith and a gregarious life of hedonism subsidized by his wealth. During his college years, he was spotted frequently in Beirut's nightclubs, drinking, fighting, and seeking the attention of women. At the same time, he also joined King Abdul Aziz University's Muslim Brotherhood, an Islamic group.

Nineteen seventy-nine, the year he graduated from college, was a momentous year in the Muslim world—especially for the increasingly ideological bin Laden.* In January, the Shah of Iran was overthrown. In March, Egypt and Israel signed a peace accord at the White House. And then in December came the Soviet invasion of Afghanistan.

Bin Laden would later claim that his father was keen on having at least one of his sons fight against the enemies of Islam, and it seems that the young man found himself and his calling in the battle for Afghanistan.[4] He would later say, "One day in Afghanistan counted for more than a thousand days praying in a mosque."[5]

In 1985, the battle in Afghanistan began to escalate, and the Pakistani intelligence service, again with the support of the CIA, began recruiting radical Muslims from around the world to come to Pakistan and fight alongside the Afghan mujahedin. Spending his own money, "bin Laden financed the recruitment, transportation, and arming of thousands of Palestinians, Tunisians, Somalians, Egyptians, Saudis and Pakistanis to fight the Russians. Grizzled mujahedin fighters still tell of the young man who rode the bulldozers himself, digging trenches on the front lines."[6]

By the end of the Soviet occupation, an estimated 35,000 Muslim radicals from forty-three Islamic countries had joined the fight.

In 1987, Osama bin Laden was introduced to a leader of Egypt's Jihad group, Ayman al-Zawahiri. At the time, al-Zawahiri was serving in Peshawar, Pakistan, as a doctor at a field hospital for Afghan refugees. Although he was working as a healer, he was also a killer. His Jihad group was behind the 1981 assassination of Egyptian president Anwar Sadat, and it was his organization that would later become bin Laden's muscle.

On August 11, 1988, bin Laden held a meeting in which he discussed the establishment of a new military group—al-Qaeda.

One of the initial reasons for the formation of al-Qaeda was logistical. Bin Laden was frustrated by the fact that there was little documentation to give the families of those missing in Afghanistan. To solve this problem, he set up al-Qaeda—"the Base"—to track those who were full-fledged mujahedin, those who were involved only in charity work, and those who were simply visitors. He toured hospitals where Afghan

---

* Some sources say bin Laden graduated in 1979 with a degree in civil engineering, others that he graduated in 1981 with a degree in economics and public administration.

and Arab fighters had been brought, giving out gifts of chocolate and cashews and carefully noting each man's name and address. Weeks later, the man's family would receive a check. Many of these fighters would remember the tall (bin Laden is over six-foot-four), mysterious man with the gentle manner and quiet voice, and he became known as the Good Samaritan or the Saudi Prince.[7]

There was, however, another aspect of al-Qaeda. Bin Laden saw the success of money and logistical support from around the world in giving political power to the mujahedin. He was particularly taken with the ability of Saudi Arabia to support these efforts. In notes from that 1988 meeting, he wrote, "We took very huge gains from the country's people in Saudi. We were able to give political power to the mujahedin, gathering donations in very large amounts, restoring power."[8]

In February 1989, the Soviet forces withdrew from Afghanistan, leaving a puppet government in place. Within nine months of the withdrawal, the Berlin Wall fell and the Soviet Union was in a spiraling decline. Osama bin Laden returned to Saudi Arabia as a triumphant hero and reentered the family construction business. He would later say that the victory over the Soviets "cleared from the Muslim minds the myth of superpowers."[9]

When Saddam Hussein's Iraq invaded Kuwait in August 1990, bin Laden offered the Saudi government his thousands of mujahedin fighters. Rather than accept his offer, Saudi Arabia instead allowed U.S. soldiers on its soil to serve as its defenders. This decision infuriated bin Laden, and he began to criticize the Saudi regime openly. When the American troops remained after the victory, bin Laden grew even more incensed. In the words of one analyst, "In his mind, the United States had become to Saudi Arabia what the Soviet occupation had been to Afghanistan: an infidel occupation force propping up a corrupt, repressive, and un-Islamic government."[10] Bin Laden had gone from being an ally of both the United States and Saudi Arabia to being their enemy; in 1991, the Saudi government expelled him. Seeking to protect its construction business, which prospered on the generosity of Saudi government contracts, bin Laden's family also disowned him.

In 1992, frustrated and unwelcome in Saudi Arabia, bin Laden relocated to Sudan, and, for the first time, became active in transnational terrorism. His initial involvement was as a financier. While he didn't actually run operations, people came to him and asked for money. In helping to build his family's business, he had enlarged his personal fortune. Although estimates vary widely, it is believed that his fortune had grown to well over $100 million, so he was able to be a generous underwriter.

During this time, bin Laden also became a major financial backer of Hassan al-Turabi, Sudan's hard-line leader, as well as of Islamist causes from Algeria to Afghanistan.

Bin Laden used his base in the Sudan to finance three terrorist training camps in the northern part of the country, and to begin to form links between al-Qaeda and both al-Itihaad al-Islamiya, a Somali group, and the Islamic Jihad Movement of Eritrea. He also reached out to his old acquaintance Ayman al-Zawahiri and linked al-Qaeda with al-Zawahiri's Egyptian Islamic Jihad group. This marked bin Laden's transition from a financier to an operator. His organization is credited with a December 1992 explosion in a hotel in Aden, Yemen, that killed two tourists and narrowly missed a number of U.S. soldiers who had just left the hotel for Somalia. That bombing is now seen as bin Laden's first act of terrorism against Americans.

Also in 1992, the Soviet-backed regime in Afghanistan collapsed, throwing Afghanistan into a chaos of competing warlords.

In 1994, Saudi Arabia officially stripped bin Laden of his citizenship in punishment of his "irresponsible behavior that contradicts the interests of Saudi Arabia and harms sisterly countries."[11]

Also in 1994, the Taliban movement began in Afghanistan, in dramatic fashion. A small force led by Mullah Omar marched into Kandahar, where it captured and hanged from the barrel of a tank a fellow commander guilty of raping two girls. To many, the Taliban (Arabic for "Students" or "Knowledge Seekers"), with its fierce religious ideology, looked like the group that could impose order on a lawless land. Within two years, the Taliban had taken over 80 percent of Afghanistan.

In that same year, 1996, the Sudanese government, under pressure from the United States and Saudi Arabia, asked bin Laden to leave. Bin Laden packed two military transport planes with some of his wealth, his four wives, and around a hundred of his Afghan-Arab fighters, and returned to Afghanistan. The timing was fortuitous for bin Laden. He needed refuge, and the Taliban needed money.

The Taliban's acceptance of violence and strict interpretation of Islam made Afghanistan an appealing place for bin Laden to set up camp. Under the leadership of Mullah Mohammed Omar, women were required to be covered from head to toe and were forbidden to work or attend school. Listening to nonreligious music was forbidden, as were dancing, photography, and television. The Taliban ruled by fear and intimidation, frequently using Kabul's soccer stadium for public executions.

The ideological bond between the Taliban and the al-Qaeda forces for whom Afghanistan would provide safe haven was deepened by a financial one: upon arrival, bin Laden gave Mullah Omar an initial payment of $3 million.

Bin Laden's funds helped the Taliban continue their push across Afghanistan. They were able to capture Jalalabad, and, ten days later, the capital city of Kabul. In a hint of the brutality to come, when they seized Kabul, Taliban fighters seized the former Soviet-friendly ruler from a UN compound, castrated him, and dragged him by Jeep to a traffic post, where they hanged him.[12]

The financial relationship was soon to be deepened by a familial one: Mullah Omar married one of Osama bin Laden's daughters. Osama bin Laden was now not only a resident of Afghanistan, he was its leader's father-in-law.

On August 23, 1996, from his base in Afghanistan, bin Laden issued a Declaration of Jihad, outlining his organization's goals: to drive U.S. forces from the Arabian Peninsula, to overthrow the government of Saudi Arabia, to "liberate" Muslim holy sites, and to support Islamic revolutionary groups around the world. He further declared that Saudis have the right to strike at U.S. troops in the Persian Gulf.[13] He would later say, "Hostility toward America is a religious duty, and we hope to be rewarded for it by God. . . . We do not differentiate between those dressed in military uniforms and civilians; they are all targets in this fatwa."[14]

Al-Qaeda had declared war on America.

5

A Gathering Storm

A Failure to Communicate

On June 10, 2000, Khalid al-Mihdhar, frustrated at his lack of progress in aviation, left California for Germany and then Yemen. His trip was more than a homecoming, though. He had an assignment—to recruit the musclemen who would control the crew and passengers while the pilots directed the hijacked aircraft to their targets. To accomplish his task, al-Mihdhar traveled extensively through the Middle East, Southeast Asia, and Afghanistan.

During his thirteen months out of the United States, al-Mihdhar's multiple-entry visa expired. In June 2001, he went to the consular office in Jeddah, Saudi Arabia, to apply for a new one. He presented a different passport than the one he had used to enter the United States in January 2000. On his visa application, he checked "no" in response to the question of whether he had ever been in the United States. As the CIA, almost a year and a half after the summit meeting in Kuala Lumpur, had

yet to watch-list al-Mihdhar or inform U.S. law enforcement agencies of
its suspicions, the consular office at Jeddah stamped him a new visa.

The sixth opportunity to interdict the tragedy of September 11 had
been missed.

Throughout the summer and fall of 2000, other eventual hijackers
began to arrive in the United States. The man who would become the
face of the terrorists, Mohammed Atta, began that peripatetic year in
Afghanistan. In February, he passed through Pakistan en route to Hamburg, Germany, a city that would become a nexus for the September 11
hijackers. Atta spent the spring contacting U.S. flight centers in Lake-
land, Florida, and Norman, Oklahoma, securing information and seeking admission. In May, Atta, still in Hamburg, obtained both an Egyptian
passport and a U.S. entry visa. In June, he took a bus from Hamburg to
Prague; from the capital of the Czech Republic, he flew to Newark.

Once in New York, Atta reunited with one of his Hamburg associates, Marwan al-Shehhi, a 22-year-old born in the United Arab Emirates. A sergeant in the UAE army, al-Shehhi was sent to Germany for
technical training. As a civilian, he returned in 1997 to study English
and electrical engineering.

In July of 2000, Atta and al-Shehhi settled in Venice, Florida. They
opened a joint account at SunTrust Bank with a $7,000 deposit and
began flight training at Huffman Aviation in Venice. Between July 18
and September 18, 2000, the joint account would receive over $100,000
in wired funds.

Atta and al-Shehhi proved to be more trainable aviators than their
San Diego colleagues. At the cost of $27,300 each, they were able to com-
plete their primary training. On December 21, 2000, they received in-
strument certifications and commercial pilot licenses through Huffman
Aviation.

One week later, Atta and al-Shehhi took six hours of advanced
instruction at a Boeing flight simulator in Opa-Locka, Florida. A
post–September 11 FBI report would note that both men "requested
training on executing turns and approaches" but not takeoffs or land-
ings.

Atta and al-Shehhi were not the only Saudis seeking aviation training in Florida. Ziad Jarrah, a 25-year-old Lebanese man who had also

been in Hamburg, had attended a technical institute studying aircraft construction and maintenance. Using a five-year B1/B2 multiple-entry visa, Jarrah entered the United States on June 27, 2000, and proceeded immediately to Venice, Florida, to begin training at another Venice flight school, the Florida Flight Training Center. On September 11, Jarrah is believed to have taken the controls of United Airlines flight 93, which crashed in a field in Pennsylvania.

The final three September 11 pilots were now in the United States preparing for their mission.

★

One recurring theme in American intelligence is the failure of the CIA and FBI to communicate with one another. The agencies' troubled relationship goes back to J. Edgar Hoover, who, as a turf-conscious FBI director, tried to torpedo the CIA before it even got started. Through a campaign of leaks and innuendo, Hoover attempted to convince President Harry Truman that in peacetime, the OSS (the forerunner to the CIA) would be an "American Gestapo."[1] When the CIA came into existence, Hoover's animus only grew. For a period, FBI Director Hoover simply didn't speak to CIA Director Richard Helms. Hoover also expressly forbade FBI agents to communicate with the CIA, thus forcing any FBI agent who wanted to have a discussion with a CIA operative to do so clandestinely.

In some ways the dissonance between the FBI and CIA is understandable. First of all, they have different missions. The CIA is an intelligence agency, the FBI a law enforcement one. The FBI is used to stepping into situations after a crime has occurred. The CIA hopes to get information in advance of threats. The CIA prefers to continue investigations for as long as possible in the hopes of digging out more information—after all, its mission is intelligence gathering, and once a suspect is arrested the information flowing to and from that person stops abruptly. The FBI, on the other hand, likes to bring an investigation to an end by charging someone and prosecuting him. This also makes sense, as the Bureau's function is primarily law enforcement.

These two agencies are also divided by jurisdiction. The CIA has neither law enforcement nor subpoena power within the United States, a denial of authority it failed to follow in the 1960s, and for which it paid a large price in terms of public perception. The FBI is allowed to operate wherever American interests are at stake. In the last decade, the Bureau has established a number of legal attachés (known as legats) outside the United States, and today operates in fifty-two countries. While the FBI's jurisdiction is limited to law enforcement and intelligence operations inside the United States, the legat system was established to support the Bureau's investigation of foreign-based crimes that have been committed, or might be committed, against U.S. citizens.

While the CIA cultivated the image of its agents as dashing sophisticates, the FBI's culture was one of blue-collar competence—heroic G-men battling larger-than-life criminals.

And the FBI is better able to market its successes. While the CIA's greatest successes are the ones that it can never reveal, the FBI usually has an opportunity—after an arrest or an indictment—to trumpet its victories.

More recently, technical problems have added a layer of difficulty on top of the cultural ones. For example, until very recently, the FBI's communications system was set up in such a way that it was nearly impossible for agents to send classified e-mails among one another or to other agencies, including the CIA. Even now, the FBI refuses to build its new systems on the CIA platform, which is widely recognized as a successful standard, choosing instead to start from the ground up, a plan that doesn't guarantee either success or system compatibility. A report by the Justice Department's inspector general found that the FBI's Trilogy project, a $458 million effort to replace the agency's outdated computers and data networks, was plagued by uncertainties about timing, cost, and the ability to achieve technical goals.[2]

Finally, both organizations operate on a need-to-know basis: information is disseminated only to those who someone determines needs it. If there's one thing I've realized in my time serving on the Senate Intelligence Committee, it is that people *like* possessing information that is secret. They *like* not disclosing information to others. It creates a mystique—that you know something too important to share—and allows you to create an aura of knowledgeability without actually having to share any knowledge. The same is true within the CIA. Ronald Kessler's book *Inside the CIA* chronicles the complaints of Nancy McGregor, who served as an assistant to former DCI William Webster: "the directorates were not eager to share information with each other.* While some secrecy was necessary, Webster and his assistants found it was often used to enhance people's own importance, hampering everyone's work. Despite the fact that they had clearances for virtually every program, the assistants were sometimes prevented from knowing what they felt they needed to know. 'Very few people [at the CIA] know the whole picture because very few are allowed to know it.' "

That problem is not exclusive to the CIA. For example, the State Department, which operated the TIPOFF terrorist watch list prior to September 11, did not allow state and local law enforcement access to that list. Its argument was that local law enforcement didn't need to know who was on the watch list because the purpose of the watch list was to catch people before they entered the country. So, by the State Department's logic, no people on the watch list were present in the United States. Of course, as we learned on September 11, that was not a correct assumption.†

On five separate occasions, September 11 hijackers came into contact with local law enforcement—once voluntarily.

On April 1, 2001, five months before the hijacking, Nawaf al-Hazmi was ticketed along Interstate 40 in western Oklahoma, driving 85 miles per hour in a 70-mile-per-hour zone. He had a valid California driver's license and an address in San Diego. Al-Hazmi mailed in his ticket and the $138 fine in money orders.

Also in April, Mohammed Atta received a traffic ticket in Broward County, Florida. By that time, he had overstayed his visa, important information to which the officer didn't have access.

In May, now in Fairfax, Virginia, al-Hazmi brought himself to the attention of the authorities. He had been the victim of an attempted street robbery. He went to the Fairfax police to make a report, although he later declined to press charges.

In July, Atta was pulled over again in Broward County, this time for speeding. Not only did the officer who stopped him not have the infor-

---

* The CIA is divided into four directorates, or divisions. Each reports to the Director of Central Intelligence (DCI). The Directorate of Operations does the human spying, the Directorate of Science and Technology controls satellites and other technical tools, the Directorate of Intelligence provides analysis, and the Directorate of Administration provides the support needed to do it all.
† There is now an effort under way, headed by the FBI's Terrorist Screening Center, to unify and improve the content and use of our watch lists.

mation that he had overstayed his visa, that officer also didn't have the information that there was now a bench warrant for Atta because he had failed to appear in court for his previous violation.

And on September 9, two days before the hijacking, Ziad Jarrah, who is believed to have been at the controls of United flight 93 when it crashed in Pennsylvania, was stopped by a Maryland state trooper on I-95 going 90 miles per hour in a 65-mile-per-hour zone. He was given a ticket with a $270 fine. The trooper determined that Jarrah's license and rental car registration were in order. The citation was later found in the glove box of the rental car left at Newark Airport.

Had local law enforcement been able to run the names of Jarrah and Atta against a watch list, it is likely that they would have been arrested and detained, and at least one team of hijackers would no longer have had a pilot. A system that tracked people who had overstayed their visas and placed their names in a criminal database would have achieved the same result.

As we work to address the failures of communication between agencies, we need to recognize that these problems are currently being compounded by two significant internal failings.

First, neither the FBI nor the CIA has proved adept at changing in response to changing circumstances.

For example, although the threats we face are no longer limited to the Soviet Union and its satellites, the CIA has been slow to recruit agents who "look like" and understand the world we need to observe—something I saw firsthand during a visit to Haiti in 1987.

I've been going to Haiti since I became governor of Florida in 1979. Florida is home to more than 300,000 Haitian immigrants, who have a personal and political stake in the success of the first independent black republic, so to Floridians like me, what happens in Haiti is practically a domestic policy concern. The first time I was able to get a CIA briefing on intelligence activities in Haiti was in 1987, after I was sworn in to the Senate.

On one of my trips to Port-au-Prince, I met with our ambassador and a number of intelligence agents. As I looked around the table, I realized that everybody there looked just like me. They were white, middle-aged men. I asked them, "How do you get good intelligence in a country that's 99.9 percent Afro-Caribbean if your people all stand out like lightbulbs?" The answer was they didn't, and that answer was validated by the next seventeen years of Haitian history. Over that time, dictatorship dissolved into military tyranny; a democratically elected president was deposed and then returned to office with the support of 20,000 U.S. troops; chaos, violence, and poverty continued; and recently U.S. troops presided over the dismissal of the very president those troops' predecessors had returned to office ten years earlier. Our intelligence agents had predicted almost none of this.

Haiti is emblematic of our post–Cold War human intelligence collection; indeed, the CIA's homogeneity presents an even greater liability as we work to gain better information from the Arab world.

Similarly, the FBI has been slow to apply new approaches to new threats, instead relying on methods it has used for decades.

That became clear to me during a briefing of the Senate Intelligence Committee. The subject was the scale of al-Qaeda's presence in the United States. The witness was the FBI's assistant director for counterterrorism. I wanted to ask him for an estimate of how many al-Qaeda operatives there were in the United States, so in an attempt to establish a baseline number, I first asked, "What is the FBI's estimate of the total number of al-Qaeda, worldwide?"

The assistant director's answer was precise: "Two hundred and thirty-seven."

I was stunned. "God damn, the CIA has told us that there were between fifteen thousand and twenty thousand al-Qaeda recruits who went through the Afghanistan training camps in the 1990s. At most, two thousand of them were killed in Afghanistan. How could it be there are only two hundred and thirty-seven operatives?"

"It's a matter of definition," the assistant director replied. "Like the Cosa Nostra, full al-Qaeda membership entails swearing an oath of fidelity to the leader, in this case Osama bin Laden, and having that commitment recorded. We have found the records, and they contain about two hundred and thirty-seven names."

I was stunned. While I was aware of the practice of *bayat*—the oath of loyalty and the signing of the book—how would terrorists trained worldwide and spread across many countries even get to "the book" to sign it?

Because of its experience and success in battling organized crime, the FBI was trying to apply a model with which it was familiar—the Mafia—to a threat about which it knew far less—al-Qaeda. I would have found this comical if it weren't so deadly serious.

Whatever relevance the Cosa Nostra practice might have had in fighting organized crime, it was totally unrelated to the capabilities of al-Qaeda. The ridiculousness of that approach and that membership estimate was bad enough by itself. But the FBI's unwillingness to communicate with other agencies compounded the problem. If the CIA, the NSA, and the immigration service had known what the FBI was telling the President as to the scale of the al-Qaeda presence in the United States, the other agencies might have been in a position to challenge the absurdly low number and the assumptions upon which it was based.

Information from the CIA and a projection of al-Qaeda's global capabilities and intentions targeted on the United States would have produced a more credible assessment of the al-Qaeda presence *in the United States alone*—which, based on information I have received, I estimate to be several orders of magnitude higher than the figure the FBI briefer suggested for the organization's *worldwide* membership.

Second, often U.S. intelligence organizations fail to communicate *internally.*

Again, this problem was most glaring in the FBI. In July 2001, in an investigation discussed more fully in the next chapter, the Bureau's Phoenix office sent a memo voicing its concern that bin Laden might be using U.S. flight schools to infiltrate America's civil aviation system. That memo was ignored by superiors and, in particular, it never reached the FBI's Minneapolis field office—which, a month later, arrested a French-Moroccan flight student named Zacarias Moussaoui.

This tendency of information to move only upward within organizations, never laterally within or between organizations, came to be called stovepiping—and stovepiping became one of the causes of the tragic failure that was September 11.

6

Hanjour Joins al-Hazmi

A Memo Is Missed

The first hijacker pilot came to the United States in 1990. Hani Hanjour came to the United States when he was eighteen in order to visit a brother in Tucson and enroll in an eight-week English language program at the University of Arizona. Whatever level of English proficiency he attained, his short experience in Tucson was transformative. By the 1990s, Tucson had a close-knit and well-established community of Islamic militants. For several years in the 1980s, Wadih el-Hage, an Osama bin Laden lieutenant who was ultimately convicted for his role in the 1998 African embassy bombings, lived in Tucson. Another group dedicated to recruiting Muslim fighters to repel the Soviet invasion of Afghanistan, al-Kifah, had one of its three American offices there, and when the Afghan mujahedin ultimately repelled the Soviets, it is believed that al-Kifah was folded into Osama bin Laden's new organization, al-Qaeda.

Whether the young Hani Hanjour had any contact with the organization is unknown. What is known is that when he returned to Saudi Arabia in 1992, his brother described him as a "different person." He had grown a full beard and ended his previous social relationships; he worked on the family farm by day, and spent most of his free time reading books on religion and airplanes.

Hanjour next returned to the United States in April 1996. He lived for a month in Florida before moving to Oakland, California, where he took another English language course and began primary flight training. In September, he moved again, this time to Scottsdale, Arizona, where he continued his flight training. He left the United States again for Saudi Arabia in November 1996, but would return twice more for flight training.

By all accounts, he was only a slightly better student than al-Mihdhar and al-Hazmi. One former instructor said that in the cockpit Hanjour was unsure of himself, even frightened, particularly during exercises in which an engine is turned off in flight so that a pilot can practice righting the plane and restoring power.[1] However, by virtue of his sheer doggedness and the number of flight hours he accumulated over multiple years in a series of schools, he was able to earn an FAA commercial pilot certificate, dated April 15, 1999.

Hanjour's final visit to the United States began in September 2000. After a stop in Florida, Hanjour moved on to San Diego, where he met Nawaf al-Hazmi for the first time. Abdussattar Shaikh, the FBI informant, remembers seeing al-Hazmi with a man fitting Hanjour's description a number of times, but because al-Hazmi wasn't known to the FBI as a person of interest, Shaikh was never asked about al-Hazmi or his associates. The seventh opportunity to open a window on the September 11 plot was missed.

In December 2000, al-Hazmi and Hanjour traveled together to Mesa, Arizona. It was another short but intensive stay. While al-Hazmi continued his bumbling attempts to master the skills of an aviator, Hanjour took advanced courses (on a simulator) in the skills necessary for flying a Boeing airliner—skills beyond those required for a commercial license. Hanjour's instructors thought he was so bad a pilot and spoke such poor English that they contacted the FAA to check if his license was a fake.[2] It wasn't. In piecemeal fashion, Hani Hanjour had earned a valid commercial pilot's license with a multiengine rating.

★

Kenneth Williams arrived in Arizona, fresh from the FBI Academy, the same year Hani Hanjour did: 1990. The son of a retired New Jersey police officer, Williams had served for three years with the San Diego Police Department. In 1990, Williams quit the San Diego force and joined the FBI bureau in Arizona as a sniper. He eventually became a counterterrorism specialist; his partner, George Piro, was the only Arabic-speaking agent in the Phoenix office.[3]

By all accounts, Agent Williams is exactly the type of person the FBI and the federal government need—smart, dedicated, loyal, and hardworking. He also had developed an intense interest in counter-terrorism.

In an interview with the staff of the Joint Inquiry, Special Agent Williams traced his interest in counterterrorism—and, specifically, aviation-related terrorism—to the early 1990s, when he found himself working on two cases in which Libyans with suspected terrorist ties were working for U.S. aviation companies. One of the individuals he was investigating had a master's degree in a technical field yet had worked first as a skycap and then as a baggage handler. The other person was working as a technical officer for a domestic airline. That person's job involved overseeing the complete overhaul of aircraft and checking the planes' structural integrity. To Williams, the fact that possible terrorists were probing airport security and achieving easy access to aircraft conjured up nightmarish visions of the 1988 bombing of Pan Am flight 103, which killed 259 people on the plane and 11 people on the ground in Lockerbie, Scotland. Williams's primary concern was that Islamic extremists could be learning how to evade airport security and to hijack or destroy aircraft.

In 1994, Williams was introduced to a man named Harry Ellen, who would offer him a window into the local Arab community. Harry Ellen had converted to Islam in 1990 and befriended the leaders of a number of Arab factions—including four groups that were on the U.S. government's terrorist list—who shared his passion for an independent Palestinian state. Some of their other activities, however, concerned Ellen, and in 1996 he relayed those concerns to Agent Williams. Specifically, he told Williams that there were some Arabs in the local mosque who were involved in aviation training.[4] In part as a result of that warning, Williams and other Phoenix agents began spending more time looking at Arabs who they suspected had ties to international terrorist groups.

In April 2000, Agent Williams decided to interview one of the people he had been watching, a man named Zakaria Mustapha Soubra. Soubra was a Lebanese national who was studying aeronautical safety at Embry-Riddle Aeronautical University's Prescott, Arizona, campus. He had also founded the Arizona chapter of al-Muhajiroun, an organization that advocates Muslim rule, espouses the killing of American citizens, and condemns U.S. support for Israel.

On April 7, 2000, Agent Williams showed up at Soubra's apartment to interview him. Williams told the Joint Inquiry that in his experience foreign nationals were at least somewhat intimidated by their first contact with the FBI. Soubra wasn't intimidated. He was defiant. He told Agent Williams that he considered the U.S. government and military legitimate targets of Islam. Tacked to the walls of his apartment, he had photocopied photographs of Osama bin Laden and one of wounded Chechnyan mujahedin fighters. According to Soubra, Williams told him, "You are free to say whatever you want as long as you don't support financially or materially any terrorist organization."

As Williams left the apartment, he saw Soubra's car outside and noted its license plate. When he ran the plates, he found that Soubra was not the car's actual owner; that was a man named Mohammed al-Qudhaeein. Al-Qudhaeein and a friend had been detained in 1999 for trying to get into the cockpit of an America West flight from Phoenix to Washington, D.C. They explained to the FBI that they thought the cockpit was the bathroom and sued the FBI, accusing it of racism. During the course of the depositions, it was discovered that Mohammed al-Qudhaeein and his friend were traveling to Washington to attend a party at the Saudi embassy, and that their ticket had been paid for by the government of Saudi Arabia. Gun-shy perhaps because of the civil case, and perhaps because of the special status accorded Saudi nationals by the U.S. government, the FBI chose not to prosecute the two men, or even to investigate them further, and al-Qudhaeein left the country.

A year later, after intelligence information was received indicating that he might have received explosives and car bomb training in Afghanistan, Mohammed al-Qudhaeein's name was added to the State

Department's watch list. In August 2001, al-Qudhaeein applied for a visa to reenter the United States but as a result of the watch-listing was denied entry. Despite the FBI's failure to follow up on the attempted cockpit entry, the watch list worked, and a potential terrorist was denied entry to the United States.

In early 2001, Williams's investigation of Middle Eastern flight students was interrupted when he was pulled from his work in counterterrorism to investigate a high-profile arson case, a switch that was deeply frustrating to him.[5] The fact that the Phoenix office would take its best terrorism investigator and assign him to an arson case is another example of the FBI's consistent prioritization of law enforcement over counterterrorism intelligence, and Agent Williams had no choice in the matter.

In May 2001, with the arson case closed, Williams returned to his work on international terrorism matters. To get back up to speed, he reviewed his case files, becoming further convinced that the number of individuals of potential investigative interest enrolled in aviation training demanded action. He began writing an electronic communication (EC) to FBI headquarters in Washington, a hauntingly prescient document that came to be called the Phoenix memo.

Meanwhile, the continuing investigation of Soubra led to the opening of investigations on six of his associates who were also involved in aviation training.

What Williams did not know at the time is that Soubra knew Hani Hanjour through a local religious center and occasionally carpooled with him to flight school. In fact, on at least five occasions prior to 2001, Soubra and Hanjour were at flight school on the same day, and on at least one of those days they used the same plane, with Hanjour flying and Soubra observing—something that the rules of the flight school indicate would only happen if the pilot, Hanjour, approved Soubra's presence in the cockpit.

In July 2001, Williams completed his electronic communication and sent it the Counterterrorism Division at FBI headquarters.

The Phoenix memo, sections of which were declassified as part of the Joint Inquiry, began: "The purpose of this communication is to advise the bureau [headquarters] and New York of the possibility of a coordinated effort by Usama bin Laden to send students to the United States to attend civil aviation universities and colleges. Phoenix has observed an inordinate number of individuals of investigative interest who are attending or who have attended civil aviation universities and colleges in the state of Arizona. The inordinate number of these individuals attending these type of schools and [the] fatwas [they have issued] . . . gives reason to believe that a coordinated effort is underway to establish a cadre of individuals who will one day be working in the civil aviation community around the world. These individuals will be in a position in the future to conduct terror activity against civil aviation targets."

Agent Williams then made four specific recommendations:

1. FBI headquarters should develop a list of civil aviation universities and colleges around the country.
2. FBI field offices should establish liaisons with these schools.
3. Headquarters should discuss the theories in Williams's memo with the CIA and other components of the intelligence community.
4. Headquarters should consider securing authority to obtain visa information on persons seeking to attend flight schools.

While the memo's final paragraphs are still classified, one of Williams's concluding points is that "Phoenix believes that it is more than a coincidence that subjects who are supporters of UBL [bin Laden] are attending civil aviation universities/colleges in the State of Arizona. As receiving officers are aware, Phoenix has had significant UBL associates/operatives living in the state of Arizona and conducting activity in support of UBL. . . ."

Under the FBI system, electronic communications contain a "lead," which is a system through which the office sending a communication can request that the receiving office or offices take some follow-up action or conduct additional investigation. In the lead section of the communication, the sending office can outline exactly what action or investigation the receiving office should conduct. Once the lead has been completed—"covered," in FBI vernacular—the receiving office will inform the sending office what action was taken, or what the result was of the investigation.

It is important to note that in the FBI's antiquated system, an electronic communication is not the same as an e-mail. The FBI's electronic system is not designed to ensure that everyone a communication is addressed to actually receives it. Rather, the electronic communication is sent to the larger unit and then forwarded only to the individual to whom the lead is assigned. What's more, the system is only capable of recognizing units if they are exactly and accurately designated in the lead section; otherwise the communication will be dumped into the Counterterrorism Division's main electronic folder, where it will sit until a secretary checks the folder and forwards it on to the appropriate unit. In fact, the system is considered so unreliable that many agents use e-mail as a backup system. In the course of the Joint Inquiry's investigation, we found that within the FBI's Counterterrorism Division, as of mid-2002, there were 68,000 outstanding and unassigned leads dating back to 1995. Since the electronic system is so antiquated that it is often circumvented, there is no way of knowing how many of these leads have actually been covered.*

In Agent Williams's communication, the lead requested that both the Radical Fundamentalist Unit (RFU) and the Usama bin Laden Unit (UBLU) consider implementing his four suggested actions. The FBI divides its work into two basic spheres—operational units investigate specific crimes; analytic units include headquarters-based agents who focus on areas whose significance is longer-term and strategic. Kenneth Williams's communication went to two separate operational units, but not to an analytic unit.

What happened next was a game of bureaucratic hot potato. The message was referred to an intelligence operations specialist (IOS) in the RFU, who concluded that the project should be handled by someone in the UBLU. A representative of the UBLU didn't want the lead transferred to that unit but agreed to take responsibility for its response. A number of agents in the UBLU discussed whether Agent Williams's fourth suggestion, that the FBI secure authority to obtain visa information on persons seeking to attend flight schools, constituted racial profiling. The intelligence operations specialist also decided to forward the electronic communication to an FBI intelligence analyst in Portland, Ore-

* In late June 2004, the FBI admitted that it was far behind schedule in creating and putting in place a system called Virtual Case File. The goal of the system is to allow agents to share information easily. As of this writing, four years and $500 million into the project, the problems that plagued Agent Williams largely still remain.

gon, who was known throughout the agency to have an interest in terrorists and airplanes, with a note saying that Williams's document "basically puts forth a theory of individuals being directed to come here to study aviation and their ties to extremists. Nothing concrete or whatever, but some very interesting coincidences. I thought it would be interesting to you considering some of the stuff you were coming up with in PD [Portland]."

This was an example of how, in the FBI, the strategic focus on the larger picture took a backseat to operational matters—to considering whether the memo could help one agent work on one case. The analyst in Portland, because she had been sent the memo only for her information, didn't take any action on it or share it more widely. My colleague Senator Dick Shelby called this attitude "the tyranny of the case file": an overriding focus on closing specific cases created no incentive to look at larger trends.

On August 7, 2001, five weeks before the September 11 attacks, the intelligence operations specialists in both the RFU and the UBLU to whom the EC had been directed decided that the lead should not be sent up to their superiors or referred to an analytic unit, and should instead be closed. A week later, Agent Williams received an electronic notice that the lead was "covered—consulted with UBLU, no action at this time, will reconvine [sic] on this issue."

One month later, it was too late.

By the day in July when Williams sent the memo, al-Hazmi and Hanjour had already completed their aviation training. However, had Williams's recommendations been acted upon promptly, liaisons with the flight schools would have found at least one and perhaps as many as three other hijackers still developing their flying skills.

Had the FBI developed the liaisons with flight schools that Agent Williams had suggested, and had the Bureau sought information from the CIA and shared its information with that agency, again, the plot might have been derailed. This was the eighth such opportunity.

Kenneth Williams was one of the first in the FBI to link the severity of the threat to the number and sophistication of international terrorists living in and around Phoenix. However, he was not the first member of the FBI to express concern about Middle Eastern or Arab men training at U.S. flight schools.

In 1983, the then Immigration and Naturalization Service had asked the FBI for assistance in locating Libyan nationals engaged in aviation or nuclear-related education.

In 1998, the head of the FBI's Oklahoma City Field Office contacted headquarters to express concern about the large numbers of Middle Eastern males at Oklahoma flight schools. The fear was that light planes could be used to spread chemical or biological agents, so the communication was not sent to the Radical Fundamentalism Unit but instead to the office's "Weapons of Mass Destruction" file.

In 1999, the FBI received word that a terrorist organization was planning to send students to the United States for aviation training. The purpose of the training was unknown, but intelligence indicated that the terrorist organization's leaders saw the training as "particularly important" and were reported to have approved a blank check to ensure its success.

In response, the Counterterrorism Division at FBI headquarters sent a communication to twenty-four field offices, asking them to pay close attention to Muslim students from the target country who were engaged in aviation training in their area. It requested that field offices "task sources, coordinate with the INS, and conduct other logical inquiries, in an effort to develop an intelligence baseline" regarding the group's use of students. There is no indication that the FBI field offices conducted any investigation in response. The analyst who drafted the communication did receive a number of phone inquiries. Some were to ask for more guidance. Others raised concerns about the Buckley Amendment implications of investigating at schools.* To address these concerns, the FBI sent a letter to the INS explaining the intelligence they were working from and requesting a database search for individuals from the target country studying in the United States. Information from the INS would then be sent to FBI field offices, which would work with local INS agents to follow up. The INS never responded to the request, and in November 2000 the investigation was dropped.

Special Agent Williams's communication joined this list of intiatives and investigations left to drop. Williams would later say that although

---

* The Buckley Amendment, part of the 1974 Family Education Rights and Privacy Act, bars postsecondary educational institutions that receive federal funding from releasing students' personal information without their written consent.

the FBI officially classified counterterrorism as a priority, he often felt that counterterrorism and counterintelligence were the Bureau's "bastard stepchild"; the lack of effort by headquarters to disseminate intelligence information to the field left him feeling like he was "out on an island."

And yet, somehow, being out of the bureaucratic trees allowed Agent Williams to see the forest. On September 11, upon seeing the news of the attacks, he walked outside to his patio and wept.[6]

Agent Williams's analysis could have been particularly helpful to the Minneapolis office of the FBI—had that office seen it.

Zacarias Moussaoui entered the United States at Chicago's O'Hare Airport on February 23, 2001. He was traveling on a French passport, which allowed him to stay in the United States without a visa for ninety days. Five months earlier, he had e-mailed the Airman Flight School in Norman, Oklahoma, expressing his interest in learning to fly a small Cessna aircraft. The school indicated that he would be welcome when he arrived, and on February 26, 2001, he began flight lessons there.

In short order, it became clear that Moussaoui was unhappy with the training at Airman. At the end of May 2001, he contacted Pan Am International Flight Academy in Minneapolis. While Airman Flight School provided lessons in piloting Cessnas and similar small aircraft, Pan Am provided ground training and access to a Boeing 747 flight simulator used by professional pilots.

In his e-mail to the Pan Am International Flight Academy, Moussaoui wrote that he wanted to "pilot one of these Big Bird." Even though he didn't have a private pilot's license, he described flying airliners as "my 'Goal' my dream." Though he admitted his qualifications could be better, he implored the school, "I am sure that you can do something, after all we are in AMERICA, and everything is possible."[7]

Most of Pan Am's students are either newly hired airline pilots who use the flight simulator for initial training, or active airline pilots who use the equipment for an update or refresher training. Although anyone can sign up for lessons at Pan Am, the typical student has a pilot's license, is employed by an airline, and has logged several thousand flight hours. Moussaoui had none of these qualifications. However, it was not un-heard of for schools like Pan Am to be contacted by people who had the money and the desire to spend a few Walter Mitty hours in a flight simulator.

The Zacarias Moussaoui who arrived at Pan Am on August 13 was not the student the school had expected, given his sweetly patriotic e-mail.

For example, during his initial ground training session, Moussaoui asked about the protocols for communicating with flight towers. Pan Am found suspicious his extreme interest in the operation of the plane's doors and control panel. Further, Moussaoui reportedly said that he would "love" to fly a simulated flight from Heathrow Airport in London to John F. Kennedy Airport in New York. Also suspiciously, he paid by pulling a wad of cash—$6,800—out of a satchel he was carrying.

The day after Moussaoui's first classroom session, the Pan Am office held its monthly meeting of instructors and administrators, and Moussaoui's name came up. Instructors wondered why he was so interested in learning the protocol for communicating with flight towers. They discussed the amount of fuel on a Boeing 747-400, and the damage such a plane could do if it were to hit something. One of the managers at the meeting said he would be willing to contact a friend who was an agent at the local FBI office. Indeed, on August 15, after Moussaoui's second day of classroom instruction, a representative of the Pan Am flight school contacted the Minneapolis field office of the FBI.

The FBI's Minneapolis field office is part of a Joint Terrorism Task Force, or JTTF.* As part of the JTTF, agents of the then Immigration and Naturalization Service shared space and worked closely with the FBI in Minneapolis. This proximity allowed the agencies to determine immediately that Moussaoui had been authorized to stay in the United States only until May 22, 2001. Thus, he was "out of status," and the INS had a reason to detain him.

The same day the Minneapolis field office learned about Moussaoui, it asked both the CIA and the FBI's legal attaché in Paris for any information they had or could get on him. At the same time, they also informed FBI headquarters of the investigation. FBI headquarters suggested that Moussaoui be put under surveillance, but the Minneapolis office did not have enough agents to do that. Also, the Minneapolis

* JTTFs are groups of local, state, and federal officials working together on a regional basis to fight terrorism.

agents believed that it was more important to prevent Moussaoui from getting any additional flight training.

After conducting a series of interviews at the flight school, the FBI agents, along with two INS agents, went to Moussaoui's hotel. The INS agents temporarily detained Moussaoui and his roomate, Hussein al-Attas, while checking whether they were legally in the United States. Al-Attas had a valid student visa and agreed to allow the agents to search his property in the hotel room.*

Moussaoui showed the agents his passport case, which included his passport, a British driver's license, a bank statement showing a deposit of $32,000 in cash to an Oklahoma account, and an application to extend his stay in the United States. The INS agents determined that Moussaoui had not received an extension to allow him to stay in the United States beyond May 22, 2001, so they took him into custody.

Though Moussaoui was cooperative, he refused to allow the agents to search his belongings. When the agents told him that he would be deported, Moussaoui agreed to let the agents take his belongings to the INS office for safekeeping. The agents packed Moussaoui's belongings, noticing that among them was a laptop computer.

The agents interviewed Moussaoui at the INS office in Minneapolis. Moussaoui told them that he had traveled to Morocco, Malaysia, and Pakistan on business, although he could not provide any details of his employment. Neither could he convincingly explain the $32,000 bank balance. After Moussaoui's detention, the Minneapolis supervisory agent called the office's legal counsel and asked if there was any way to search Moussaoui's possessions without his consent. He was told he had to obtain a search warrant.

It is important to understand that the FBI had two choices in the type of warrant it could pursue. The first was a standard criminal search warrant, which requires the law enforcement agent seeking it to go before a judge with evidence that establishes probable cause to believe that a crime is being, has been, or will be committed.

The second is a Foreign Intelligence Surveillance Act (FISA) search

---

* As of this writing, al-Attas has been convicted of making false statements to the FBI regarding statements by Moussaoui and the extent of his relationship with Moussaoui. He remains in custody as a material witness.

warrant, issued by a secret Foreign Intelligence Surveillance Court (FISC). Under FISA, the FBI can obtain a court order authorizing a physical search or electronic surveillance, such as a wiretap, if it can demonstrate that the subject (1) is an agent of a foreign power, which can be a foreign country or an international terrorist group; and (2) is, among other things, engaged in international terrorism or activities in preparation for terrorism on behalf of that foreign power. Court orders issued under FISA are classified.

The existence of these two types of warrants is a consequence of "the Wall"—the barrier between law enforcement and intelligence. In truth, the Wall is not a single barrier, but rather a series of restrictions on activities between and within agencies constructed over sixty years of legal, policy, and institutional decisions. In the words of the Joint Inquiry's summary report, "These walls separate foreign from domestic activities, foreign intelligence from law-enforcement operations, the FBI from the CIA, communications intelligence from other types of intelligence, the Intelligence Community from other federal agencies, and national-security information from other forms of evidence."

The division between foreign intelligence and law enforcement is seen most clearly in the different procedures that have been developed regarding law enforcement and foreign intelligence electronic surveillance and searches.

The Fourth Amendment to the U.S. Constitution requires a judicial warrant for most physical searches for law enforcement purposes. In 1967, the Supreme Court extended that protection to electronic surveillance, but did not address the question of whether electronic surveillance for foreign intelligence required a warrant. In 1972, the Court held that a domestic group could not be subjected to warrantless electronic surveillance unless a connection was established between the group and a foreign power.*

However, the 1975 Church Committee found numerous instances of warrantless electronic surveillance of citizens who were not agents of a foreign power, and of warrantless physical searches intended to identify subversives and protect intelligence sources and methods. These find-

---

* The FBI lawyers interpreted the phrase "foreign power" to mean "recognized foreign power"— and thus set for themselves a higher threshold of evidence than the FISC requires.

ings led to the enactment of the Foreign Intelligence Surveillance Act of 1978.

During the Church Committee inquiry, some argued that the judiciary was simply not equipped to review requests for foreign intelligence surveillances. FISA established a special court to review these requests. The Act also recognized that intelligence and law enforcement interests would necessarily coincide in some cases where foreign intelligence surveillance is appropriate, such as espionage and terrorism investigations. In those cases, the Act permits information produced by surveillance to be shared with law enforcement. However, to ensure that the division between foreign intelligence surveillance and law enforcement surveillance was maintained, the Act required a certification that "the purpose" of a proposed FISA surveillance was to collect foreign intelligence information. The reason for these technical distinctions is that it is more difficult to meet the constitutional standards for a criminal search warrant than it is to meet the statutory requirements for a FISA warrant. This raises the concern that law enforcement agencies, lacking the evidence they need to get a criminal warrant, will be tempted to disguise their real intentions and seek a FISA warrant. Thus, the Wall was erected.

This was the decision that confronted the FBI as they sought to unlock Moussaoui's computer. They knew that they had in custody a suspicious character, clearly up to no good. They were worried that they didn't have enough in the way of "probable cause" to justify a criminal search warrant. And they feared that if they tried to get a standard criminal search warrant and failed, they wouldn't be able to get a FISA warrant, because the attempt to obtain a criminal warrant would suggest that "the purpose" of the proposed surveillance was a criminal investigation and not intelligence. That would disqualify the request for a warrant in the FISA court.

Over the following days, the Minneapolis agents considered which kind of warrant to pursue, or whether they should simply deport Moussaoui to France after arranging for the French authorities to search Moussaoui's possessions and share their findings with the FBI. It was urgent that they choose a course of action, because the INS felt it could defensibly hold Moussaoui for only seven to ten days.

On Saturday, August 18, Minneapolis sent a detailed memorandum to FBI headquarters describing the Moussaoui investigation and stating that Moussaoui's "possession of weapons and his preparation through physical training for violent confrontation" gave Minneapolis reason to believe that he, al-Attas, "and others yet unknown" were conspiring to seize control of an airplane.

The question was how to learn who the "others yet unknown" were and what exactly they planned. The FBI's Minneapolis office decided that given what they already knew of Moussaoui's travels, the best approach would be to try to link him with a foreign power and go for a FISA warrant.

However, the FBI case agent in Minneapolis was becoming increasingly frustrated with what he perceived as a lack of assistance from the Radical Fundamentalist Unit (RFU) at FBI headquarters. Even in mission-centered bureaucracies, there are personality conflicts, and the FBI case agent in Minneapolis had had previous conflicts with the RFU agent over FISA issues. The personality conflict inflamed the case agent's belief that headquarters was not being responsive to the threat Minneapolis had identified.

At the suggestion of a Minneapolis supervisor, the Minneapolis case agent contacted an FBI official who was detailed to the Director of Central Intelligence's Counterterrorist Center (CTC). The Minneapolis agent gave the official a detailed description of the Moussaoui investigation and asked for any information that the CTC could provide to strengthen the case linking Moussaoui to international terrorism.

On August 21, 2001, the Minneapolis case agent sent an e-mail to the supervisory special agent in the Radical Fundamentalist Unit who was handling the matter: "[It's] imperative that the [U.S. Secret Service] be apprised of this threat potential indicated by the evidence. . . . If [Moussaoui] seizes an aircraft flying from Heathrow to NYC, it will have the fuel on board to reach DC."

On August 23, two FBI agents assigned to the Oklahoma City field office's international terrorism squad visited the Airman Flight School, where Moussaoui had first attempted to learn to fly. One of the agents had actually visited the school two years earlier, in September 1999. He had been assigned a lead from the Orlando field office to visit the school on a case concerning an individual who had received training at Airman and been identified as Osama bin Ladin's personal pilot. Here he was, investigating two radical Islamic terror leads, two years apart, at the

same flight school. His two visits to Airman were to do with two separate cases, rather than with one larger investigation, so they were not
linked in his mind, or in the Bureau's. Had they been, the investigation
might have taken on some urgency. Another result of the tyranny of the
case file.

One day earlier, on Wednesday, August 22, the FBI legal attaché's office in Paris had provided a report stating that Moussaoui had been in
Chechnya assisting Chechen rebels. That fact alone could have been
enough to secure the FISA search warrant the Minneapolis field office
was hoping to get. However, because of a misinterpretation of the FISA
requirements, it provoked a series of discussions between Minneapolis
and the Radical Fundamentalist Unit at FBI headquarters focusing on
whether a specific group of Chechen rebels was a "recognized" foreign
power. Ideally, the FBI wanted Moussaoui identified with a foreign
power that had been recognized by the State Department as a terrorist
group and for which the Foreign Intelligence Surveillance Court had
previously issued warrants, like al-Qaeda.

The Radical Fundamentalist Unit agent believed that the Chechen
rebels were not a "recognized" foreign power and that even if Moussaoui was linked to them, the FBI could not obtain a search warrant
under FISA. The RFU agent told the Minneapolis agents that they
needed to connect Moussaoui to al-Qaeda, which he believed was a "recognized" foreign power. This led the Minneapolis agents on a search
for information showing that the Chechen rebels were connected to
al-Qaeda.

An FBI lawyer mistakenly thought that Moussaoui had to be connected to an organization on the State Department list of foreign terrorist organizations—a "recognized" foreign power. Though this would
have prevented the lawyer from having to break new ground in FISA
court, it was not a FISA requirement. Somehow, the word "recognized"
had been added to a rule that didn't include it. During the Joint Inquiry,
North Carolina senator John Edwards asked Marion "Spike" Bowman,
the deputy general counsel of the FBI, whether any of his lawyers had
given any mistaken advice on the law. Bowman said that they hadn't.
He was wrong.

Because of his lawyers' misinterpretation, Minneapolis spent the better part of three weeks trying to connect the Chechen group to al-Qaeda

in the hopes of establishing a connection between Moussaoui and a "recognized foreign power" and thus allowing them to see what was on his computer.

The Minneapolis case agent, hamstrung and now completely frustrated, once again contacted the CTC, asking for additional information concerning connections between the group and al-Qaeda; he also suggested that the Radical Fundamentalist Unit agent contact the Counterterrorism Center as well, so that together they could create two points of pressure pushing for the same information. The RFU agent responded that he had all the information he needed and requested that Minneapolis work through FBI headquarters when contacting the CTC.

Ultimately, the RFU agent agreed to submit Minneapolis's FISA request to the attorneys in the FBI's National Security Law Unit (NSLU) for review.

In the course of the Joint Inquiry's investigation, our staff interviewed a number of FBI attorneys whom the Radical Fundamentalist Unit agent had asked about the Moussaoui case. All of them confirmed that they had indeed told the RFU agent that there was insufficient evidence to link Moussaoui to a foreign power. However, the attorneys also told our inquiry staff that had they seen the Phoenix memo, which was knocking around the FBI's system at the same time, it would have changed the context of the Moussaoui investigation and made a stronger case for the FISA warrant. However, the point was moot: the only analyst who saw both memos had not made the connection.

Rather than work with the Minneapolis field office to help their investigation, headquarters was getting increasingly frustrated at their persistence. During a conversation on August 27, 2001, the Radical Fundamentalist Unit agent told a Minneapolis supervisor that he was getting people "spun up" over Moussaoui.

According to his notes and his statement to the Joint Inquiry staff, the supervisor replied that he *was* trying to get people at FBI headquarters "spun up": he was trying to make sure that Moussaoui "did not take control of a plane and fly it into the World Trade Center."

The Minneapolis agent said that the headquarters agent replied, "[T]hat's not going to happen. We don't know he's a terrorist. You don't have enough to show he is a terrorist. You have a guy interested in this type of aircraft—that is it." The headquarters agent claims not to remember this exchange. The Minneapolis supervisor—stunned, in retrospect, that in his frustration he had blurted out exactly the attack that would take place, told our staff on the Joint Inquiry that he had no reason to believe that Moussaoui was planning an attack on the World Trade Center; he was just trying to get headquarters' attention by illustrating how dramatic a threat a hijacked aircraft could be.

Headquarters continued to throw up one bureaucratic hurdle after another. On August 28, 2001, after reviewing the request for a search warrant, the RFU agent edited it and returned it to Minneapolis for comment. His major change was the removal of information about connections between the Chechen rebels and al-Qaeda, which he told the Minneapolis agent was insufficient.

After the edit was complete, the RFU agent briefed the FBI's deputy general counsel, Spike Bowman. Bowman told our staff that he agreed with the RFU agent that there was insufficient information to show that Moussaoui was an agent of a foreign power. Following that briefing, the RFU agent e-mailed Minneapolis to say that the information was even less sufficient than he had previously thought, and that he wouldn't recommend going forward with the request.

The quest for a FISA warrant was over.

Still hoping to unlock the secrets held in Moussaoui's computer, the Minneapolis office now focused on arranging for Moussaoui's September 17 deportation to France, and the agreement that French officials would search his possessions and provide the FBI with their findings. No one thought of attempting to obtain a criminal search warrant, even though the primary reason that that had not been tried in the first place was the concern that it would prejudice a future request under FISA.

The commission investigating the September 11 attacks would later conclude that had the FBI announced Moussaoui's arrest, or made public its fears that he intended to hijack airplanes, the publicity might have been enough to disrupt the plot. This was the ninth such lost opportunity.[8]

Instead, the last weeks of August and the first week and a half of September went by with final preparations being made for Moussaoui's deportation.

7

Teaming Up

A Historic Election

Yemen had been of great interest to Osama bin Laden since the early 1990s. From his point of view, it had several important assets: a strategic location at the tip of the Arabian Peninsula; political instability; and dire poverty. In addition, over a third of the county was beyond the control of the Yemeni government. Perhaps the fact that bin Laden's father was Yemeni gave the country some sentimental appeal as well.

The United States also had an interest in Yemen. We hoped that President Ali Abdullah Saleh would institute reforms that would help Yemen move away from its anti-Western past as a Soviet satellite and improve relations with the United States. As a gesture of goodwill, and because of Aden's location on the route between the Mediterranean Sea and the Indian Ocean, the U.S. Navy set up a refueling operation in the port of Aden. Even before that agreement was reached, however, Osama bin Laden had been planning maritime attacks against U.S. naval vessels calling in Yemeni ports.

His first opportunity occurred in early January 2000, when a U.S. destroyer, *The Sullivans,* arrived in the port of Aden.* As *The Sullivans* moored, an explosives-laden boat slid from its dockage and headed for the ship. It never reached the destroyer: the weight of the TNT it carried caused it to take on water, capsize, and sink.

One of the organizers of the failed attack was Muhammad Omar al-Harazi, an al-Qaeda operations chief in East Africa and one of the plotters of the Nairobi embassy bombing. Al-Harazi was personally humiliated by the failed attack. Two days later, he headed to Kuala Lumpur for the terrorist summit that the CIA knew was taking place. As I explained earlier, Malaysia's inability to get a listening device into the meeting and the CIA's unwillingness to do so prevented the conversations from being monitored, but it is widely assumed that the escape of *The Sullivans* was discussed, and that planning for a second attempt on an American vessel in Yemen was moved from theoretical to operational.

The U.S.S. *Cole,* a 505-foot-long, 8,600-ton guided missile destroyer, made its first port call in Aden on the morning of October 12, 2000—the thirteenth such visit by an American ship under the military agreement between the United States and Yemen.

As the *Cole* moved slowly into the deep natural harbor, framed by thousand-foot hills, and headed for the fueling dolphin—a facility in the middle of the harbor that allows ships to take on fuel without having to dock—it was approached by two of three ships that had been contracted to bring food and remove waste.

Though the *Cole*'s refueling stop had not been publicly announced, the U.S. embassy had notified the Yemeni government of the visit about ten days in advance, and by the day before the *Cole*'s arrival, the various merchants who would be removing trash, providing fresh food, and aiding in the fueling operation were aware that the ship was on its way.

At 8:45 A.M., the *Cole* began to tie up to a mooring point near the fuel dolphin, a process that takes about an hour. Some of the crew was working to handle the refueling, a number of sailors stood on watch on the deck above, and many were having a meal. The crew had had training

---

* The U.S.S. *The Sullivans* is named for George, Francis, Madison, Joseph, and Albert Sullivan, five brothers from Iowa who were killed when their ship, the U.S.S. *Juno,* was torpedoed during World War II.

in repelling an overt attack from a small boat, and extra sailors were on watch, but there was nothing suspicious about the two small tender craft circling the *Cole*. The only anomaly was that one of the expected three boats hadn't arrived. Then another small boat, a fiberglass-hulled skiff, approached from across the harbor and pulled up alongside the *Cole*. The crew members who saw it assumed it was the missing tender ship expected as part of the port stop operation. The two men aboard the skiff stood erect, as if to salute, and then the *Cole* was rocked by a blast so powerful it flipped over cars onshore.

The blast hit amidships, and the explosives were sophisticated enough in their composition and arrangement that the energy of the explosion was directed below the waterline, blowing a forty-by-forty-foot hole in the half-inch-thick steel plates of the armored hull. The explosion ripped into an engine compartment, flooding it. The force of the explosion drove the ship's mess upward into the deck above it, trapping and crushing sailors between the metal. Seventeen sailors were killed and thirty-eight injured.

The *Cole* is one of the Navy's most advanced destroyers, equipped with Tomahawk cruise missiles and the Aegis battle-management system, a network of computers and radars capable of simultaneously tracking more than 100 targets on land, on the sea, and in the air. It was later rumored that Osama bin Laden had a particular animus against the *Cole* because it was one of the ships that had launched the cruise missiles against his Afghan camps in 1998 as retaliation for the embassy bombings in Kenya and Tanzania. It is more likely that the *Cole* was a target of opportunity: the ships involved in that attack were never publicly identified by name, so one of bin Laden's loyalists would have had to read the hull markings of vessels engaged in those attacks, and al-Qaeda would have had to receive advance word of the *Cole*'s arrival. (This terrifying and unlikely prospect would force us to significantly revise our assessment of al-Qaeda's sophistication and its penetration of our military.) Still, the question remains as to how the attackers got enough advance warning of the port stop to substitute their boat— which had been specially built so that the explosives were part of its structure and would have been undetectable upon search—for the expected one.

Also unknown is whether these suicide boaters had received training at a Hezbollah training camp for underwater demolition in northern Lebanon.

The bombing of the *Cole,* another result of that fateful meeting in Malaysia, was the worst attack on American armed forces since the 1996 bombing of an Air Force barracks in Saudi Arabia. Al-Qaeda's toll of American lives had reached fifty, and a slow stream of terrorists had entered the United States, or were about to do so, in the hopes of making it climb much, much higher.

It was shortly after the *Cole* attack that Nawaf al-Hazmi settled in Mesa, Arizona, with Hani Hanjour to resume their aviation training.

Ziad Jarrah, who had flown into Atlanta, Georgia, on June 27, 2000, had moved to Venice, Florida, where he began flight training at the Florida Flight Training Center.

Also during the summer of 2000, Mohammed Atta and Marwan al-Shehhi arrived in Florida and began flight training at Huffman Aviation in Venice. Marwan al-Shehhi was known to the CIA—or, at least, his first name was. In March 1999, German intelligence officials passed on to the CIA al-Shehhi's first name, and a telephone number in the United Arab Emirates.[1] According to German sources, German intelligence obtained that phone number by monitoring the telephone of Mohammed Zammar, an Islamic extremist in Hamburg. The Germans then asked the CIA to track "Marwan" and, though the CIA claims to have tried the phone number, it seems the lead wasn't followed further.[2] Al-Shehhi arrived at Newark Airport on May 27, 2000, unhindered and untracked: the tenth missed opportunity to tap into the September 11 plot.

November 2000 found three of the hijacker pilots nearing the completion of their training in Florida.

★

That same month, America's attention was also centered on Florida, but for an entirely different reason. Vice President Al Gore and Texas governor George W. Bush were engaged in what was looking to be the closest presidential election in modern history, an election that was increasingly likely to be decided in my home state.

From Election Day through mid-December I found myself drawn

into the bizarre events played out in the media, the streets, the courts, and the nondescript county offices where beleaguered local officials try-ing to reconcile hanging, dimpled, or pregnant chads knew that their decisions might determine who would lead the world's only super-power. On December 12, the U.S. Supreme Court ordered the Florida recount stopped and thus effectively brought an end to the election of 2000. George W. Bush would be America's forty-third President.

As the drama around the presidential election unfolded, so did a less-noted passage in the U.S. Senate, one that would result in the Senate being divided 50–50 for the first time in history and would ultimately re-sult in my being the most senior member of my party on the Senate Se-lect Committee on Intelligence.

Before the 2000 election, Republicans enjoyed a 55–45 advantage in the Senate. Virtually every Democrat speaking to a national audience that year had said, "We're going to win the presidency, and we're go-ing to take back the House and the Senate." Of those three goals, taking back the Senate seemed the least realistic: not only did the Republicans outnumber us by five to begin with, but also Bob Kerrey (Nebraska), Frank Lautenberg (New Jersey), and Pat Moynihan (New York) were retiring. However, several Democratic Senate challengers won— Hillary Clinton (New York), Tom Carper (Delaware), Jon Corzine (New Jersey), Bill Nelson (Florida), Ben Nelson (Nebraska), Mark Day-ton (Minnesota), and Jean Carnahan (Missouri). Debbie Stabenow, in Michigan, and Maria Cantwell, in Washington, were locked in races too close to call. On November 8, Debbie Stabenow was declared the winner in Michigan; the race between Maria Cantwell and Slade Gorton, which was being recounted, would decide whether we'd have a first-ever 50–50 Senate. On December 1, Cantwell was declared the winner by 2,229 votes. With the presidential election still undecided, that event went largely unnoticed. This led to an interesting paradox. If Al Gore won the presidency, Senator Joe Lieberman of Connecticut would become Vice President and vacate his seat, leaving his successor to be appointed by his state's Republican governor. Therefore, if we ended up with a Democratic President, we would have a Republican Senate. However, if Bush became President, Lieberman, who had won reelection in Con-necticut, would take his seat, giving Democrats parity in the Senate. When Al Gore conceded on December 13, that is exactly what we faced.

Because George W. Bush wouldn't be sworn in for the first two weeks of the 107th Congress, for two weeks the Senate was under Democratic control, with Vice President Gore casting the tie-breaking votes. After the inauguration ceremonies on January 20, 2001, Dick Cheney assumed the vice presidency and the Republicans held what could be the tie-breaking vote in a 50–50 Senate.

The agreement reached by Senate Democratic Leader Tom Daschle of South Dakota and Senate Republican Leader Trent Lott of Mississippi as to how the evenly divided Senate would be organized left some of the most controversial and significant issues to be fought through by the ranking Republican and Democrat on each committee.

I had joined the Intelligence Committee in 1993, and for the next eight years I gradually worked my way up the seniority ladder. Unique among Senate committees, the Intelligence Committee has an eight-year term limit. By 2000, in what I expected would be my last year on the committee, I was the third-ranking Democrat, behind Senator Carl Levin of Michigan and Senator Charles Robb of Virginia. I was ready to complete my term and move on.

But in an electoral upset, Senator Robb lost his seat to the former governor of Virginia, Republican George Allen. Senator Levin was faced with the choice of exercising his ranking position on the Intelligence Committee or the Armed Services Committee, on which he was also the most senior Democrat. He chose the latter. Now I was not only the ranking Democrat but also the only Democrat in line for ranking status who actually had any experience serving on the Committee.

With some measure of self-interest, and also in the belief that the committee and the party would be ill served if the ranking Democrat were a rookie, I asked Tom Daschle for a waiver to allow me to serve two more years. Senator Daschle agreed.

Because I was the ranking Democrat on the committee, there were some particularly sensitive matters for Senator Richard Shelby, the committee chairman, and me to negotiate. Due to the classified nature of much of the information with which the Senate Select Committee on Intelligence deals, the engagement of a member of a senator's personal staff, which would be normal for all other committees, is not possible. Therefore, a committee staff member is designated to assist and represent each of the committee's seventeen members; the staffers are known as liaisons, and each one has his or her own area of expertise. Frequently a close bond develops between the member and his or her liaison staff member.

Throughout its twenty-five years of existence, the Intelligence Committee has had a unified staff. This is at stark variance with the other Senate committees, where frequently the most partisan disputes are not among the members but among their ambitious and aggressive staffers. In the Intelligence Committee, given the nature of the work, this had long been held to be inappropriate. However, the charter of the committee had been written with an escape clause: should the minority party feel that its needs are not being served, it can unilaterally demand a partisan division of the committee, with the majority controlling two thirds of the committee budget and staff and the minority the balance. This was a parliamentary grenade whose pin had not been pulled for a quarter of a century.

Senator Shelby started the discussions with the proposal that the Democrats would have the right to designate two of the approximately twenty-five professional positions on the Intelligence Committee staff—the Democratic staff director and a deputy. Senator Shelby would select all the rest, including the staff liaisons for Democratic senators. I knew this was a nonstarter and told Dick as much in our first negotiation session. The Democrats wanted to select their own liaisons, and as a group we wanted to have our own counsel to advise us on legal matters. We were in gridlock for more than two weeks. There were several Democratic members who wanted to throw the grenade.

As other committees were resolving their differences, the Intelligence Committee became one of the last holdouts. Failure to reach an agreement would mean that the resolution of our committee's internal structure would be taken from our hands and settled by Senators Daschle and Lott. Neither Shelby nor I wanted that to happen.

Finally, we were able to reach a compromise. The Democrats would have three general staff positions—director, deputy director, and counsel—and would select the eight staff members who would serve as liaisons to the eight Democrats on the committee. Senator Shelby would select the balance of the professional staff and all the support staff. Recognizing the tenuousness of the 50–50 Senate, we further agreed that should the Democrats come into control during the 107th Congress, the staff would continue as originally selected, but any new hires necessitated by staff resignations would be filled by the Democrats, subject to the liaison rule. This arrangement seemed to be as fair as we could make it, and it assured continuity of the committee's work should some change in the makeup of the Senate occur.

Besides enjoying the prestige of being the highest-ranking member of my party on the committee, I was now a member of the "group of eight." This group comprises the eight members of Congress—the chairs and ranking members of both the House and Senate Intelligence Committees, as well as the leading Democrat and Republican in each body—who, by law, must be consulted by the President when a highly sensitive covert action is to be undertaken. The tradition is that an objection from a substantial portion of the group of eight—no majority vote is required—is enough to sidetrack the President's wishes. The power granted to the group of eight over these sensitive covert operations is one of the most executivelike powers granted to anyone in the Congress, and a solemn responsibility with which I was now entrusted.

8

Terrorists on the Move

A Senate Upended

In March 2001, al-Hazmi and Hanjour completed their Arizona flight training and relocated to Falls Church, in northern Virginia. The area had a significant Saudi community, including the recently arrived imam of San Diego, Anwar Aulaqi. Al-Hazmi and Hanjour began attending Aulaqi's mosque. A member of the congregation helped them find an apartment; that same person would later drive Hanjour to Paterson, New Jersey, where he would purchase his ticket for American Airlines flight 77.

On April 23, Walid al-Shehri and Satam al-Suqami arrived in Orlando, Florida. Over the following three months, all of the other hijackers who were not pilots arrived in the United States in pairs.

These men came from varied backgrounds. Some came from wealthy families and had good educations. Others came from poor families and had virtually no education. Some had exhibited a great deal of religious commitment; some had not. Some had struggled with depression or alcohol abuse; others seemed simply to be drifting in search of a purpose. For all their differences, there were some significant similarities as well. All of them had been exposed to extremist ideas through family, friends, or clerics, and had become radicalized as a result of that exposure. All of them, once committed to militant Islam, had traveled to Afghanistan to train in the camps of the exiled Osama bin Laden. Nearly all were joined in America by at least one male relative. They were young: all but one were under 30, and nine were younger than 23. Of the nonpilots, all but one were Saudi.

The last pair of hijackers, Salim al-Hazmi (Nawaf al-Hazmi's brother) and Abd al-Aziz al-Umari, arrived in New York on June 29. Khalid al-Mihdhar, having recruited many of the new arrivals as the muscle in the hijackings, waited to see that his charges were safely in America, and then, on July 4, he returned as well. Days later, Omar al-Bayoumi, the man who had helped the first two future hijackers get settled in San Diego, left America for Birmingham, England.

All of the September 11 hijackers were now in the United States.

On May 24, Marwan al-Shehhi flew from New York to San Francisco on a Boeing 767, the first in a series of scouting flights the hijackers began taking between the northeastern United States and California.

★

On that same day, May 24, 2001, the diligently negotiated power sharing of an equally divided U.S. Senate fell apart. Senator James Jeffords of Vermont, speaking from the city of Burlington, announced he was changing his party affiliation from Republican to Independent and would be voting with the Democrats to reorganize the Senate.

As a result, I became chairman of the Senate Select Committee on Intelligence on June 6, 2001, the day Senator Jeffords's switch became effective.

This was my first chairmanship since I had become a member of the Senate, and I was excited at the potential not only to direct the committee but also, through it, to push the intelligence community in new directions.

The primary means by which the Congress influences the policy of the intelligence agencies is the annual intelligence authorization bill.

The committees of the Senate may be divided into two groups: the Appropriations Committee, and everybody else. A ritual of "everybody else" is to pass an annual authorization bill, which, theoretically, sets congressional policy for the executive agency over which the committee has jurisdiction. It outlines that agency's budget and broadly describes how Congress feels that money should be spent. When it comes time to appropriate, or actually spend, the money that's been authorized, the Appropriations Committee members step in. This is the point at which the appropriators can direct money to pet projects in their home states or districts, taking control away from the authorizers and sometimes ignoring their directives.

Again, the Intelligence Committee differs from its fellow committees. The rules that govern it state that the appropriators cannot direct expenditures for the intelligence agencies unless those expenditures have been authorized by the Intelligence Committee and are consistent with the policies in the intelligence authorization bill. In other words, when the Intelligence Committee authorizes, it does so with live ammunition.

After a decade of service on the committee, I came to the chairmanship with a clear concept of what the intelligence agencies' priorities should be in the post–Cold War era. I decided that during my tenure as chairman, I would focus on four key areas: counterterrorism; rebuilding the intelligence community's human intelligence capabilities; reforming the National Security Agency, which is responsible for code making and breaking and for international electronic eavesdropping; and improving our measurement and signature intelligence (MASINT) capability, a cutting-edge technology.

Traditionally, there have been three basic ways in which America gathers intelligence, with an agency that roughly corresponds to each.

First, there is gathering intelligence by human means, or HUMINT, and that is handled largely by the CIA.

Second, there is signals intelligence (SIGINT): gathering and analyzing the secret communications of our foreign adversaries. The agency chiefly concerned with signals intelligence—with both understanding the secret communications of other countries and protecting our own—is the National Security Agency (NSA).

Third, intelligence may be obtained through imagery. The imaging intelligence function is handled mainly by the National Geospatial-Intelligence Agency, which, along with the National Reconnaissance Office, is responsible for the operation and maintenance of our nation's satellite fleet.

Now there is a fourth, the more and more important source of intelligence I mentioned above, MASINT. Detecting radioactive material is a form of MASINT, as is tracking the speed of submarines or missiles.

While on the committee, I wanted to do as much as possible to strengthen our human intelligence.

I once asked an experienced British intelligence officer what he saw as the most urgent necessity facing his nation's intelligence community. His answer: "Penetration, penetration, penetration. We were able to understand the Soviets from the outside. We are not able to master the capabilities and intentions of the terrorists without getting inside their tents. And the only way to do that is to be able to penetrate the tents."

The challenge of getting inside those tents is a daunting one. The number of on-the-ground case officers, especially those with the skills to recruit and manage or "run" the foreign nationals who are most likely to be accepted into a tent, shrank during the last years of the Cold War. And it hasn't gotten appreciably better in the new era. Because the intelligence community's budget is a proportion of the defense budget, when the peace dividend was distributed after the fall of the Soviet Union, the intelligence community became an involuntary contributor. The cuts led the CIA, for instance, to reduce its HUMINT staff by approximately 20 percent during the early and mid-1990s. This was accomplished through an open-ended early-retirement policy. The unintended consequence of this policy was that many of the younger and more employable agents left for the private sector, leaving the Agency with fewer agents, many of whom were focused on the Soviet Union. As a result, the CIA was even more deficient in the skills necessary to take on new threats. An expanded corps of case officers and analysts who speak the languages of the Middle East and Central Asia and have cultural empathy with those regions has emerged as a critical requirement in understanding the terrorists. In testimony, George Tenet told the committee that it takes the CIA five years to train and place a case officer. To me, that seemed too long. I felt that we needed to reform the composition of the intelligence community to better coincide with the threats facing America, and we needed to do so quickly.

This challenge is exacerbated by two others. First, the CIA is a "career" agency, focused on recruiting people straight out of college and keeping them for a lifetime. But nowadays, young people expect to jump from job to job; the Agency must find ways to employ people who don't intend to stay for the life of their careers, and to utilize the skills and talents of people who are interested in coming to the CIA in mid-career. This is an area where former DCI George Tenet made a serious commitment, and the agencies are beginning to see results.

Second, the Muslim community perceives an anti-Muslim bias at the CIA. That bias actually doesn't exist. The problem is that the CIA's background checks involve speaking to friends, neighbors, and family members, and many American Muslims have family in countries that America finds suspect. That factor complicates the security review process.

These two problems are keeping America from tapping its greatest intelligence asset. We are one of very few countries to have loyal, patriotic citizens who understand and speak the languages of countries and groups about which we seek knowledge. Although much of the discussion of intelligence reform is focused on moving the boxes on an organizational chart, and I agree that some of those shifts would be advantageous, I believe new personnel policies will be a far greater contributor to the modernization of the intelligence community.

The most immediate challenge we faced, however, concerned another of my priorities, NSA modernization. On January 24, 2000, the NSA's computer system had crashed for four days, paralyzing the agency. This was not your garden-variety computer crash; it was a full shutdown of the largest computer system in the world. For the next three days, as hundreds of engineers and technicians worked around the clock to restart the complex network, trillions of bytes of data were being collected daily but not analyzed. The NSA sought to minimize the damage, pointing out that the information hadn't been lost, it just wasn't being analyzed. In their words, "we may have lost timeliness, but we have not lost intelligence." Porter Goss pointed out the flaw in that logic: "We are extraordinarily fortunate that this incident did not take place in the midst of an escalating international crisis—lives may well have been lost because of it."

The first good news we got after the NSA crash was that it was not caused by terrorism, malfeasance, or some turn-of-the-millennium problem. The breakdown was caused by the failure of NSA's systems to keep pace with the rapid change in computer and telecommunications technology, the greater complexity of collecting that information, and the expanded target (during the Cold War, 60 percent of the data collected concerned the Soviet Union; by 1993 that proportion was down to 15 percent). Simply put, the NSA's system was outdated. Given the volume of information it was collecting, it was as if the system were trying to drink from a fire hose; it couldn't keep up. Over the years, the Intelligence Committee, and I personally, had criticized the NSA for failing to modernize quickly enough. A crisis was needed to goad the agency into change. One of my first experiences as chairman of the committee was having the head of the NSA, Air Force Lieutenant General Michael Hayden, come before the committee to ask, somewhat sheepishly, for the money necessary to fix the problems and upgrade the NSA systems. News reports have put that request at over $100 million. In truth, it was over $1 billion.

Our first authorization bill increased funding to accomplish the goals I had laid out, including funding a revitalization of the NSA, investments in correcting our deficiencies in human intelligence, and a commitment to rebuild a research and development program for cutting-edge technologies such as MASINT. At Senator Shelby's insistence, it also asked for further study about the problem of leaks of classified information.

I was happy—Senator Shelby and eventually the full committee had accepted my reprioritizations—and proud. Within three months of becoming chairman, we had passed the authorization bill and sent it to the full Senate. In a statement, I said, "While the end of the Cold War warranted a reordering of national priorities, the continued decline in funding has left us with a diminished ability to address the emerging threats and technological challenges of the 21st Century. The Intelligence Community is our nation's vital early warning system and we must support its mission to the fullest extent possible."

The date was September 6, 2001.

9

Final Preparations

Missed Signals

Throughout June and July 2001, the NSA noticed a rise in threat activity, the third such rise since that winter. Analysts noted that something was afoot, and speculation centered on whether the target was abroad. Sufficiently concerned that an attack would occur on the Arabian Peninsula, the U.S. military declared ThreatCon Delta and sent all ships in the area to sea. At the same time, Attorney General John Ashcroft began traveling exclusively by government jet, as opposed to the commercial aircraft attorneys general normally take, despite the fact that senior FBI and CIA officials knew of no specific threat against the Attorney General.[1]

Meanwhile, in the course of investigating the attack on the U.S.S. *Cole,* the FBI had developed information that an individual known as Khallad was Khallad bin Attash—a principal planner of the *Cole* bombing—and that two other participants in that bombing had delivered money to him around the time of the January 2000 Malaysia meeting.

The FBI shared this information with the CIA, whose analysts were prompted to take another look at the meeting in Malaysia. They discovered that Khallad had indeed been present. This information was significant, because it meant that the other attendees, including al-Mihdhar and al-Hazmi, had been in direct contact with a key planner in bin Laden's terrorist network. Still, the CIA did not add al-Mihdhar and al-Hazmi to the State Department's watch list. Had the Agency done so, al-Mihdhar, who was abroad at the time, would have been denied reentry into the United States.

On June 11, FBI headquarters representatives and CIA representatives met in New York with the FBI agents handling the *Cole* investigation. The New York agents were shown but not given copies of the photographs taken in Malaysia. When the FBI agents asked why these people had been photographed, the CIA agents wouldn't tell them, reasoning that they would not share information outside the CIA unless authorized to do so and unless that was the purpose of the meeting. Nothing other than internal policy prevented them from sharing this information. Again, the CIA did not tell the FBI agents anything about al-Mihdhar's U.S. visa or al-Hazmi's travel to the United States, although they would later claim that this information had already been sent to the FBI. The CIA analyst who attended the June 11 meeting told the Joint Inquiry that the information "did not mean anything" to him, because he was focused on terrorist connections to Yemen. This needless refusal to share information cost the nation its eleventh opportunity to disrupt the September 11 plot.

On June 13, al-Mihdhar went to the U.S. consulate in Jeddah, Saudi Arabia, and applied for a new visa. His passport was not the one he had used to enter the United States on January 15, 2000. The application asked whether he had ever been in the United States; he checked no. On July 4, al-Mihdhar reentered the United States.

A week later, a CIA officer who had been assigned to the FBI and was searching through the CIA's electronic database found the CIA cable saying that Khallad had attended the meeting in Malaysia. Deeply troubled, the CIA officer sent an e-mail from FBI headquarters to the Director of Central Intelligence's Counterterrorist Center saying of Khallad, "This is a major league killer, who orchestrated the Cole attack and possibly the Africa bombings."

That e-mail launched a review of all of the earlier cables concerning the Malaysia meeting, a task that fell to an FBI analyst assigned to the CTC. On August 21, that analyst put together two key pieces of information contained in earlier cables: the CIA's knowledge that al-Mihdhar had a multiple-entry visa to the United States, and the information that al-Hazmi was already here.

Working with an Immigration and Naturalization Service representative who had been assigned to the CTC, the analyst found that al-Mihdhar had been in the United States, had left, and had reentered the country just six weeks earlier. This information, combined with the joint arrival of al-Hazmi and al-Mihdhar in Los Angeles in January 2000—around the time that Ahmed Ressam's "millennium bombing" plot to destroy Los Angeles International Airport was foiled by an alert customs official at the Canadian border—finally put the men under serious suspicion.

On August 23, eighteen months after it had obtained information identifying al-Mihdhar and al-Hazmi as suspected terrorists carrying visas for travel to the United States, the CIA sent a cable to the State Department, the INS, the U.S. Customs Service, and the FBI requesting that "Bin Laden related individuals" al-Mihdhar, al-Hazmi, and two other attendees of the Malaysia meeting be immediately placed on their various watch lists and denied entry into the United States. (Although the CIA believed al-Mihdhar was in the United States, his presence on the watch lists would empower authorities to detain him if he attempted to leave.)

On August 28, the FBI's Usama bin Laden Unit sent the New York field office a document recommending it open an intelligence investigation "to determine if al-Mihdhar is still in the United States." The New York FBI agents tried to convince headquarters that, given the importance of the search and the limited resources available to the Bureau, they should open a criminal investigation, which would allow them to pursue al-Mihdhar with greater urgency. Again, this was an example of the elevation of criminal investigations over counterterrorism intelligence. However, misunderstanding the applicable law, FBI headquarters refused the request, saying that al-Mihdhar could not be connected to the ongoing *Cole* investigation without using some intelligence information.

On August 29, the Bureau of Diplomatic Security (BDS) at the State Department gave the FBI al-Mihdhar's and al-Hazmi's visa information. Al-Mihdhar had written on his application that he would be staying at a Marriott hotel in New York City. The FBI did not ask the BDS to use its extensive means of tracking down visa violators to help locate the two, something that representatives of the BDS told the Joint Inquiry they would have been capable of doing had they only been asked. Similarly, the INS, not having been asked to search for the two on an urgent or emergency basis, put the names al-Mihdhar and al-Hazmi into the queue with other, more routine name searches it was running at the time. The FBI did not even canvass its own counterterrorism sources, among whom was the informant in San Diego who knew both of the men and had housed one of them. Had the Bureau simply sent a directive to all its field offices, telling them to check the two names with their sources, it is quite possible they would have come across vital information and been able to interdict the attack. Thus was lost the twelfth such opportunity.

(Also on August 29, one of the FBI agents in New York, frustrated at the languid efforts to overcome the criminal/intelligence Wall, wrote an e-mail to headquarters: "Someday someone will die—and wall or not— the public will not understand why we were not more effective and throwing every resource we had at certain problems.")

On September 5, an FBI agent determined that al-Mihdhar had not registered at any New York–area Marriott hotel. On September 10, the FBI's New York City field office prepared a request that the FBI office in Los Angeles check registration records at a number of hotels where they thought the two might have stayed and that it ask the airlines United and Lufthansa, on which al-Mihdhar and al-Hazmi had entered and left the United States, for travel and alias information.

Also on September 10, CNN would later report, the National Security Agency intercepted two cryptic communications from Afghanistan. One said "the big match" was scheduled for the next day. The other referred to the next day as "zero hour." Neither message was translated until September 12.[2] The leak of these messages during the course of the

Joint Inquiry would become a major disclosure, and ultimately trigger an FBI investigation of the Joint Inquiry.

In August, training completed, the terrorists began their final preparations for the attack. On August 1, Khalid al-Mihdhar and Hani Hanjour met an illegal immigrant from El Salvador named Luis Martinez-Flores in the parking lot of a 7-Eleven in Falls Church. Al-Mihdhar withdrew $100 from an ATM there and gave the cash to Mr. Martinez-Flores, who then rode with them to a nearby state government office and signed forms falsely attesting to their permanent residence in Virginia—all that is required to obtain a state identification card.

With official state identification cards in hand, the very next day Hanjour and al-Mihdhar were able to sign attestation forms for fellow hijackers Salim al-Hazmi and Majid Muqid at a different government office, in Arlington.

On August 4, at the international airport in Orlando, an immigration official named Jose Melendez-Perez was in the process of clearing passengers in the international baggage area of the Orlando airport when he noticed that one new arrival stood out. As Melendez-Perez said, "When I began to ask him routine questions, he gave me a dirty look." The arrival was Mohammed al-Qahtani. A Saudi national, al-Qahtani had arrived from London with no return ticket or hotel reservation. Melendez-Perez, thinking that someone lacking these basic travel documents was possibly a hit man because hired killers are rarely told where they are going or whom they are meeting, wanted to question him further, and told the other customs agents he needed an interpreter and a supervisor.

Many of the other agents thought Melendez-Perez was risking his career because, as he later told me in an interview, it is made clear to customs officials in their training that Saudis are different. He told me he was taught that a Saudi encountered in the course of duty is to be treated with deference and special respect. Supervisors feared that the initiation of enforcement action against a Saudi would get them fired. Still, Melendez-Perez's supervisor assented to the further questioning.

When they sat for the interview, Melendez-Perez noticed that al-Qahtani was impeccably dressed, and well built.

"From where will you be returning to Saudi Arabia?" Melendez-Perez asked.

"I don't know," al-Qahtani answered through the interpreter. "I am meeting a man with whom I have a business arrangement. When he picks me up we are going somewhere, but I don't know where. I'll be going back in six days."

Melendez-Perez was less concerned with the substance of the answer than he was with al-Qahtani's disposition. As Melendez-Perez would later say, it appeared as if al-Qahtani had been trained to handle interrogation. He grew increasingly defiant during their ninety-minute interview, and Melendez-Perez concluded that he should be barred from entry to the United States and returned to Saudi Arabia. Still, his fellow inspectors told him that he was "crazy" to deny entry to a Saudi.

Melendez-Perez's instincts proved correct. Waiting outside the airport for al-Qahtani's arrival was Mohammed Atta. It is not known whether al-Qahtani was intended to be the twentieth hijacker, or whether he was to be part of a different attack, but he was later captured by U.S. troops in Afghanistan and is now being held at Guantánamo Bay in Cuba.[3]

On August 13, Mohammed Atta flew from Washington to Las Vegas on a Boeing 757, his second surveillance flight. The same day, Hanjour and al-Hazmi flew from Dulles to Las Vegas via Los Angeles. Though it is unclear whether they met up with Atta or others in Las Vegas, FBI director Robert Mueller testified to the Joint Inquiry that al-Hazmi and Atta were now meeting regularly. Also interestingly, Hanjour and al-Hazmi returned from Las Vegas to Baltimore with a layover in Minneapolis, an unlikely itinerary except that Minnesota was where Zacarias Moussaoui had started flight lessons the day before. It is not known whether they met up with Moussaoui, but their pattern of travel was beginning to indicate that the terrorists were linking up with one another as they finalized their plans. Had intelligence officials been observing any one of the conspirators during this crucial period, they might have opened a window onto the plot.

On August 25, hijacker Ziad Jarrah, the man who would take the controls of United Airlines flight 93, the only flight not to hit a building, purchased a global positioning device.

Also in late August, al-Mihdhar and al-Hazmi signed on to Travelocity.com to order tickets for United flight 77 from Dulles. In placing those orders, they would have viewed a screen showing a seating diagram and allowing them to choose their seat assignments on the Boeing jet they would eventually hijack.

Meanwhile, in Paterson, New Jersey, Majid Muqid and Hani Hanjour went to the ATS travel agency to buy Hanjour a seat on American Airlines flight 77, but Visa declined to approve the transaction. The pair returned later and purchased the ticket with $1,842 in cash. Muqid, doing the talking for the two, asked that Hanjour be seated as far forward as possible. Hanjour was assigned first-class seat 1B near the cockpit.

On Saturday, September 8, Fayiz Ahmad, accompanied by another man, arrived at the Milner Hotel in Boston. There Ahmad subsisted on canned food and pizza until the morning of September 11, when he boarded United Airlines flight 175.

The next day, Marwan al-Shehhi, the man who would pilot United flight 175 into the South Tower of the World Trade Center, and Mohand al-Shehri, one of his muscle men, became the last of at least seven of the hijackers to leave the Panther Motel in Deerfield Beach, Florida. Curious about what the pair had left behind, the proprietor, Richard Surma, dug into the motel's dumpster and found a black tote bag containing aeronautical maps of the eastern United States, a protractor, a German-English dictionary, and three martial-arts books.[4]

Sometime in the morning of Monday, September 10, Mohammed Atta was in New York City. The FBI believes that Atta, too inexperienced to handle the airliners without use of a global positioning device, visited the World Trade Center to obtain coordinates for such a navigation device.[5]

During the day, Atta called Khalid Shaikh Mohammed, the operational planner of the attacks, in Afghanistan. Mohammed gave him final approval to launch the attacks.

Meanwhile, Hamza al-Ghamdi, another of the United flight 175 hijackers, checked into the Days Hotel in Brighton, Massachusetts. On his last night alive, the Days Hotel guest watched a pornographic movie on the in-house video system.

Atta also arrived in Boston that afternoon, then rented a blue Nissan sedan and headed to Maine. At around 6:00 that evening, Atta and Abd al-Aziz al-Umari checked into the Comfort Inn in South Portland, Maine.

Also on September 10, Osama bin Laden telephoned his mother in

Syria to tell her that he would be unable to meet her there because "something big" was going to happen that would end their communications for a long time.[6]

★

President Bush's administration had gotten off to an up-and-down start. He had passed a major tax cut, but lost Jim Jeffords and the Senate in the process. He had made progress on his education reforms, but stumbled badly in other areas. For example, on the environment he broke a campaign promise by announcing that the U.S. would not regulate carbon dioxide emissions, a main cause of global warming. He alienated our allies by abandoning the Kyoto agreement to fight climate change and caused an uproar at home by trying to kill regulations that would have lowered dangerously high levels of arsenic in our drinking water. On foreign policy, the Bush administration seemed simply to be withdrawing from treaties, and withdrawing from the world. And Bush's stewardship of the economy was beginning to raise doubts. By his sixth month in office, 75 percent of America's projected $5.6 trillion surplus was gone, and America had begun to hemorrhage jobs.

I didn't know George W. Bush well, but he and I had met years before—not surprisingly, at a baseball game. The person who brought us together was the late, great sportswriter Shirley Povich, of *The Washington Post.*

Shirley and I had a tradition of at least once a year going to see a game together; in 1992, the game we attended was between the Rangers and the Orioles at Baltimore's new Camden Yards. The then owner of the Orioles, Eli Jacobs, invited us to come up to his box. George W. Bush, an owner of the Rangers, was there. My first impression of him was that if central casting had wanted someone to play the principal owner of a Texas Major League Baseball team, Bush would have been the guy. In my memory, he was wearing a blue blazer, khaki pants, and a pair of cowboy boots.

He was not jovial, though—rather, he struck me as withdrawn, even standoffish. Despite the convivial atmosphere of the box, he made no effort to go around and introduce himself. Certainly, it wouldn't be fair to judge a man by one impression—he may simply have been intent on watching his team play—but he was clearly unlike his father, George H. W. Bush, who was always cordial.

By the summer of 2001, Bush was being berated in the press for not being a particularly hard worker, a chorus that intensified when he announced in July that he would be taking a thirty-one-day vacation beginning in August and lasting through Labor Day. *The Washington Post* calculated that by that date, President Bush would have spent 42 percent of his time in office either on vacation or on his way to vacation.

Scrambling to respond, the White House began calling President Bush's Crawford, Texas, residence the Western White House and billing his time away as a "Home to the Heartland Tour." In addition, his advisers scheduled some policy work for August, including a decision on whether to allow federal funds to be used to pay for embryonic stem cell research. The President also continued to be kept up-to-date on matters of national security through receipt of a President's Daily Brief, or PDB.

The PDB is one of the most highly classified documents in the U.S. government. Six days a week, it provides the President and a very limited number of his closest advisors the intelligence communities' assessment of the most significant events of the past twenty-four hours. Compiled by a small unit of intelligence analysts within the CIA's Directorate of Central Intelligence with input from other intelligence agencies, the PDB may be thought of as a daily top-secret newspaper reporting on current developments around the world as well as broader trends. The PDB itself is clipped into a loose-leaf notebook, and regardless of whether the President is in Washington or traveling, it is presented to him in person by a CIA official. The purpose of the PDB is not to make policy but to enhance the judgment of decision makers by providing them with information not available to the general public.

On August 6, 2001, the President's Daily Brief was presented to him by John McLaughlin, George Tenet's deputy at the CIA. One section bore the headline "Bin Laden Determined to Strike in U.S."

In the following pages, the brief stated,

> *Clandestine, foreign government, and media reports indicate Bin Ladin since 1997 has wanted to conduct terrorist attacks in the U.S.* Bin Ladin implied in US television interviews in 1997 and 1998 that his

followers would follow the example of World Trade Center bomber Ramzi Yousef and "bring the fighting to America."

After US missile strikes on his base in Afghanistan in 1998, Bin Ladin told followers he wanted to retaliate in Washington. . . .

. . . *Al-Qa'ida members—including some who are US citizens— have resided in or traveled to the US for years, and the group apparently maintains a support structure that could aid attacks.* (italics in original)

The second-to-last paragraph of the brief said, ominously: "FBI information since that time [1998] indicates patterns of suspicious activity in this country consistent with preparations for hijackings or other types of attacks, including recent surveillance of federal buildings in New York."

And, the PDB noted, "The FBI is conducting approximately 70 full field investigations throughout the US that it considers Bin Ladin–related."

Aircraft hijacking as a political tool dates back more than seven decades. The first reported airplane hijacking occurred in Peru in 1931, when a Pan American mail plane was taken over by a revolutionary political faction that wanted to use it to drop propaganda leaflets. The first hijacking of a U.S. plane occurred in 1961, when Puerto Rican–born Antuilo Ramierez Ortiz used a gun to force a National Airlines plane bound for Key West to reroute to Havana, where he was given asylum. In the 1970s and 1980s, hijacking was adopted as a means of terror and a bargaining tool by the Palestinian Liberation Organization, Hezbollah, and other anti-Israel terrorists. Between 1968 and 1970 alone, nearly 200 hijackings took place. "Traditionally," hijacked airplanes have been used for either economic or political purposes. If you belonged to a political group, some of whose members were incarcerated, and you wanted to free them, you might hijack an airplane of the incarcerating nation and use the passengers as collateral. Because of this history, the standard training for pilots was not to resist hijackers or try to deal with them in flight, but rather to acquiesce, to get the plane on the ground, and then to let professional negotiators take over.

That practice presupposed, of course, that the hijackers had an interest in living through the ordeal. And although, after September 11, members of the Bush administration would claim that nobody could have imagined that planes might be used as weapons, during the course of our inquiry we found that the possibility had been imagined, investigated, and interdicted more than once, and that in one case the Pentagon had been a target.

In December 1994, Algerian terrorists tried to fly an Air France plane into the Eiffel Tower. Their plan was foiled in Marseilles when a French SWAT team stormed the plane as the hijackers waited for it to be filled with three times as much fuel as was needed for a flight to Paris.

In 1995, Filipino authorities uncovered a plot known as Project Bojinka. The plot was to blow up eleven planes simultaneously in the air, crashing a twelfth into CIA headquarters and a thirteenth into the Pentagon. An informant, Abdul Hakim Murad, who had trained at a flight school in Norman, Oklahoma, told Filipino police that the plan was to have someone "board any American commercial aircraft pretending to be an ordinary passenger, then he will hijack the aircraft, control its cockpit and dive it into CIA headquarters. There will be no bomb or any explosive that he will use in its execution. It is a suicidal mission that he is very much willing to execute."

And in August 2001, the intelligence community obtained information regarding a plot to either bomb the U.S. embassy in Nairobi from an airplane or crash an airplane into it. The intelligence community also learned that two people who were reportedly acting on instructions from Osama bin Laden met in October 2000 to discuss this plot.

Whether the President was aware of any of this is unknown. What is known is that the President clearly did not take the August 6, 2001, PDB as an urgent matter. No directives were issued for further exploration or consideration of options, much less for any action.

President Bush would later claim that the PDB contained no "actionable intelligence": "There was not a time and place of an attack. It said Osama bin Laden had designs on America. Well, I knew that. What I wanted to know was, is there anything specifically going to take place in America that we needed to react to."[7]

However, the President could have taken any number of actions.

If he or a member of his staff had taken the not unreasonable step of notifying the Federal Aviation Administration of the possibility that aircraft might be hijacked, that agency could have been on higher alert for suspicious passengers. If someone had taken a further step and considered the fact that hijackings as al-Qaeda saw them were not the same as "traditional" hijackings, the FAA could have modified its protocols requiring pilots not to resist. The flight crews of the first three aircraft hijacked on September 11 apparently did not resist, and as a result they were killed and replaced with flight-trained hijackers. Not until the passengers and crew on the fourth aircraft became aware of what had happened to the three previous flights did they fight back.*

The PDB is not the only daily briefing prepared. Senior members of the intelligence community are also given a daily Senior Executive Intelligence Brief, or SEIB. The SEIB is circulated to roughly 300 people, including the Senate Intelligence Committee. As a general rule, the SEIB covers the same developments as the President's Daily Brief.

The August 6 SEIB, however, did not. While the PDB contained a number of paragraphs of contemporary intelligence at its conclusion, the SEIB, consistent with the PDB in all other respects, omitted those paragraphs. As a result, Congress and other senior intelligence officials were left ignorant of the chilling information about the potential attacks. These people were therefore unable to correct erroneous information or act on information that would have surely rung alarm bells had they seen it.

For example, the Federal Aviation Administration—which is a daily recipient of the SEIB—never read the words "F.B.I. information . . . indicates patterns of suspicious activity in this country consistent with preparations for hijackings or other types of attacks, including recent surveillance of federal buildings in New York."

Had its officials seen this sentence, the FAA might well have considered immediately alerting commercial airlines that airliners might be hijacked and used as weapons, not as tools of political or economic pressure. Increased surveillance of passengers—including the use of a national watch list for screening—would have kept at least three hijackers off their flights. But no one apart from the President and his closest advisors saw that sentence and therefore nobody acted on the information.

The assertion in the PDB that the FBI was engaged in seventy full

---

* At a June 2004 hearing of the Senate Commerce Committee, Patricia Friend, the president of the Association of Flight Attendants, testified that flight attendants are *still* being trained to cooperate with hijackers.

field investigations of the presence of al-Qaeda cells and operatives within the United States was, at the very least, a great stretching of the truth.

During the Joint Inquiry, we asked for the August 6 PDB and were denied official access by the White House. However, representatives of the intelligence community did accurately describe the PDB's content. When the White House learned that we had that information, the CIA refused to allow us to tell the American people what information had been given to the President, claiming that to do so would disclose classified information. We would be allowed to see the information, but not allowed to say that the President had seen it. This decision flew directly in the face of the rules regarding classification: protection of sources and methods is a reasonable rationale for keeping something classified, but protecting an individual from embarrassment is not. Only in 2004 was another commission, the independent 9/11 Commission, officially given the PDB. Even then, the White House delayed releasing the information to the public, declassifying it only after much of it had been previously released.

As of this writing, nobody has been held accountable for the misinformation in the PDB (the mythical seventy full field investigations), nor has anyone adequately worked to identify what the PDB described as al-Qaeda's United States–based *"support structure that could aid attacks."* Sadly, I would later find this failure to investigate al-Qaeda's American support network consistent with the administration's lack of curiosity about a potential terrorist infrastructure also within the United States supported by a foreign government.

★

In the early summer of 2001, I organized an oversight trip for members of the House and Senate Select Committees on Intelligence—we would visit key hot spots around the world and, I hoped, get valuable insights for the United States' intelligence efforts. Senator Jon Kyl of Arizona and Porter Goss, the Republican chairman of the House Permanent Select Committee on Intelligence, joined me on the trip, which would take us from the mountainous borderlands that were the realm of al-Qaeda to a high-tech surveillance center in northern England.

On our first stop, Vienna, Austria, we focused on the increasing sophistication of communications systems and the difficulty of monitoring them. Until the late 1990s the most advanced communication regularly used by terrorist organizations was the satellite telephone. For example, Osama bin Laden seemed to be under the impression that his signal from his satellite phone could not be traced or intercepted; because of his false sense of security, we were sometimes able to pick up his conversations.

However, before September 11, that information was accidentally leaked; bin Laden promptly stopped using his satellite phone and instead communicated in face-to-face meetings, by written messages, and through personal couriers.

We also visited London. Like Vienna, London has long been a crossroads for shadowy individuals and groups; England has been the repeated target of terrorist attacks, mostly by the Irish Republican Army. In part because of this experience, the British had been developing a strong and increasingly effective domestic intelligence system, MI-5, at a time when we in the United States thought that two oceans would do the job of protecting us. In a meeting at our embassy, members of MI-5 presented us with a slide show explaining how they assessed vulnerabilities, got information to the private sector, and informed those private-sector actors of when to pick up the phone and report things to them. It was an impressive display of cooperation between the government and the private sector.

We peppered the speakers with questions about how they go about protecting vulnerable infrastructure. MI-5 performs continual security audits, using the intelligence they are able to gather about the tools available to various terrorist groups and the targets they've shown a desire to attack. On the basis of that information, MI-5 makes recommendations to the targeted sectors. For example, if it's known that a terrorist group wants to target the chemical industry, MI-5 will inform the industry of the terrorists' intent and describe the most sophisticated attack the terrorists are likely to pull off, and then will give that industry a recommendation for protecting itself. A similar procedure applies to railroads, airports, seaports, and other vulnerable systems. It seems straightforward enough, yet, incredibly, no single entity in the United States in 2001 had a similar capability; no entity has it even now.

Our next visit was in northern England. In an idyllic landscape of small farm plots, stone walls, tailored hedgerows, and postcardlike villages, we came upon an incongruous sight, a white structure bristling with antennae, satellite dishes, and geodesic domes of varying sizes, looking like something out of *2001: A Space Odyssey*. The facility we were looking at was Menwith Hill. Run jointly by the United Kingdom's Government Communications Headquarters and America's NSA, Menwith Hill—"Big Ears"—is believed to be the largest signals intelligence center in the world.

Inside the facility were a series of wide-open spaces occupied by several hundred people grouped into mission-based clusters of roughly twenty-five people. Within each cluster, the workers were divided into two areas. The technicians tended the sophisticated monitors and computer systems that were collecting the information, and the analysts were prioritizing and analyzing the data. As we toured the complex, we saw analysts poring over data that was streaming in from thousands of miles away, including real-time observations of events that merited the observation of the Menwith Hill staff. To them, the significance of the pictures they were assembling was self-evident. Of course, it wasn't that obvious to us. A worker would punch a button and say, "Look at this!" We'd see a series of squiggly lines, which for the Menwith staff contained a world of information. Such information may well be more important than armaments in this new century.

Every stop was a learning experience, but for me the two most compelling experiences occurred at our second stop, Pakistan.

Upon arriving in Islamabad, we met with President Pervez Musharraf. The main topic of discussion was the United States' fear that continued hostilities between India and Pakistan would trigger a nuclear conflagration. Earlier, we had received intelligence information indicating that things could get out of control very quickly. Pakistan and India were neophytes; they had put immense national energy into developing the weapons, but had invested far less thought in the system safeguards that more mature nuclear nations had adopted.

To us, President Musharraf seemed to want to be more closely aligned with the West. Specifically, he wanted us to lift our sanctions, particularly those restricting access to United States replacement military parts. The president said the sanctions were also having a crippling effect on military-to-military contact. He told us that during his training to be a soldier, he had worked alongside Americans, and that that experience had opened his eyes to America. He feared that Pakistan's young soldiers now were being denied the opportunity not only to get the best training, but to have the experience with America that would make a new generation more favorably disposed to our country.

Since President Musharraf had come to power in a coup, we asked when he would be holding open elections. He reminded us that when he came to power, he didn't suspend civil rights or the judicial system, and—knowing that wasn't the answer we wanted to hear—allowed that "we will have an election, but I will retain an element of power."

Finally, we asked him for his help in going after Osama bin Laden. He told us about his difficulty in exerting any control on Pakistan's western border, but seemed to want to be helpful.

From Islamabad, we went to Kashmir to see the Line of Control between India and Pakistan and discuss the small-arms skirmishes occurring there, and the effect of those skirmishes on the two nations' tense nuclear standoff.

Following a helicopter trip, we took a small four-wheel-drive vehicle over treacherous mountain switchbacks to the Line of Control, where we were met by Pakistani military officers who showed us the bunkered firing positions that faced Indian soldiers on the other side of a narrow gorge. That gorge, separating two nuclear powers, couldn't have been more than a quarter-mile wide and 500 feet deep. In fact, the Indian soldiers, having figured out that we were Americans, had gotten up from their firing positions and were waving at us.

In Islamabad, we had encouraged President Musharraf to continue negotiations with India. At the Line of Control, we saw how negotiations took place on the front lines: they were shouted across the muddy river below.

From the Line of Control we returned to Islamabad; the next day saw another helicopter trip, to the mountainous borderland between Pakistan and Afghanistan. This area was considered to be extremely sympathetic to both the Taliban and al-Qaeda, and only loosely controlled by Pakistan. It was notable that the Pakistani military officers serving as our guides were taking greater security precautions than they had at the Line of Control. At the Line of Control, the threat of nuclear war and random shelling hung over everyone, but American individuals were as safe there as anybody else. Meanwhile, in these lands, our guides feared that we would be tempting targets.

The official boundary between Pakistan and Afghanistan, the Durand Line, runs a thousand miles and was drawn by the British envoy Sir Henry Mortimer Durand in 1893. It has largely been ignored ever since. The real boundary is a natural one, the mountains of the Safed Koh range. One side of the mountains is clearly in Afghanistan; the other side is clearly in Pakistan. But in a swath up to 100 miles wide in between are the Pashtun tribal areas, where national allegiance is a secondary concern and survival is the first.

The Khyber Pass is the most famous crossing point between the two countries, connecting Peshawar, Pakistan, with Jalalabad, Afghanistan. There are actually about 800 passes through the mountains, which helps explain why it is so difficult to fully control movement between the two countries, but the Khyber is the lowest and most accessible.

From above, the Khyber Pass looks a little like a football—a bowl-shaped area in the mountains with openings to the east and west, at the two narrow ends of the football. The pass itself is in Pakistan, but from where we were standing, we could see the border control point in Afghanistan just down the road.

What was once a caravan path through the pass is now a paved two-lane road; that afternoon, it was choked with truck traffic. Many of the trucks, marked with the distinctive blue "UN" of the United Nations, were bringing food aid and supplies to the people of Afghanistan, who were suffering tremendously from famine, drought, and the brutal reign of the Taliban.

In the hills rising to our north and south, and in the lands that lay beyond the border, was what we had come to see: the place that al-Qaeda now called home.

For hundreds of years, the region has been home to tribal skirmishes and blood feuds, battles of expansion and invasion, from the Moguls, to the Sikhs, to the British, to the Soviets. The traces of that violent history can be seen everywhere—in the fortified dwellings that many Pashtuns call home; in the rail line that was such an engineering feat to build and has now been left to decay; in the British-built prison sitting just down the hill from the fort where we sat to have our lunch; in the pockmarked hillsides that have absorbed mujahedin and Soviet munitions, and would, within months, absorb American ones as well.

The weather was warm and dry, rather like August in Denver, about 80 degrees during the day but dropping into the 50s at night.

On the south slope of the Khyber Pass, we visited a fort called the Michni Post, built of stone coated with something like adobe. The fort's most memorable feature wasn't its architecture, though, but was a story posted on its exterior wall. In 1842, an injured surgeon named William Brydon, the lone survivor of a massacre of British soldiers in Kabul, staggered into the Michni Post, having traveled 140 miles by foot. His story was a stark reminder of the distrust of outsiders this place bred.

Dr. Brydon's grim story reminded me of a poem Rudyard Kipling wrote about the place in 1890. "The Ballad of the King's Jest" has mostly been understood as a commentary on the fact that those who suffer the most horrible fates are not the open enemies of authority, but those who seek to pacify power with flattery and obsequiousness. It begins:

When spring-time flushes the desert grass,
Our kafilas wind through the Khyber Pass.
Lean are the camels but fat the frails,
Light are the purses but heavy the bales,
As the snowbound trade of the North comes down
*To the market-square of Peshawur town.**

The penultimate thought is ominous:

"Heart of my heart, is it meet or wise
To warn a King of his enemies?
We know what Heaven or Hell may bring,
But no man knoweth the mind of a King.
Of the grey-coat coming who can say?†
When the night is gathering all is grey.
Two things greater than all things are,
The first is Love, and the second War."

---

* Kafilas are caravans; frails are baskets for holding fruit; Peshawur is Peshawar, twenty miles east of where we were standing.
† The reference to "grey-coat coming" is a reference to a Russian invasion.

As I stood there, looking into Afghanistan, my gaze settled on a small village on the horizon. I was struck by how primitive and undeveloped the region looked. Even after millennia of habitation, it was desolate.

Notionally part of a nation-state, these were really tribal lands; it was hard to conceive that such a place—barren, arid, sparse, harsh, and forbidding—could harbor a significant enemy to any nation, let alone the United States of America.

Perhaps that was why people like Dick Cheney, Donald Rumsfeld, and Paul Wolfowitz would refuse to believe that out of Afghanistan could come an attack as coordinated and deadly as the one that occurred on September 11, 2001, or that nonstate terrorism is the biggest threat that the United States faces.

To this day, I am haunted by the fact that two weeks before the attacks of September 11, my colleagues and I—looking into a land that had seen battle after battle over the centuries—were also looking at the place that would become the focal point in the first great battle of the twenty-first century.

10

Zero Hour

A Day Unlike Any Other

Early on the morning of September 11, Khalid al-Mihdhar and Nawaf al-Hazmi left their Laurel, Maryland, hotel for Dulles Airport. On their way, they dropped a duffel bag at the neighboring mosque. The note attached to it read, "For the brothers."[1]

At 5:33 A.M., Mohammed Atta and al-Umari checked out of the Comfort Inn in South Portland, Maine. With computer bags slung over their shoulders, they arrived at Portland International Airport in time for the last-minute boarding of a 5:45 A.M. flight to Boston. In Boston, they made their connection to American Airlines flight 11 with minutes to spare. Atta's bag, however, did not.

It was later found to contain a four-page letter and will in Arabic, with fifteen directives on how Atta was to prepare for death on his "last night." The document includes Muslim prayers, as well as practical reminders to bring "knives, your will, IDs, your passport," and, finally, "to make sure that nobody is following you."

The document urges the hijackers to crave death and "be optimistic." At the same time, it starkly addresses their fear on the eve of their suicide mission: "Everybody hates death, fears death," according to a translation of highlights of the document. ". . . But only those, the believers who know the life after death and the reward after death, would be the ones who will be seeking death." A section entitled "Last Night" reads:

Remind yourself that in this night you will face many challenges. But you have to face them and understand it 100 percent. . . . Obey God, his messenger, and don't fight among yourself where you become weak, and stand fast, God will stand with those who stood fast. . . . You should pray, you should fast. You should ask God for guidance, you should ask God for help. . . . Continue to Pray throughout this night. Continue to recite the Koran. Purify your heart and clean it from all earthly matters. The time of fun and waste has gone. The time of judgment has arrived. Hence we need to utilize those few hours to ask God for forgiveness. You have to be convinced that those few hours that are left you in your life are very few. From there you will begin to live the happy life, the infinite paradise. Be optimistic. The prophet was always optimistic.[2]

At 7:45 A.M., Atta and al-Umari boarded American Airlines flight 11.

Before 7:59 A.M., Atta called Marwan al-Shehhi, who was aboard United Airlines flight 175. Both planes were sitting on the runway at Boston's Logan Airport.

At 8:13 A.M., the control tower had its last routine communication with flight 11. Within minutes, the four hijackers got up from their seats and stabbed the passenger Daniel Lewin, a former member of the Israeli Defense Forces. A flight attendant, Amy Sweeney, called an American Airlines ground manager and reported that two flight attendants had been stabbed and a passenger's throat had been slashed. She said the hijackers seemed to be of Middle Eastern descent, and she gave their seat numbers.

At approximately the same time, flight 175 took off from Logan Airport, and flight 77 departed from Dulles. Meanwhile, United Airlines flight 93, with Ziad Jarrah and three other hijackers aboard, was delayed on the runway at Newark. It would not take off until 8:42.

Aboard flight 11, pilot John Ogonowski activated a "talk-back" device enabling Boston controllers to hear a hijacker on the flight set, saying, "We have some planes. Just stay quiet and you will be okay. We are returning to the airport."

A controller responded, "Who's trying to call me?" The hijacker was heard to say, "Everything will be okay. If you try to make any moves you'll endanger yourself and the airplane. Just stay quiet."

At 8:28 A.M., Boston flight control radar saw flight 11 making an unplanned 100-degree turn south. Five minutes later, flight controllers heard a hijacker on flight 11 say to the passengers, "Nobody move, please, we are going back to the airport. Don't try and make any stupid moves."

At 8:40 A.M., Boston flight control notified the North American Aerospace Defense Command (NORAD) that flight 11 had been hijacked.

Two minutes later, United Airlines flight 93 took off from Newark International Airport, bound for San Francisco.

All four flights were in the air, and three were under the control of the hijackers.

★

In Washington, D.C., September 11 dawned blue and cloudless.

As I walked to work in the Senate from my Capitol Hill town house, I picked up *The Washington Post*. The *Post* is read by many Washingtonians, of course, and I also have a personal connection to the paper. My half-brother, Phil, became publisher of the *Post* at the request of his father-in-law, Eugene Meyer, in 1946, and helped transform the paper from one that was respected but financially shaky into a newspaper that came to play a vital role in politics and civic affairs in Washington. After Phil's death in 1963, his widow, Katharine, became the publisher and helped guide the *Post* to greatness.

The news that morning was not good for the President. The lead story reported the Environmental Protection Agency's advocacy of a regulation tightening the standard for the amount of arsenic permitted in America's drinking water. In this the EPA was partially reversing an earlier decision for which the President had caught hell. A story directly below that featured the results of a *Washington Post*–ABC News national survey showing that 57 percent of Americans supported reducing the size of the President's recently passed tax cut in order to handle the shrinking surplus. Less than half of those polled approved of President Bush's handling of the economy, with 81 percent saying that Bush's tax cut had either hurt the economy or done nothing. The poll also showed that more Americans now trusted the Democrats in Congress to deal with the economy.

In addition, an editorial declared, "when it comes to foreign policy, we have a tongue-tied administration. After almost eight months in office, neither President Bush nor Secretary of State Colin Powell has made any comprehensive statement on foreign policy. It is hard to think of another administration that has done so little to explain what it wants to do in foreign policy." Three quarters of a year into his term, President Bush was foundering.

★

My first meeting of the day was in the House Intelligence Committee's conference room. The committee is housed on the east side of the fourth floor of the Capitol, just under the roof. The ceilings in the conference rooms and the offices are low—less than eight feet—adding a touch of claustrophobia to the clandestine purposes of these suites. Occupying the former offices of the Joint Committee on Atomic Energy, one of the most secretive and powerful committees ever to exist in Congress (it was disbanded in 1977), the rooms are designated a sensitive compartmented information facility (SCIF). Sensitive compartmented information (SCI) is classified information either about, or obtained from, sources, methods, or analytical processes so sensitive that the information must be handled only by people with the highest security clearances and only in a secure environment. A SCIF is that secure environment—a specially designed facility in which the information can be used, stored, processed, or discussed. SCIFs must be certified as meeting dozens of stringent security requirements: for instance, walls must be of a certain thickness and construction; there must be an alarm system that will summon a response force within minutes; the air ducts must be secured and sound-baffled; the number of entrances and exits must be limited;

and the facility must have access-controlled doors that are either metal or solid wood clad with metal.

Because of the soundproofing and the nearly airtight doors, when you enter a SCIF it feels as if you've entered a hushed environment. The everyday noise of the outside world is notable for its absence. It is almost as if the gravity of the information contained and the business transacted there permeates the air.

This is particularly true of the House Intelligence Committee's conference room, with its deep brown paneling, lithographs from the Revolutionary and Civil Wars, and a five-by-twelve-foot mahogany conference table.

To get there, you ascend a narrow staircase, where an electronic eye beams an image of you to a guard on duty inside the door. Upon entering, you walk down a narrow hallway decorated with World War II propaganda posters urging discretion—from the famous "Loose Lips Might Sink Ships," to an image of a soldier drowning under the caption "Someone Talked," to a picture of Uncle Sam with his finger to his lips, to one poster featuring a 1776 quote from George Washington that reads, "There is one evil I dread, and this is, their spies. I could wish, therefore, that the most attentive watch be kept."

My meeting there that morning was the breakfast with General Mahmood Ahmed of ISI, the Pakistani intelligence service, that I described in the introduction to this book, and that broke up when we got word of the attack. I ran down three flights of stairs to my hideaway office on the first floor of the Capitol. With me were Bob Filippone, my national security advisor, and Al Cumming, the staff director on the Intelligence Committee.

On that Tuesday morning, my then chief of staff, Buddy Shorstein; my two deputy chiefs of staff, Buddy Menn and Mark Block; my communications director, Paul Anderson; my legislative director, Bryant Hall; my scheduler, Sage Newman; and my operations director, John Provenzano, all having seen the news, were already at the hideaway, awaiting our morning meeting.

This office is near the part of the Capitol called the Crypt, a room where the forty Doric columns stand, supporting the Capitol's nine-ton iron dome. The office windows look out over the eastern front lawn of the Capitol.

My staffers were gathered in front of the television, watching smoke pour from the crippled buildings.

Still not having quite grasped what was happening in New York, I decided that the best course of action was to try to get down to business. I asked Bob Filippone, who was standing closest to the phone, to call the Senate cloakroom to find out what votes would be taking place that day.

Bob later told me that the woman who answered the phone said, "Votes? We're evacuating." At which point Bob turned around and looked out the window to see Capitol Police officers running across the lawn, away from the building. We had also begun to hear a commotion in the halls.

Before Bob could say anything, Buddy Menn spoke up, saying, "Senator, given the fact that it looks like everyone is fleeing the building, I think whatever business we have can wait."

At that moment, there was a pounding on the doors. It was the Capitol Police, yelling at us to evacuate.

We streamed out of the room into a crush of people fleeing the building. The police were shouting, "There's a plane coming for the Capitol, run, get out, you've got to run!"

Though there are a number of building exits on that floor, including one just feet from my office, the police were urging people into the basement. This didn't seem so unreasonable: the Capitol basement is connected by a series of tunnels to the three Senate office buildings, so maybe we could get back to my office in the Hart Building. A couple of my staffers didn't think this was a good idea; they turned around to the building exit, but I was swept downstairs, into the tunnels.

The pandemonium had separated me from all of my staff but Paul Anderson and John Provenzano, who flanked me as we ran through the low-ceilinged subterranean hallway. We and many of the others fleeing headed for the Senate subway, which ferries members from the office building to the Capitol, but a Capitol Police officer told us that we couldn't use the tunnels to get back to the office buildings.

The crowd, being told that it had to get out because there was a plane bearing down on the building, but that the exit route they had chosen was barred, was scared and frustrated. We doubled back into another hallway, and, finding a set of stairs back up to the Capitol's ground floor, managed to get outside through an exit directly underneath the ceremonial stairs that lead up to the Senate chamber.

Outside, too, confusion reigned. With no serious evacuation plans in place, the entire Capitol—members of Congress and staff, the press, and visitors alike—had emptied onto the East Lawn, the grassy expanse between the Capitol and the Supreme Court.* People were punching their cell phones, vainly trying to get through to friends and families.

No sooner had we gotten out to the lawn than we heard a low rumble overhead, which caused screams and fearful looks skyward. Some thought it was another attack. We later realized that the sound was the sonic boom from the fighter jets that had been scrambled from Falmouth, Massachusetts, and Langley Air Force Base in Virginia. Those planes had been dispatched to the World Trade Center, and then were rerouted to the skies over Washington. At each location, they showed up too late to prevent the hijacked planes from hitting their targets.

Rumors were running rampant outside. We heard, incorrectly, that a bomb had gone off at the State Department. We also heard, but didn't know whether to believe, that the Pentagon had been hit. Within minutes, we were able to see the smoke from across the river, and had to assume that those reports were true.

Nawaf al-Hazmi and Khalid al-Mihdhar, whose mysterious, circuitous, destructive journey to America began on January 15, 2000, ended that journey at 9:37:30 a.m. on September 11, 2001, when flight 77 from Dulles smashed into the southwest side of the Pentagon.

As smoke rose from the Pentagon, Senator John Breaux of Louisiana asked me where I was planning on going and whether I had somewhere to meet up with staff. I told him I didn't. He responded, "Well, this is probably the stupidest place we could be."

He was right. Instead of having hundreds of people in a secure but potentially threatened building, we now had hundreds of people in a nonsecure and equally threatened public space.

At that point, I decided to head back to my town house, and tried to put out the word that my whole staff was welcome to join me there. About ten of them ultimately did. As we crossed First Street, U.S.

---

* The East Lawn is now a construction site, soon to be home to the new Capitol Visitor Center.

Supreme Court Police held us up while two black Suburbans whipped by. The Supreme Court was being evacuated.

We arrived at the town house at 10:00 A.M.

At first, both Buddy Menn and John Provenzano wondered whether we should be at my house at all. I don't make much of a secret of where I live, and they were worried that I could be a target. (Their fear that my address was known was humorously confirmed that afternoon, when Jennifer Sergent, a reporter from Scripps Howard News Service, showed up at my door to talk to me.) Even if I were not an individual target, Buddy and John pointed out, my house is close to both the Capitol and the Supreme Court; it could also be an unintended target were there to be another plane attack. Suzanne, the second youngest of my four daughters, lives in Great Falls, Virginia, and John recommended we go there—the same recommendation my wife, Adele, would make when I was finally able to get her on the phone.

At that point, however, we were seeing images of choked roads and bridges leaving Washington, and so the impossibility of getting there, combined with my desire to stay in the place where I was comfortable, and which, importantly, had a secure phone line, led me to decide that it would be best to stay put.

Whereas cell phones were working only sporadically, land lines were functioning better, so almost immediately we began working the phones, trying to get information about what was happening. Senators and their staffs began calling me, assuming that the chairman of the Intelligence Committee would have more information than they did.

The first thing I did was try to get messages to my wife and four daughters that I was safe. Adele had been planning to fly to Washington that morning to join me for a "Texas-style barbecue" at the White House. By the time I reached her, at our home in Miami Lakes, Florida, she had seen the news and wasn't even attempting to get to the airport.

Next I put in a call to George Tenet, trying to find out what was happening and how to relay that information to the Senate. He and I managed to connect late in the morning, at which point he told me that the CIA didn't know much yet.

Al Cumming, the staff director on the Intelligence Committee, came over and spent the day keeping in touch with various intelligence agencies and officials.

Meanwhile, senators were clamoring for information. The evacuation of the Capitol was unplanned, unprecedented, and chaotic, and now these leaders, people used to being briefed constantly, were scattered around the city, left worried and out of touch. This was particularly true for New York's senators, Charles Schumer and Hillary Clinton, because their state had suffered the most severe attack. Senator Schumer's chief of staff soon phoned, and a member of Senator Clinton's staff came knocking on my door in person. The news media, too, were desperate for official information, especially because President Bush, after taking off from Florida, had basically disappeared. But I still knew hardly more than anyone else.

Everyone speculated about who might be behind the attacks. In the course of the afternoon, I heard people suggest that Palestinians, Hezbollah, or Cuban terrorists were responsible. With the advantage of my fresh memories of the Khyber Pass, and with General Ahmed having just described to us the mentality of the Taliban and al-Qaeda, I came early to the judgment that this looked like an al-Qaeda operation. I wasn't the only one. Orrin Hatch, of Utah, said on television that he suspected Osama bin Laden was behind the attacks.

I wasn't confident enough of my suspicions to express them publicly. But much potentially incorrect information was being promulgated, and the President was absent. The chaos was compounded by the fact that Senators Daschle, Lott, Reid, and Nickles, as well as House Speaker Dennis Hastert, had been evacuated. Even my counterpart in the House, Porter Goss, had been evacuated shortly after Hastert at the Speaker's request. Everybody in the chain of command—both executive and legislative—had scattered. I felt that I had a duty to calm, inform, and restrain the rampant speculation that was already erupting.

That afternoon, there was a meeting at the Capitol Police headquarters. On the seventh floor of the headquarters, I found the Senate's sergeant-at-arms, Al Lenhardt, who was the Senate's chief security officer (and who had only been on the job for about a week). Together we found a secure phone, where I placed another call to DCI Tenet. He still knew little about the attacks. I brought up the idea of opening the Capitol the next day, something that I thought would be symbolically important. "George, do we have any reason to believe that this threat is a continuing one?"

No, Tenet replied; he believed that we had seen all we were going to see.

After that call, I walked into the senators' meeting. Senators Daschle and Lott were "attending" through a conference call to the secure location where they had been evacuated. The mood was tense. A number of senators told Daschle and Lott that they had to get back to Washington, especially with the President absent. The two told us that, now that every commercial or private plane in American airspace had been accounted for and grounded, they would fly back to the Capitol that evening.

I then presented what I knew about the continuing nature of the threat and reported that we'd probably be able to open the Capitol the next day. Some in the room wanted a display that evening, to demonstrate that our democracy hadn't been shut down. There was some talk of everyone going to the steps of the Capitol in a show of unity, an act the Capitol Police thought was ill-advised. It was decided that just the four House and Senate leaders would go, so as to make a symbolic statement without creating a security risk.

Apparently, after I left the meeting and Senators Daschle and Lott returned to Washington, many of the House members decided they wanted to participate in a show of resolve on the Capitol steps. Senator Daschle convinced a number of senators not to join him because he had been told the House members weren't joining Speaker Hastert. When the Senate members saw the House members walking over to the Capitol steps, many of them joined in as well.

I was waiting to give a television interview when I saw the moving footage of many of my colleagues bursting into a spontaneous rendition of "God Bless America." That lovely moment showed the sense of unity and common purpose that would fuel our work in the days ahead.

Later that evening, I drove downtown for a final interview, this one with CBS News. After that was finished, I called Adele and my daughters one last time and went to bed. It was midnight. September 11 had become September 12. One of the worst days in American history was over.

Part II

★

AFTER

11

The Aftermath

Never in the nation's history had such an attack within the continental United States taken place.

As we saw the smoking wreckage of the Twin Towers and the west side of the Pentagon, the scope of the tragedy began to sink in; for many, it became more personal, as well.

One of the 125 people who died in the Pentagon was Terrence Michael Lynch, 48, a former Senate Intelligence Committee staff member. Terry had left government service in 1999 to become a consultant, and was in a meeting at the Pentagon when the plane hit.

We describe the Senate as a family; the realization that Terry had died in the attack made us realize that the attack had struck close to home, not only physically but emotionally as well. At Terry's memorial service at Christ Church in Alexandria, Virginia, I was particularly struck by a reading from the book of Revelation:

And God shall wipe away all tears from their eyes;
and there shall be no more death, neither sorrow, nor crying,
neither shall there be any more pain;
for the former things are passed away (Rev.: 21:4)

The tragedy brought out a massive outpouring of sympathy from around the world, with candlelight vigils, flowers laid outside our embassies, and the French newspaper *Le Monde* even declaring in an editorial, "We are all Americans."

The attacks brought with them, too, the realization that two oceans were not enough to separate us from the horror we saw so often in other parts of the world. All of a sudden, an unattended bag sitting on a park bench was a threat, a crowded outdoor event seemed an invitation to danger, a low-flying plane was no longer dismissed with nonchalance. Our long-held "splendid isolation" was gone forever. In one fateful day, all of America had been awakened to danger. The question was how we'd be called to action.

By the time I arrived for work on September 12, the Capitol building, "the people's house," had been closed to the public and was beginning to resemble an armed fortress, with heavily armed guards stationed around its perimeter.

The Congress, normally slow to act, recognized that urgent action was required: New York and the Pentagon would need funds to rebuild and recover, the President would need new powers to fight terror, we would have to get our airlines flying again, we'd have to find out exactly who had attacked us, and we'd have to authorize the President to use force against those people, groups, or nations. It's impossible to overstate the sense of unity and common purpose we felt. Every issue that had divided us as people and as parties seemed trivial in comparison with what we were now facing.

By the evening of September 12, the Bush administration sent the Senate leadership a draft of the language it wanted in a resolution authorizing the President to use force against the perpetrators of the attacks. The draft included this clause:

Resolved by the Senate and the House of Representatives of the United States of America in Congress assembled,

That the President is authorized to use all necessary and appropriate force against those nations, organizations, or persons he determines planned, authorized, harbored, committed, or aided in
the planning or commission of the attacks against the United States
that occurred on September 11, 2001, and to deter and preempt any
related future acts of terrorism or aggression against the United
States.

Despite our overriding feeling that whatever the President requested, he should get, the clause "and to deter and preempt any related
future acts of terrorism" gave a number of us pause. This was asking
Congress to give the Bush administration (and every future administration, for that matter) a blank check to go to war with anyone it deemed
capable of carrying out an attack.

Was this an overstatement born of the heat of the moment, or a delib-
erate overreach in the hopes that Congress's instant unity and heated desire to give the President the tools he needed could be leveraged to
achieve a longer-term goal? Time has shown that the latter may be true;
still, concerns voiced by both Senators Robert Byrd and Tom Daschle
were enough to get the language edited. Instead, we granted the President the authority to use force against those nations, organizations, and
persons that were learned to be connected to the tragedy of September 11. In making that change, we made clear that al-Qaeda and those
who harbored and helped it were not only our bull's-eye, they were the
totality of the target. By Friday, September 14, we had passed the "use of
force" resolution.

In short order, we had also authorized billions of dollars in aid to help
New York and other affected areas recover and begin to rebuild, and
provided emergency aid to keep the airlines in business.

On September 13, as we were working out the draft language of the
joint resolution authorizing the President to use force against those responsible for September 11, the President was holding a meeting with
Saudi Arabia's ambassador to the United States, Prince Bandar bin Sul-
tan bin Abdulaziz, more commonly called Prince Bandar. Bandar had
been informed the night before by a high-ranking CIA official that fifteen of the nineteen hijackers were Saudis, and that it looked increasingly as if Osama bin Laden, an exiled Saudi, might have been its

mastermind. Presumably, this information created a difficult situation for both Prince Bandar and President Bush. Prince Bandar, a scion of the Saudi royal family, had to maintain a relationship with America—a country that purchased hundreds of billions of dollars in Saudi oil and supplied Saudi Arabia with hundreds of billions of dollars of weaponry—although many of the people his family ruled saw America as a mortal enemy.* President Bush owed a debt to a family that had been an ally in the 1991 Gulf War, funneled millions of dollars to his own family through an investment group, and, stunningly, would reportedly propose, more than a year later, to lower the price of oil to "prime the U.S. economy for 2004."[1]

Neither the President nor Prince Bandar has disclosed what was discussed in that meeting. But later that day, something strange began to happen. Although the FAA had ordered all private flights grounded, a number of planes began flying to collect Saudi nationals from various parts of the United States. For example, a ten-passenger Learjet picked up three young Saudi men in Tampa and flew them to Lexington, Kentucky, where a Boeing 747 was waiting for some Saudi horse-racing enthusiasts. (For nearly three years, the White House and other agencies insisted that these flights never took place, confirming their existence only under investigation by the independent 9/11 Commission.)[2]

By September 19, more than 140 Saudis—including several members of the bin Laden family—had been flown out of the United States. Certainly, the majority of the travelers were innocent of any crime. However, at least one is thought to have had terrorist ties, and even the innocent members of bin Laden's family could probably have provided some insight into his funding and operations. The FBI interviewed none of them.

The FBI claims that it did not grant permission for those planes and their passengers to leave. Prince Bandar claims otherwise. Richard Clarke, then the White House's counterterrorism czar, told me that he was approached by someone in the White House seeking approval for the departures. He did not remember who made the request, and he allowed that he was understanding of it, having had to evacuate Americans from other countries in times of crisis. But first, he wanted the FBI

---

* Saudi Arabia has 262 billion barrels in proven oil reserves and was exporting 8 million barrels a day in 2001. Nearly a quarter of America's oil comes from Saudi Arabia, a situation that I believe gives another country far too much control over America's national security and economy.

to review a list of passengers and make sure that none of them were people of interest. Though the FBI claims it did not authorize the flight, it also claims that none of the passengers were needed for interviews, so the flights were allowed to leave. The remaining question is where in the White House the request originated, and how. The only people who know what was discussed in their meeting on that day are George W. Bush and Prince Bandar.

★

Long before the September 11 attacks, I had noted with interest the work of the independent commissions that reviewed the issue of terrorism, especially the U.S. Commission on National Security/21st Century, headed by former senators Gary Hart and Warren Rudman. The so-called Hart-Rudman Commission was put together in 1998 by then President Bill Clinton and then House Speaker Newt Gingrich, of Georgia, to make sweeping strategic recommendations for U.S. security in the new century.

After two and a half years of study, the commission concluded that "the combination of unconventional weapons proliferation with the persistence of international terrorism will end the relative invulnerability of the U.S. homeland to catastrophic attack." A direct attack against American citizens on American soil was likely during the next quarter century, the commission said, and Americans would likely die on American soil, possibly in large numbers.

The commission also unanimously approved fifty recommendations, including the formation of a Cabinet-level office to combat terrorism. According to the commission's executive summary, which was released on January 31, 2001, the proposed National Homeland Security Agency would have "responsibility for planning, coordinating, and integrating various U.S. government activities involved in homeland security."

Many of these recommendations conformed to a report released in June 2000 by the National Commission on Terrorism, chaired by Ambassador Paul Bremer, who would later be named to head the Coalition Provisional Authority in Iraq. The Bremer Commission had looked into terrorism specifically and called for a number of changes in our laws and our methods of defense. It advised targeting states that support terrorism (Afghanistan, Iran, Syria, and North Korea were mentioned specifically; Iraq was not), cutting off terrorist funding, and reforming our government agencies to ensure that there is a comprehensive American antiterror plan.

Unlike most blue-ribbon panels, which are appointed to deal with politically difficult or unpalatable issues and whose recommendations often wither when presented to an apathetic White House and Congress, these two commissions had a big impact in Congress. I, along with my colleagues Jon Kyl and Dianne Feinstein, began working on legislation based on their reports.

Upon entering office, President Bush didn't seem to feel a similar sense of urgency in converting these well-examined recommendations into policy. Rather than embrace the recommendations, he announced in May that he would have Vice President Cheney study the potential problem of domestic terrorism, and in the meantime responsibility for the issue would be handed to the Federal Emergency Management Agency (FEMA)—something the Hart-Rudman report specifically recommended against.

By the late summer, my staff had worked the recommendations of Hart-Rudman and Bremer into legislation that was finished but languishing on September 11.*

On September 20, the President delivered a stirring address to a joint session of Congress. I was particularly heartened to hear him say that our antiterror efforts needed to be coordinated at the highest level and would reach beyond al-Qaeda. "Our war on terror begins with al-Qaeda, but it does not end there. It will not end until every terrorist group of global reach has been found, stopped, and defeated."

The next day, I introduced two bills. The first was a series of measures to enhance our ability to infiltrate terrorist cells, to collect information necessary to guarantee America's security, and to better share information by breaking down some of the walls that separated intelligence from law enforcement.

---

* Also languishing on September 11 was my bill to increase security at America's seaports, something I had been pursuing since 1997, when a visit to Port Manatee in Florida opened my eyes to the fact that millions of cargo containers were entering the United States uninspected and unsecured upon arrival. That bill passed in December 2001, but it has since been left underfunded and largely ignored by the Bush administration.

The second bill was to have the President appoint, and the Senate confirm, a director of a newly created National Office for Combating Terrorism, whose purpose would be to make sure that all federal agencies were pursuing a common set of antiterror objectives.

While the President had called the night before for the creation—by executive order—of a White House staff position addressing homeland defense, I felt that unless we went a step further and made that position a statutory one, with genuine authority to plan and direct the war on terror, and control programs, budgets, and personnel in that plan's execution, whoever held the office (and the President had stated that it would be Governor Tom Ridge of Pennsylvania) would be little more than a glorified advisor. Senator Joe Lieberman wanted to go a step further yet, creating a National Department of Homeland Security. I was not comfortable that we knew enough about the enemy we were facing to cast our response in stone and create a new department. I felt that a statutory office would provide greater focus until we fully understood how best to change our security posture.

Our proposals—each going beyond what the President wanted—prompted one of my post–September 11 White House meetings, on October 24.

At that meeting, the President made it immediately clear that he wasn't interested in either one of our proposals, that he thought an "assistant to the President," with the President's support, would be able to do whatever was necessary with respect to counterterrorism or homeland security. President Bush's attitude was somewhere between dismissive and distracted—so much so that at one point Senator Lieberman turned his head toward me and rolled his eyes. Given the President's strong language in his speech to Congress about the need for greater coordination, this was not the considered engagement I had expected. Regrettably, the President maintained his position until the summer of 2002, when, under intense public pressure, he became an advocate of a Department of Homeland Security. The President's procrastination over those eight months gave us the worst of both worlds—inadequate immediate enhancement of the defense of America from subsequent attacks, and no focus or thoughtful analysis of homeland security for what would surely be a protracted war on terror.

I was also surprised to see that the President seemed much changed since the first meeting I had had with him as President. In that meeting, which occurred shortly after he took office, he had invited a number of centrist Democrats, mainly members of the Senate Finance Committee, to the White House so that he could try to sell us on his tax plan. At the time, I was struck by how informed, animated, and convincing he was.

After the terrorist attacks, he seemed subdued, withdrawn, and uncertain. Despite the commanding display he had put on just days earlier, before a joint session of Congress, President Bush now was nearly silent. On questions directed to him, he deferred to Dick Cheney and National Security Advisor Condoleezza Rice.

I wasn't sure whether he was tired or felt out of his depth, but this was a sea change from the President Bush who earlier had been thrusting, parrying, and ultimately convincing a number of centrist Democrats to join him on the issue of tax cuts.

Despite President Bush's opposition to a department—or even a Senate-confirmed director—of homeland security, the meeting was amicable and suffused with a sense that we were working together.

Though in retrospect the President's refusal to consider our proposals and his overreaching attempt to gain extraordinarily broad authority to use force seem somewhat suspicious, the truth is that we all felt that whatever disagreements we were having were minor when set against the challenges America now faced. A common comparison was to America after Pearl Harbor.

The legislative efforts I have just described were not the only ones being made. Also in the works was an effort to reinterpret—and in some cases rewrite—a number of our antiterror laws that had become grossly outdated. As Orrin Hatch put it, "Laws written in the age of rotary phones were insufficient to deal with the complexities of information sharing and communication over cell phones and the Internet."[3]

Interestingly, the first proposals released by Attorney General John Ashcroft for what would later become the USA Patriot Act, on September 23, seemed to have been written largely by the criminal division at the Department of Justice. The draft included a provision enabling the federal government to detain indefinitely any noncitizen suspected to have a connection to terrorists, with no requirement that formal charges be brought or proven.

It allowed the unrestricted sharing of grand jury and eavesdropping data throughout the government. It permitted Internet service providers and employers to unilaterally allow the FBI to tap e-mail. While the proposals that received the most attention were the controversial ones, I was more concerned with what was *missing* from the bill, namely the recognition that there was a role for the intelligence community in fighting terrorism. In fact, it seemed that intelligence community hadn't been consulted at all.

We decided to bring to the negotiations language mandating that intelligence information that's found in a criminal case must be shared with the intelligence community. We had to wade right into the negotiations. The future Patriot Act was not moving through the slow, stately, committee process of hearings and amendments we learned about in our eleventh-grade civics book. Everyone who had something to contribute to the bill was working out of the Judiciary Committee's hearing room in the Dirksen Senate Office Building. It looked more like the floor of the New York Stock Exchange than it did the legislative process, with ten different clusters of people negotiating ten different parts of the bill, furiously scribbling amendments on sheets of loose-leaf paper. In one corner were the folks working on the immigration sections, in another were the people working on the financial crimes section.

And in our corner were the intelligence folks, who had been told for years by both the Justice Department and the intelligence community that everything was fine, that the information sharing was going great, that their agencies were working "cheek by jowl." Now those claims rang hollow. Still, it was hard to get anybody to embrace the concept of true information sharing. The Justice Department saw terrorism as a criminal problem; as prosecutors of terrorist crimes, they didn't want to share anything with anybody. The Department of Justice was concerned about any sharing that would affect the evidentiary value of information the FBI had unearthed. Meanwhile, the intelligence community didn't want to have to open up more of its workings to the Justice Department. The intelligence professionals seemed to feel that too much collegiality could risk public disclosure of sources and methods of intelligence collection. In that room, we were seeing a microcosm of the very problem we were trying to solve.

In the end, we were able to put into law the idea that all intelligence information found in a criminal case must be shared with intelligence officials—and we used almost exactly the language of the bill I had introduced on September 21. That idea became the Title IX provision of the USA Patriot Act. In typical Washington fashion, that section, which encountered so much resistance, is now pointed to as one of the signature accomplishments of the act.

The Patriot Act also signaled the beginning of a partisan fracture. It began when Attorney General Ashcroft demanded on September 17 that the bill be passed by September 21, although he hadn't given us any of his legislative language and wouldn't for an additional two days. The split was exacerbated when Ashcroft claimed that if the bill were not passed immediately, the responsibility for more attacks would rest at the feet of Democrats.

That seemed unhelpful and unnecessary. The truth is that we were moving with extraordinary speed: the Patriot Act was passed on October 25—forty-four days after September 11—and signed into law the next day.

At that time, a number of things were being said about the attacks. The first was that it was a surprise, a bolt from the blue. The second was that no one could have imagined such an attack carried out in such a manner. The third, that since no one could have envisaged the use of commercial aircraft as a weapon of mass destruction, no one could be held accountable. The forth was that for all of the devastation, the attack was basically quite simple, requiring nineteen people and a sum of money estimated at between $175,000 and $250,000.

I believed that all of these statements—which were fast on their way to becoming truisms—were wrong.

First, the attack was not a bolt from the blue. Our intelligence agencies had been picking up increased "chatter" about an impending terrorist attack; this rise in threat activity elicited President Bush's fateful August 6 briefing.

Second, we had been able to imagine such an attack. We had known that the World Trade Center was a terrorist target ever since the World Trade Center bombing in 1993, and over the course of the Joint Inquiry we collected at least twelve instances in which our intelligence officials had found information outlining a terrorist desire to use planes as weapons.

Third, the idea that nobody should be held responsible for this "unimaginable" act was particularly frustrating to me. President Bush voiced this attitude when he said, "What I wanted to know was, is there anything specifically going to take place in America that we needed to react to."[4] Here he revealed a stunning lack of understanding about how both intelligence and leadership work. Intelligence is very hard and frequently dangerous work. We all wish intelligence could tell us exactly what is going to happen, when, and where. But really what intelligence can do is present an accurate picture of the threats, targets, and methods. It is incumbent on the consumer of intelligence, be it a congressional staffer or the President, to make policy judgments and recommendations based on that intelligence. I have identified twelve instances prior to September 11 in which the plot could have been interdicted. That it wasn't is, by definition, a failure. It amazes me to this day that no one— not one single person—has been held accountable for the intelligence and other lapses that contributed to the failure to interdict the attack. Neither has any superbly competent performance, such as that of Kenneth Williams in Arizona, been specifically recognized. Once you realize that the attacks of September 11 were very much imaginable, it is important that people be held accountable. None have been.

As for the attack's complexity, it is true that September 11 was underwritten at a relatively small cost, less than a quarter of a million dollars. That misses the point. A central question of September 11 is whether the nineteen terrorists acted in a vacuum, or whether they were assisted by an infrastructure of terrorism. In the events leading up to September 11, such as the facilitation of al-Hazmi and al-Mihdhar's lives in San Diego, I find a pattern of substantial logistical, personnel, and skills development and financial support consistent with what the President was told in his fateful August 6 briefing. I further suspect that the pattern of such support was more pervasive than is currently known or acknowledged.

It is also not true that the plot was simple. In testimony before a closed session of the Joint Inquiry (which was later declassified), George Tenet noted that the plot was actually quite professional. The hijackers entered the United States at staggered intervals, from different countries, and through different cities. The plotting was also compartmented. Bin Laden himself, in a videotape found in Afghanistan after the attacks, said that even some members of his inner circle, and some of the hijackers themselves, were unaware of its full scope. Finally, Tenet noted that the plot was resilient: it was not thwarted by al-Hazmi or al-

Mihdhar's inability to learn how to fly, by the arrest of Zacarias Moussaoui, or by al-Qahtani being turned back from the United States when he arrived in Orlando.

When anyone describes the attack to me as fundamentally simple, I ask them to imagine it this way: You are sent to a foreign country where you speak little, if any, of the language and look different from most of the people. Your job is to rendezvous with a team, many of whom you've never met, to learn a skill that is not commonly taught, to refine, practice, and execute a plan to destroy a national monument, and to do all that without arousing any suspicion. I would submit that if nineteen Americans were sent to Yemen to do something akin to what the September 11 terrorists did here, they wouldn't get very far before people started asking questions.

From the beginning, I believed almost intuitively that the terrorists who pulled off this attack must have had an elaborate support network, abroad and in the United States, to funnel them money and provide the other support they needed. To me, this is where the real costs of the attack lay—not in the $250,000 provided directly to the terrorists but in the significant and sustained cost of maintaining an infrastructure. For that reason, as well as because of the benefits that come with the confidentiality of diplomatic cover, I began to hypothesize that this infrastructure of support was probably maintained, at least in part, by a nation-state.

In carrying out their plot, the terrorists had killed themselves. It is not easy to stop terrorists who are willing to give their lives in an attack. In fact, the only way to do so is a sustained offensive in which we and our allies work to destroy their networks at home and abroad, while also dealing with the conditions that have nurtured and radicalized new generations of terrorists. It seemed to me that this would be our post–September 11 challenge.

★

It was apparent to me from the outset that there would be a legitimate call for an inquiry to shed light on how such an event could have occurred, who was responsible, and how the nation could be better prepared to reduce the chances of a repetition of September 11. The questions were, Who would conduct such an inquiry? Would it be an independent commission? Would every committee simply exercise its oversight authority?

My first instinct was to turn to a friend in the House, the Republican chairman of the House Permanent Select Committee on Intelligence, Porter Goss. I had known Porter for more than twenty years and had great admiration for his intellect, experience, objectivity, and character.

Porter began his career in government as a CIA agent, and in many ways he embodies that agency's culture and makeup. The son of a wealthy Connecticut family, Porter entered the CIA after graduating from Yale. The Goss family had enjoyed a vacation on Sanibel Island, off the southwest coast of Florida; when Porter left the CIA due to health concerns, he retired to Sanibel for reasons of both climate and familiarity. Sanibel also happens to be a popular place for retired CIA agents. Porter got together with two of his former colleagues, and they decided to start a newspaper in Sanibel, the *Island Reporter*.

Porter ran for and was elected to the first Sanibel city council in 1974 and was named mayor by his fellow councilmembers. Because of Goss's election and the many retired CIA staff living on Sanibel, one national story ran with the headline "Ex-Spooks Take Over Island."[5]

In 1982, an airport construction scandal rocked Lee County, with three of the five members of the county commission indicted for corruption. I was governor at the time, so it was my responsibility to suspend the indicted commissioners from office until the charges against them were resolved, and to appoint their replacements.

There were a lot of Democrats in Lee County who wanted to be appointed, but Porter had a superb reputation, so even though he was a Republican, I asked him if he could take one of these positions. He did.

Porter restored integrity to the county government and helped complete what is now the Southwest Florida Regional Airport. In 1988 he was elected to the Congress.

In the House, Porter worked his way up through the ranks of the Intelligence Committee, becoming chairman in 1997. In the aftermath of this tragedy, our lives and careers, which had intersected twenty years earlier, would intersect again.

I believed that of all of the components that enabled the September 11 attacks to succeed, the most significant was intelligence, so it would make most sense for the congressional intelligence committees to lead the investigation.

Porter Goss had been thinking along the same lines, so I presented the idea that our two committees—his in the House and mine in the Senate—might conduct a joint inquiry into the attacks.

Porter was immediately amenable to the idea. We'd need to get our cochairs and fellow committee members to agree.

In honing the idea, we decided that a joint inquiry must meet certain key requirements:

First, the work would have to be completely bipartisan.

Second, the inquiry would require the full support of the congressional leadership and the White House.

Third, since we were both chairing committees that had ongoing responsibilities, and those responsibilities could not be set aside, the work of the inquiry must be separate from the committees' other responsibilities. We would have to hire a separate staff with the sole job of conducting the September 11 inquiry. This decision produced considerable frustration among members who wanted to be briefed by their own staff, and among some committee staff, who felt shut out of this important investigation.

Still, with Porter and me in agreement that the best inquiry would be a joint inquiry, and having outlined how that inquiry would work, we were ready to go to our respective leaders to ask them to sanction the intelligence committees as the lead investigating committees.

On the afternoon of September 25, after having secured the agreement of Senator Shelby and several other members of my committee, I met with Senator Daschle, the majority leader of the Senate, and Senator Harry Reid, of Nevada, the assistant majority leader, to explain our proposal for a joint inquiry on terrorism and September 11. Senators Daschle and Reid were polite but skeptical. It was tough enough to get anything accomplished through the Senate process alone; they feared that a joint investigation would make the process even more unwieldy. I laid out the case that there was a public and congressional outcry for this investigation, and that the necessity of understanding what had happened and using that information to reduce the chance of a repetition would give us the momentum to cross any procedural hurdles. I argued

Overall, Porter and I both felt that we'd been received with more enthusiasm than we could have hoped for or expected. Up until that point, we had been hearing that the White House felt that this was an internal matter for the intelligence community and that if there were any problems that had contributed to September 11, the intelligence agencies' leadership could find and correct them.

I didn't know what accounted for the change in attitude. Perhaps President Bush, Vice President Cheney, and Dr. Rice felt that because our investigation was to be completely bipartisan, would take place largely behind closed doors, and would be confined to intelligence matters, it had relatively little potential to harm the administration. Perhaps they felt that agreeing to this one investigation would relieve the pressure to have an independent commission, which the administration clearly was resisting. Or the President might have been genuinely curious about what had happened, and interested in turning answers into action. Whatever the motivation, we were happy to have not only the approval but the support of the White House, and to be moving forward.

★

The war in Afghanistan began on October 7. Afghanistan was a battlefield that was accommodating to the things we do best, especially precision aerial bombardment. The skies over Afghanistan became home to B-52 and B-1 bombers with their payloads of joint direct attack munitions (JDAMs). There were EA-6 prowlers, used to jam enemy communications, and A-10 Thunderbolts and AC-130s for close air support. There were all manner of helicopters for support and rescue. And then there were our strike fighters, the F-15s, the F-16s, and the F-14 Tomcats and F-18 Hornets that delivered the precision laser-guided bombs. Circling the battlefield were KC-10 Extenders and KC-135 Stratotankers, which served as flying gas stations to keep the whole aerial panoply aloft.[6]

For the first time in the history of war, bombs and missiles from aircraft beyond the reach of antiaircraft weapons were directed toward specific enemy combatants on the ground. This marked a major step in the transformation of aerial warfare. In World War II, it could require 3,000 sorties to destroy a single target; in the Gulf War that number had been reduced to ten. What we saw in Afghanistan was one plane de-stroying ten targets.[7]

Also making a name for itself in the skies over Afghanistan was an unmanned aerial vehicle, or UAV, called the Predator.

The Predator is a medium-altitude, long-endurance UAV. Though ungainly looking—27 feet long, with a bulbous front turret, long, thin wings, and a rear tail that looks like an inverted "V"—it is a highly ef-fective reconnaissance aircraft. It is controlled by a pilot on the ground, using a joystick, and it can remain on station, over 400 nautical miles from its base, for twenty-four hours before returning home. It carries a surveillance package of two electro-optical cameras and one infrared camera for use at night. It also has a radar system, which allows it to "see" through inclement weather. The Predator's superlative ability to spot targets led a number of people to suggest that it be weaponized rather than having it relay target information so that other aircraft could be called in for a strike. This led to a long back-and-forth between the CIA and the Air Force. The Air Force contended that it had weapon-bearing aircraft that could perform the task at least as well as a weaponized Predator. The CIA contended that firing missiles from planes was not its business. However, in both agencies there were people arguing in favor of weaponization, and those arguments finally won out. In February 2001, the Predator became lethal, able to carry and launch a Hellfire missile. This made the Predator not only effective at reconnais-sance but also able to destroy a target that it had spotted and that might be present only temporarily. In Afghanistan, the Predator's visual feeds could be relayed directly to other aircraft, and the Predator could "paint" targets with its laser, a combination that allowed U.S. forces to strike—either with the Predator or with other aircraft—within five minutes of "acquisition."

The success of the Predator made it all the more ironic that the craft's very existence owed more to luck than to strategy. From the earliest de-velopment of the idea, there were a huge number of bureaucratic dis-putes over who should develop, own, task, and maintain the aircraft. Not surprisingly, the Air Force expressed the greatest resistance, largely because the Air Force has been historically resistant to aircraft that are not piloted. When a country faces a foe, a sense of urgency moderates bureaucratic disputes. In the absence of a foe or a threat, the bureaucratic weeds grow up, as they had around the Predator. Still, the sheer technological virtuosity and surveillance potential of the craft kept it moving forward.

Today, the Predator is owned and maintained by the Air Force, but it is tasked by the CIA.

One evening early in the Afghanistan campaign, I visited CIA headquarters in Langley, Virginia, during a Predator flight in progress over Afghanistan. I was ushered into a control room where a pilot sat at a joystick, in front of several screens. One screen showed what a pilot would normally see in a heads-up display in a cockpit—altitude, bearing, and speed. Another screen brought us a live image of what the Predator was "seeing." Yet another screen tracked the aircraft's progress against a map of the region. On request, the pilot could drop the craft's altitude to take a closer look at areas of interest, and he could maneuver away from inclement weather. It was amazing to watch requests made in Langley reflected in what the Predator was seeing half a world away.

Clearly, this was just about the perfect weapon in our hunt for Osama bin Laden. The fact that almost all of them were removed from the battlefield in early 2002 was a clear case of how the Bush administration's singleminded focus on Iraq undermined the war against al-Qaeda in Afghanistan.

The war against the Taliban was short. Kabul fell on November 13, five weeks after the beginning of the campaign. Kandahar fell three weeks later. Massive air superiority played a leading role in taking down a totalitarian theocracy and chasing al-Qaeda into the mountains.

With the Taliban defeated, the U.S. focused on rooting out al-Qaeda and finding Osama bin Laden. By the beginning of 2002, the United States had over 25,000 troops in the region. Bin Laden had been surrounded in the area known as Tora Bora. A CIA antiterrorism agent said, "We don't know his address, but we do know his zip code." I speculated at a Tallahassee press conference on October 15, 2001, that we would kill or capture Osama bin Laden within the next thirty days.

With bin Laden surrounded and al-Qaeda on the run, we had a foot on the neck of the terror network. Knowing that, and having spoken to leaders at Central Command, I believed that al-Qaeda's end was near.

12

A Meeting at MacDill

By February 2002, things were moving along well. We hadn't yet formally announced the creation of a joint inquiry, but we were beginning to lay out its framework. And our military was making progress in Afghanistan. Things were going so well that in a speech in Winston-Salem, North Carolina, President Bush declared, "We have totally routed out one of the most repressive governments in the history of mankind, the Taliban."

On February 5, calling on his countrymen to "take each other's hands" to rebuild the nation, interim Afghan leader Hamid Karzai raised his nation's new flag over the presidential palace. The flag had been originally approved in 1964 as Afghanistan's national emblem but had not flown over government offices in Kabul since the Taliban had taken over in the early 1990s.

Finally by mid-February, the United States had begun shipping al-

Qaeda and Taliban suspects to the newly opened Camp X-Ray at Guantánamo Bay in Cuba.

However, there were also disturbing signs that the war was not nearly over. February saw the resurgence of attacks on U.S. and allied peacekeeping forces, and the abduction of the *Wall Street Journal* reporter Daniel Pearl, whose death would be confirmed days later.

On January 31, Condoleezza Rice gave a speech at the Conservative Political Action Conference in which she said, "Al Qaeda is far from finished. It operates in dozens of countries around the world and it threatens many more. And the President has made clear that we and our allies will not rest until the threat from al Qaeda and the network itself is no more."

She went on to say,

We will pursue [al-Qaeda's] members by every means at our disposal. We will disrupt its plans, destroy its bases, arrest its members, break up its cells and choke off its finances. And our enemy is not just al Qaeda, but every terrorist group of global reach. This is not just our struggle; it is the struggle of the civilized world.

The United States has made clear to leaders on every continent that there is no such thing as a good terrorist and a bad terrorist. You cannot condemn al Qaeda and hug Hamas.

The United States draws no distinction between the terrorists and the regimes that feed, train, supply and harbor them. Simply put, harboring terrorists isn't a very good business to be in right now.[1]

It was exactly the type of statement I wanted to hear from the White House, and exactly the approach I felt America should be taking. The Bush administration seemed to be getting it right.

But two weeks later, I had an experience that would put the lie to those words, shatter my faith in the integrity of the Bush administration, and make me doubt the President's commitment to winning the war on terrorism.

On February 19, 2002, I visited MacDill Air Force Base in Tampa for a briefing on the status of our mission in Afghanistan.

MacDill is home to U.S. Central Command (CENTCOM), one of nine unified combat commands that are assigned operational control of our combat forces. A unified combat command comprises forces from two or more of the armed services and has a broad or continuing mission. At the time, CENTCOM was responsible for overseeing activity in the no-fly zone over southern Iraq (Operation Southern Watch) and running the war in Afghanistan (Operation Enduring Freedom).

Interestingly, the whole concept of a central command comes from congressional oversight, specifically a Pentagon reform bill called Goldwater-Nichols, which was passed in 1986 to address the concern that the various branches of the armed forces were not communicating well or working together.

When I was in Tampa, I would periodically visit MacDill in order to get a CENTCOM briefing; on this visit, I wanted to get a report on the status of the war in Afghanistan.

I had one of my staffers drop me off at the gates to the installation at about 9:00 A.M., and I was brought to the office of General Tommy Franks. As the officer in charge of CENTCOM, Franks is responsible for U.S. military operations in a twenty-five-country theater, ranging from Egypt to Central Asia. One reporter has described Franks as the "modern equivalent of a proconsul in the Roman Empire."[2]

Though it houses some of America's most advanced warmaking technologies, CENTCOM feels like the office of a large insurance company, with nondescript offices, halls, and decorations.

I hadn't met General Franks before, but I knew his biography. He had his first combat experience as an artillery officer in Vietnam, where he was wounded. He advanced steadily through the ranks, and by 1991 and Operation Desert Storm, he was an assistant division commander of the 1st Cavalry Division.

After that war, Franks's rise accelerated, culminating in June 2000 when he became a full four-star general, the highest rank possible in the U.S. Army.

Franks was very much unlike his more famous predecessor at CENTCOM, Norman Schwarzkopf, who frequently spoke to the media. And while the former Supreme Allied Commander Europe, General Wesley Clark, a former Rhodes scholar, was a smooth and polished speaker, Franks was a man of few words, and those he did speak were with a folksy drawl.

Over coffee, General Franks talked about his life in Texas. In our short conversation, I realized that he was both a good soldier and a soldier's soldier—he was willing to do what his civilian commanders asked of him, and when he did, he was deeply concerned about force protection and about using airpower to put our troops in the most advantaged situation possible.

We finished our coffee and headed for the briefing.

A CENTCOM briefing, like most military briefings, is the type of "just the facts" presentation that would make Sergeant Joe Friday proud. General Franks and I were ushered into a conference room, where we sat at a horseshoe-shaped table. Behind us was tiered amphitheater seating, which was empty. There, a well-prepared briefing officer described the status of the war in Afghanistan, beginning with its strategic purposes and then considering the specific tactics that underlay our current operations. His PowerPoint presentation, with maps, photos, and video, ended in the conclusion that things were looking good in the war on terror. Although my earlier prediction of capturing bin Laden in thirty days had stretched, by this point, to 120, the news still seemed encouraging. The briefing concluded, I thanked the briefer and got up to leave.

At that point, General Franks asked for an additional word with me in his office. When I walked in, he closed the door. Looking troubled, he said, "Senator, we are not engaged in a war in Afghanistan."

"Excuse me?" I asked.

"Military and intelligence personnel are being redeployed to prepare for an action in Iraq," he continued. "The Predators are being relocated. What we are doing is a manhunt. We have wrapped ourselves too much in trailing Osama bin Laden and Mullah Omar. We're better at being a meat ax than finding a needle in a haystack. That's not our mission, and that's not what we are trained or prepared to do."

It took me a second to digest what he had told me. General Franks's mission in Afghanistan—which, as a good soldier, he was loyally carrying out—was being downgraded from a war to a manhunt. What's more, the most important tools for a manhunt, the Predators, had been rede-ployed to Iraq at the moment they were most needed in Afghanistan.

I was stunned. This was the first time I had been informed that the decision to go to war with Iraq had not only been made but was being implemented, to the substantial disadvantage of the war in Afghanistan.

Franks continued, "We can finish this job in Afghanistan if we are al-lowed to do so. And there is a set of terrorist targets after Afghanistan. My first priority would be Somalia—there is no effective government to control the large number of terrorist cells. Next, I would go to Yemen. Its president is willing to help in the war on terrorism, but has no capa-bilities to do so. Iraq is a special case. Our intelligence there is very un-satisfactory. Some Europeans know more than we do on Iraq's weapons of mass destruction. . . ."

General Franks wasn't complaining; he was making a statement of fact. But the fact was damning. Here, General Franks, a four-star gen-eral and the commander of CENTCOM, was laying out for me how he would fight a true war on terrorism. Instead, his men and resources were being moved to Iraq, where he felt that our intelligence was shoddy. This admission was coming almost fourteen months before the beginning of combat operations in Iraq, and only five months after the commencement of combat in Afghanistan.

The more I thought about it, the more furious I became. Victory against al-Qaeda was in our grasp, and we were releasing the pressure. The redeployments were a tangible statement that not only did we not have the military or intelligence capacity to simultaneously win an ongo-ing war in Afghanistan and take on Saddam Hussein in Iraq, but also that someone in the White House had put Saddam Hussein ahead of Osama bin Laden.

The reality seemed at sharp variance with what the President had been saying publicly about rooting out terrorists wherever they exist, and with what Dr. Rice had claimed just days earlier. And though Presi-dent Bush packaged action in Iraq as part of the war on terror, the truth was that not only was it not a part of the war on terror, it actively and demonstrably detracted from the war on terror.

As I was driving away from CENTCOM, I recalled a lesson from ancient history, when the tragic blunders of Athens in the Pelopon-nesian War ultimately led to its destruction. Upon looking it up again, I was struck by how trenchant the analogy was: In 413 B.C., Athens, in the midst of a war with Sparta, decided to attempt to expand its empire by taking over Sicily. The campaign was disastrous. It led to the destruction of the Athenian navy and it weakened Athens to the point that Sparta was able to defeat it, effectively ending the Athenian empire and the classical age. As General Franks explained to me how America was shifting its efforts from Afghanistan to Iraq, I understood how Pericles must have felt when he said, "I am more afraid of our own mistakes than of our enemy's designs."

★

Meanwhile, the Joint Inquiry was coalescing as we sought to investigate another series of mistakes. Just days before my briefing at MacDill, Porter Goss, Nancy Pelosi, Dick Shelby, and I had announced that our respective committees would conduct an inquiry into the September 11 attacks, and would do it jointly.

The closest relation to what we were proposing to do was the 1987 Iran-Contra investigation, which relied on the merged staff of two special committees to conduct its investigation. Unlike the permanent intelligence committees, however, the panels were specifically established for the inquiry and disbanded upon its conclusion.

Ultimately, the historians concluded that never had the Congress done what we were trying to do: merge two full standing committees, served by a unified staff, to conduct a sensitive inquiry. As Senate historian Don Ritchie summarized it:

> Ever fearful of tyranny, the Framers of the Constitution solved the problem of concentration of power by dividing responsibilities among three branches of government, and by further dividing the legislative branch into two houses. As James Madison explained, the best safeguard against governmental tyranny was to set ambition against ambition. . . . Over the past more than two centuries, the Senate and the House have proudly established their own institutional cultures. Efforts to bridge these differing cultures have met with only limited success.

> [None] of the other congressional investigations we reviewed

involved two previously existing committees creating a merged staff to conduct an investigation jointly.

In other words, in an institution of precedents, we were doing something unprecedented. We were on our own.

The first step was to outline the scope and goals of the inquiry. We decided that the three principal objectives of the Joint Inquiry would be

to determine what the intelligence community knew or should have known prior to September 11, 2001, regarding the international terrorist threat to the United States, including possible attacks against the homeland of the United States or its interests abroad;

to identify any systemic problems that may have affected the intelligence community in learning of these attacks before they occurred, and in preventing them; and

to recommend reforms to improve the intelligence community's capacity to identify and prevent future attacks.

The Joint Inquiry would operate under two restrictions. Its charter was limited to the review of the intelligence community. This left many agencies that played a role in the events before and after September 11, particularly the Federal Aviation Administration, what was then the Immigration and Naturalization Service, and the nonintelligence components of the Department of Defense, out of our jurisdiction.

Second, the report had to be completed by the end of the 107th Congress, January 2, 2003. Dick Shelby, Porter Goss, Nancy Pelosi, and I all agreed that with thirty-seven members from across the political spectrum making up our committees, and with a huge number of important and politically sensitive decisions ahead, the most important thing was to be able to trust one another. As an indication of this trust, we decided that no decision would be made unless it was unanimous. In other words, any one of us could veto the other three. Over the course of the inquiry, this rarely happened, but the knowledge that it could reminded us that we were all in this together.

13

The Inquiry Begins

WMDs in the Refrigerator

On May 25, two weeks before we were to begin our closed hearings, I participated in a congressional trip with Senator Barbara Mikulski. Our first stop was Moscow, where we helped to mark the tenth anniversary of the Nunn-Lugar Act, named for its authors, former senator Sam Nunn of Georgia and Indiana senator Richard Lugar. One of the most visionary enactments of the post–Cold War period, Nunn-Lugar has provided approximately $1 billion a year to Russia and other states of the former Soviet Union to help them dismantle their nuclear warheads and the means of delivering those weapons—missiles, long-range aircraft, and submarines.

In recent years, Nunn-Lugar's scope has been extended to provide funds for the destruction and management of chemical and biological weapons of mass destruction. We've got a lot of work to do with the Russians to complete this process, and need to do more to protect against the theft or sale of nuclear weapons components or material. Of course, accurate intelligence about interested buyers, sellers, and traffickers of this material will be vital to this effort.

The morning following our arrival, the seventy-five participants were bused from our hotel to Pokrov, some fifty miles east of Moscow. It was a beautiful late-spring drive out of the bustle of the capital city through small villages and farm plots. This was my fourth visit to Russia, the second since the collapse of the Soviet Union in 1991. I had been impressed in Moscow at how much better the city looked and functioned—there was no more standing in three lines to buy one item. The same was true for the rural region through which we bused. You could see it in the recently acquired farm equipment in the fields and the better-kept-up farmhouses. After about an hour and a half, we arrived at the Pokrov Biologics Plant.

At one time, the plant was a campuslike cluster of almost twenty buildings made of a brownish-yellow brick. Its original purpose was to produce vaccines for agricultural use, including one for anthrax that was a chief product of the center.

During the last decade of the Cold War, Pokrov allegedly took on a more sinister task: producing anthrax bacteria and smallpox virus that could be used in a weaponized form. The newest buildings in the complex were built primarily underground, with only Quonset-hut roofs covered by vines above the surface. Despite the fact that Pokrov never officially was linked to the Soviet military or to Biopreparat, the Soviet Union's secret biological weapons program, the new buildings were hardened against nuclear attack, with thick blast doors and reinforced concrete. This is where the uglier business of Pokrov was suspected to have taken place; some intelligence officials estimate that the complex was capable of producing the smallpox virus at a rate of 200 tons a year.

All of the buildings in the complex were so poorly maintained they were falling apart, but some buildings were still in use. One of those, near the middle of the campus, was called the Museum.

This was no ordinary museum, however. Preserved inside it were samples of all the toxins that at one time had been manufactured or compounded at Pokrov.

Weeds flourished in the cracks of the concrete sidewalk, and it was obvious that the security fence had fallen or been taken down. There was no perimeter security for the building. Once inside, I asked our guide what was the protection for these lethal chemicals. He shrugged. "We used to have an electrified fence—it is now down. But, no matter, the electricity was off most of the time, so it was useless." There was more: "And we used to have an electronic alarm system. It didn't work very reliably, either, so it's no loss that it has been removed. But we do have protection now which does not require electricity." He took us up a set of steel-grate stairs anchored into poured concrete walls, to two large rooms. In both were standup commercial-sized refrigerators— that's where the products that were the heritage of the campus were stored. The refrigerators were unexceptional except for three or four that had a string wrapped around the box and anchored at the back with a soft wax seal. I asked what the string was about. The guide explained: "This is our last line of security. If any unauthorized persons enter these most dangerous refrigerators, we will know it by the broken string."

My God, I thought, the only thing between samples of the most dangerous chemicals that have ever been produced and a terrorist looking for weapons of mass destruction is a *piece of string*. My anxiety was heightened shortly after my return, when a story in *The Washington Post* about Pokrov reported that there had been break-ins, as well as attempts by mysterious "Arab businessmen" to purchase various things.[1]

It was a stark reminder of the importance of the work our committee was about to begin. If the terrorists had the will, the means, and the inclination to plot a coordinated hijacking, it could also be assumed that they would like to get their hands on these weapons—weapons that could make the loss of life on September 11 look minor by comparison.

On May 28, we flew from Moscow's Vnukovo airport to Warsaw. As we stepped off the military aircraft, I recognized my status. Senator Barbara Mikulski is more than a celebrity in Warsaw—she is royalty. Her heritage and long-time support for Polish causes such as Poland's entry into NATO have made her recognizable and loved. I just tried to not get pushed down by her admirers.

Poland had emerged as a strong ally of the United States when disputes erupted with Europe. Because of this deepening relationship and Poland's relatively long involvement, as a Warsaw Pact nation, with Iraq, Poland had been selected by the United States as its representative in Baghdad when we broke off diplomatic relations in 1991. Since that time, Poland had become our primary eyes and ears inside Iraq. As

Prime Minister Leszek Miller told us, this was something the Poles were happy to do. He saw it as part of Poland's NATO duty, and part of its integration into the Western world.

The Poles were also particularly proud of their history in the intelligence world. Polish cryptanalysts and mathematicians had helped break the German Enigma code. Though their domestic concerns centered largely on Russian gangsters and the element of drugs and lawlessness they introduced, they saw this era as another opportunity to be major players in international intelligence. Also, because of Poland's history as a Warsaw Pact nation, a number of operatives were at work there whom we weren't likely to come across in the United States—people from North Korea and other former Soviet-supported and suspect nations—and the Poles offered to cooperate in our scrutiny of them.

Both the prime minister (who has since stepped down) and the head of Poland's intelligence service told us they were eager for more exchange with the CIA, and more opportunities to be trained by Americans. We promised to pass on their concerns, and left for Hamburg, Germany, heartened at the enthusiasm of such an ally.*

Of the German cities I have visited, Hamburg is among the most handsome. Its location on the Baltic and its many interconnecting canals have earned it the title of the Venice of the North. However, Senator Mikulski and I were there to get information on the city's darker side—the side that served as a base and safe harbor for al-Qaeda. The group's Hamburg cell was the principal source of the most skilled September 11 hijackers.

Germany is divided into sixteen states, or *länder*. These *länder* have more autonomy than the states of the United States. Each state, for instance, has its own immigration and intelligence service. Hamburg is its own *land,* and it has a reputation for being among Germany's most open and liberal. Hamburg also is the home to several of the most advanced technical institutes and universities in Europe. These universities have drawn thousands of young students from Arab

---

* Poland's favorable disposition toward the United States has continued during the war in Iraq. When Secretary of Defense Donald Rumsfeld talked about "old Europe" and "new Europe," he was citing Poland as an example of the "new Europe" type of ally we wanted. Amazingly, President Bush has managed to strain relations with this closest of allies by refusing to help ease Poland's backlog of applications for U.S. visas, continuing to treat Poland like a suspect satellite of Russia rather than a true partner.

countries. Partly as a result, about 5 percent of Hamburg's 2 million inhabitants are Muslim.[2]

Roughly twenty of these students were members of an al-Qaeda cell in Hamburg—a cell that included Mohammed Atta, Marwan al-Shehhi, and Ziad Jarrah, three of the four September 11 pilots. It is believed that these men and others were recruited into al-Qaeda in a largely informal process that began by drawing them into a deeper commitment to Islam and a more rigid interpretation of it, followed by an invitation to go to Afghanistan to see what it was like, followed by a visit to the terrorist training camps, and ultimately ending in al-Qaeda indoctrination for those who seemed receptive to the idea.[3] The Joint Inquiry also found that this process was likely coordinated by a man named Mohammed Zammar, a suspected recruiter for al-Qaeda.

Our first question was why so many of the terrorists had come through Hamburg. In addition to citing the universities there and the reputation for openness, the American and German officials we met gave us two other reasons. First, they noted that ever since World War II, Germany has been wary of intruding on religion, and thus even the most militant mosques were left alone. The people we met with noted the irony that the strict privacy and religious privilege laws that the world demanded of Germany after the Holocaust had become an obstacle to investigating terrorists.*

The second reason was that Germany had created a rather robust welfare state, one in which a foreigner could get an enormous number of subsidies by doing very little.

Our people in Hamburg were devastated that so much of the planning for September 11 had taken place there. The FBI legat there was one of the most impressive operations I had seen: with little support from headquarters, it had moved away from the tyranny of the case file, reaching out to local authorities, colleges, and universities to develop a web of information that might not close one single case, but could affect many.

Our FBI agents there also noted that the German analog of the FBI had been particularly helpful in tracking down suspected terrorists after

---

* Ironically, France takes the opposite approach. Mosques are monitored, and if an imam is advocating violence and is from another country, he is deported.

September 11; however, they were worried that the decreasing number of case officers left us too dependent on the Germans, and that we had raised tensions by not sharing our information with them.

The horrors that could grow anywhere from a decaying Russia to a modern Germany only increased my resolve to harden America against a world filled with threats. Upon my return, we would begin the process of digging into what allowed one of those threats to hit America.

★

At the Joint Inquiry's first meeting, on June 4, 2002, we ratified the resolutions establishing the inquiry and gave each member of the thirty-seven-person bicameral panel an opportunity to make an opening statement.

The most memorable of these was from Congresswoman Nancy Pelosi, who eloquently reminded us that we were entrusted with a spiritual obligation to the families of the victims and offered a moment of silent prayer for the dead.

Senator Barbara Mikulski reminded us that seven months earlier, a series of letters containing anthrax had set off a national scare and taken five lives. One of the letters was addressed to Senator Daschle, and when the letter was opened in his Hart office, the resulting contamination shut down the building for three months. At the time our inquiry began, there was some suspicion that the anthrax-tainted letters were part of a second wave of al-Qaeda actions. On Senator Mikulski's motion, anthrax was added to our agenda.*

★

Most congressional hearings begin with opening statements by the chair, by the ranking member of the minority, and sometimes by the members as well. These statements are generally wandering, and frequently over-focused on the parochial concerns of the individual member. They are

---

* The inquiry would ultimately conclude that at the time the report was completed, December 10, 2002, "no connection has been established between the anthrax attacks and the terrorist attacks of September 11."

followed by a statement from whoever is testifying before the hearing. If that person is the head of an agency, the statement usually lauds that agency's accomplishments, and, if the hearing appears likely to be a hostile one, cites all the improvements the agency has made.

This statement is then followed by questioning from the members of Congress. With thirty-seven members on the Joint Inquiry panel, one of our major concerns was that the length and repetition of the questioning could get out of hand, especially given that these questions often take the form of statements with some small interrogatory at the end. The net result of the whole process is often a great deal of talk and a minimal amount of edification. If we genuinely wanted to conduct an investigation, the usual system simply wouldn't work.

Eleanor Hill, the staff director of the Joint Inquiry, suggested resurrecting a technique she had used during her time on the Permanent Subcommittee on Investigations, the "staff statement." We decided to begin each day's hearing with a staff statement—a presentation that would be read aloud before a witness began testifying. As Eleanor put it, "The way I view investigative hearings in the legislative process, the ultimate goal is fixing the problems through legislation or recommendations to agencies. First you have to build the record and marshal the evidence to show the problem. When you prosecute a case you have to do the same thing."

The staff statements accomplished their purpose in four ways.

First, they enabled the inquiry, in a coherent and comprehensive way, to give the American public a clear picture of the complex facts and circumstances that constituted the story of September 11.

Secondly, they ensured that committee members, regardless of how well they had prepared, would begin the hearings with the same foundation of knowledge.

Third, they forced the witnesses to address our concerns from the very outset. Once the staff statement was read, the witness was playing on a factual field of our making. Rather than simply tell us how wonderful their agency was and how much it was improving, they had to address the staff description we had been given of their actions and, often, their failings.

Fourth, they invigorated the staff, who would hear their work presented aloud.

After the staff statement was read, we would allow the witness to make an opening statement, in which he or she now had to respond to our findings of fact.

Following the staff statement and a presentation from the witness, the leaders would ask their questions. At that point, most committees would simply go through their membership in order of seniority. Again, we tried a different approach. For most of the hearings, we chose one person from the Senate and one from the House, one Republican and one Democrat, to be the designated questioners for that session's witnesses. Those two members would work with the committee staff to formulate a series of questions that we wanted the witness to answer on the record. This also turned out to be an effective way of getting more members to feel involved and invested in the work of the Joint Inquiry.

Only then, following the staff statement, the witness statement, the leaders' questions, and that day's designated questioners, did we open the floor to members' questions. Here we decided to use an "early bird" system, under which the members who were energetic and interested enough to show up early got an earlier shot at the witness. Managing thirty-seven members of Congress while running a deeply important investigation required order and incentives, and the system we came up with provided both.

After our June 4 business meeting, we spent the next two days hearing from members of the Joint Inquiry staff on the evolution of the terrorist threat and the response of the United States.

On June 11, we had our first witness from outside the inquiry: Richard Clarke, the man who had been the counterterrorism czar for both Presidents Bill Clinton and George W. Bush.*

Clarke had a reputation for gruffness and for having little tolerance for slow learners and less for fools. In his gravelly voice he recited, without notes, a history of al-Qaeda and of the United States government's response to the terrorist threat.

Ours was, according to Clarke, a slow and incomplete awakening.

He talked about how the CIA was given the job of determining the

* Because of the White House aversion to having staff testify as witnesses, Mr. Clarke appeared before us as a briefer, not a witness, and was thus not placed under oath.

source and size of al-Qaeda's funding, and had come up with very little information. He spoke about how the FBI simply wasn't focused on the problem, calling the efforts of fifty-five of the FBI field offices "extremely poor and not coordinated." The only organizations that escaped Clarke's brutal assessment were the New York City FBI field office—"excellent"—and the NSA: "Eighty to ninety per cent of our quality intelligence came from the NSA."

Overall, it was not a glowing picture.

On June 18, our witnesses were the director of the CIA, George Tenet, and the FBI director Bob Mueller. They were both defensive in explaining their agencies' work prior to September 11.

Director Mueller testified that "while here [in America], the hijackers effectively operated without suspicion, triggering nothing that would have alerted law enforcement and doing nothing that exposed them to domestic coverage. As far as we know, they contacted no known terrorist sympathizers in the United States."

Given the fact that one of the terrorists, Nawaf al-Hazmi, lived with an FBI informant for almost four months, and Hani Hanjour had attended flight school with another known terrorist sympathizer, this was not a very confidence-inspiring comment.

In the days following that testimony, the Joint Inquiry held eight additional closed sessions on specific intelligence issues, including the organization and coordination of the intelligence community prior to September 11, technical and human intelligence gathering, the not-for-attribution undertakings of the intelligence community known as covert action, and, importantly, the financing of terrorism. We also spent a day looking at the genesis of the use of airplanes as weapons.

We were the students in a secret, limited-enrollment seminar on the challenges of terrorism and the capability of U.S. intelligence to identify and interdict those challenges before they became another September 11.

We were also causing some political antennae to perk up. As the Joint Inquiry became more specific in its requests for witnesses and documents, we were encountering rising resistance from the intelligence agencies and the White House. For example, we felt that it was nearly useless to talk to agency directors. We wanted to talk to the people who were actually handling the information and making decisions—FBI field agents, CIA analysts, and other mid-level people who were directly responsible for obtaining and sifting through information. Both agencies were extremely resistant to what they felt was an intrusion into their work, and getting these agents to testify required daily squabbles with the agencies. We wanted access to the President's Daily Brief (PDB) of August 6, 2001—a document the administration denied us, and for an understandable reason. As we now know, that document contained a specific warning about Osama bin Laden's desire to strike within the United States and took note of suspicious people making preparations that the intelligence community found consistent with hijacking. The administration had wanted a whitewash, a validation of its stated belief that there was no way September 11 could have been avoided and therefore no one was responsible. It wasn't going to be getting one.

The agencies' resistance took smaller, pettier forms as well. For example, the inquiry staff who were investigating the FBI had managed to secure an office at FBI headquarters; however, neither the heat nor the air-conditioning in the office worked. What's more, the FBI, which promised to give its staff a way of getting in touch with the investigators should they have something to share, never did. Over at the CIA, our investigators were given an office right next to the CIA's congressional affairs office, and, in a world of secrecy, the loaner office had glass walls. As a result, anyone who voluntarily spoke to the Joint Inquiry would be doing so on public display, a significant disincentive to candor.

On June 19, the Joint Inquiry met in closed session with Air Force Lieutenant General Michael V. Hayden, the director of the National Security Agency, who, it was later reported, discussed with us messages that the NSA had intercepted on September 10 but not translated until September 12, 2001. Even had they been translated, we believed, the messages would not have provided enough information to stop the September 11 attacks; yet the statements contained in them were so bold in their intimation of an impending terrorist attack that not having translated them seemed a missed opportunity.

One of the things we didn't count on when we began our closed hearings was the intensity of the media interest. Ours was the first investigation into the tragedy of September 11, and we were conducting the first months of it behind closed doors. It seems obvious in retrospect that the media would be clamoring for any information about the goings-on inside the hearing room—and several hours after General Hayden testified, it appeared that CNN had gotten more than a little.

That afternoon, David Ensor, a CNN reporter, citing "two congressional sources," quoted phrases contained in two classified NSA intercepts from September 10, 2001. According to Ensor, who credited CNN's then Capitol Hill producer Dana Bash with the scoop, the intercepts included the phrases "The match begins tomorrow" and "Tomorrow is zero hour," and reported that the information had been presented to the inquiry by General Hayden.

The next day, splashed across the front page of *The Washington Post* was the headline "NSA Intercepts on Eve of 9/11 Sent a Warning; Messages Translated After Attacks."

USA Today's headline blared, "Heard 9/10: 'Tomorrow Is Zero Hour.' "

Virtually every major newspaper had one form or another of the story.

Though the substance of the communiqué was potent, to me it was not that important. Of greater concern was the disclosure of the methods by which the communiqué was obtained and of the fact that U.S. intelligence had a particular facility under surveillance—a fact that was not part of the initial report but was mentioned in some of the accounts that followed. One news outlet reported that the calls "came from sources—a location or phone number—that were of high-enough priority to translate them within two days but were not put in the top priority category, which included communications from Osama bin Laden or his senior al Qaeda assistants."[4]

This was a classic case of disclosing protected sources and methods, and I was livid about it.

I wasn't the only one.

The next morning, as I was shaving, I got a call at home from a very agitated Vice President Cheney. He didn't waste any time with pleasantries. "What in the hell is going on? Bob, we have tried to be as cooperative as possible, but we cannot tolerate this leakage to the press. If it continues, we will terminate our assistance to the committee."

Given the fact that the administration's support for our investigation had almost totally collapsed by that point, I thought the Vice President's comments were disingenuous and pompous. Still, I assured him that we took this episode as seriously as he did and would undertake an immediate review to determine what had happened and what to do about it. The Vice President seemed only mildly pacified.

The White House immediately jumped on the leak as an opportunity to criticize our inquiry, and to muzzle it. Later that day, a White House spokesperson said, "The selective, inappropriate leaking of snippets of information risks undermining national security."[5]

Later that morning, I spoke to Porter Goss; Cheney had called him, too, about the same time as he called me. As a former employee of the CIA, Porter is religiously respectful of classified information and the protection of sources and methods. He was at least as shaken by the leak as I was, if not more so.

We agreed that we had to take decisive action to demonstrate our commitment to security and discretion. We considered asking for the House or Senate Ethics Committee to investigate, but their jurisdiction was limited to congressional members and staff, and there had also been administration and intelligence agency staff in the room. For that reason, we felt it would be most appropriate not to have a self-investigation or an Ethics Committee investigation, but to invite the FBI to investigate the leak. Now the investigated were investigating the investigators. We believed that that approach was the only way to demonstrate our seriousness about the leak. (In typical FBI style, as of this writing—more than twenty-four months after the CNN disclosure—the investigation of the leak is still under way with no resolution in sight.)

Still, something else was gnawing at me. The leak was bad enough on its own. But the fact that the second day's newspapers were reporting more details than had appeared in the first day's story indicated that perhaps the reporters were being fed more information from elsewhere. That, combined with the White House's almost gleeful outrage and indignant hints that, merely by its existence, the Joint Inquiry was harming national security, made me think that perhaps the leak was intended to sabotage our efforts. I am not by nature a conspiracy theorist, but the fact that we were hit with this disclosure at the moment we began to make things uncomfortable for the Bush administration has stuck with me. Over a year later, I asked Congressman Goss whether he thought we had been set up. Nodding, he replied, "I often wonder that myself."

As the FBI collected phone logs and conducted interviews with every member of the Joint Inquiry, the story of the leak began to fade. The truth was that we were not about to be deterred from our goal. In fact, we were picking up steam, continuing to make investigative gains, and preparing to open the public portion of the hearings, which would begin on September 18, 2002.

14

Into the Middle East

In spite of the turmoil caused by the leak allegation, and the potential it had to slow our work and split the committee, we continued to investigate the events that led up to September 11 and to build a reform agenda from the lessons we were learning. However, even as we considered how America could confront worldwide terror organizations, the nation's attention was being drawn by the gravitational pull of Iraq.

During the recess for the Fourth of July holiday, I took what would be my last oversight trip as a member of the Intelligence Committee. With Senators Evan Bayh and Mike DeWine and our wives, we would be visiting Egypt, Syria, Lebanon, and Israel. With the potential for a war in Iraq becoming clearer and clearer, the trip's initial objective—of gathering information on counterterrorism—was being increasingly usurped by the one conversation taking place in the Arab world: Would America be engaging in a second Persian Gulf War?

Our first stop was in Egypt, a longtime U.S. ally in a region where we have a limited number of true friends. Egypt is also an example of how a majority-Muslim nation (94 percent of Egyptians are Muslim) can develop a stable secular government.

The high point of the U.S.-Egyptian relationship was reached in March 1979, with the signing of the Israel-Egypt peace accord, a signing I had the honor of attending. Egyptian president Anwar Sadat called it "a historic turning point of great significance." Israeli prime minister Menachem Begin spoke of how "Peace is the beauty of life." And President Jimmy Carter spoke of the challenges that lay ahead, saying, "Future days will require the best from us all to give reality to these lofty aspirations." Following their words, Begin and Sadat, with Carter standing between them, shook hands. To see the genuine embrace of friendship and respect infused all who were assembled there with hope. It was to be a false hope.

The dinner following the signing was held under a large white tent on the opposite side of the White House from where we had gathered five hours earlier. The tent sheltered sixty-three round tables, each with a white tablecloth anchored by a large vase of flowers. We happened to make our way to our table, ahead of everyone except an Egyptian gentleman who appeared to be in his mid-fifties. Through his translator, he introduced himself as Mr. Hassan abou-Heif, a member of the Egyptian parliament and a retired army officer. We began talking about what life had been like for our Egyptian guest leading up to that day. He told us that three times he had gone to war with Israel. The table began to fill. Seated to my left was a member of the Knesset Foreign Affairs and Defense Committee, who introduced himself as Yitzhak Rabin.

The future prime minister and martyr for peace recounted that the first time he had come to Washington was in the mid-1950s, when he was a young Israeli army lieutenant. His assignment had been to study U.S. aerial photographs of the Sinai Peninsula as part of Israel's preparation for a possible attack by Egypt. As Mr. Rabin reached this point in his personal history, the lights inside the tent were dimmed. President Carter, Prime Minister Begin, and President Sadat stood at the back of the tent as the national anthems of the three nations were played. As the last notes of "The Star Spangled Banner" wafted into the night sky and the leaders walked toward their table of honor, Rabin leaned toward me and whispered, "I never thought that the only thing which would come between me and an Egyptian military officer would be a vase of flowers."

The promise of that night has become a cold peace. There has been no armed conflict between Israel and Egypt since that March day twenty-five years ago, but there is little human interchange—commercial, cultural, educational—between the people of the two states.

The historic step taken that day saw Egypt expelled from the Arab League (it was reinstated in 1989), and helped earn Sadat, Begin, and, twenty-three years later, Carter, the Nobel Peace Prize. It also sparked riots in the streets of Kuwait and Israel's West Bank. And Sadat's willingness to make peace with Israel led to his death. On October 6, 1981, he was saluting the troops in a military parade when an assassination team ran from one of the parade vehicles and began firing weapons and throwing grenades into the reviewing stand, killing Sadat and twenty others, and wounding four American diplomats.

President Sadat's assassins were identified as members of Egyptian Islamic Jihad, the terrorist group that would later merge with al-Qaeda.

One of the people in the reviewing stand that day was Hosni Mubarak, the air force officer who would succeed Sadat as president, and with whom we were now about to meet.

★

After five hours of sleep, our congressional delegation headed for the opulent former hotel on the outskirts of downtown Cairo that now serves as the Egyptian presidential palace.

In the middle of the hotel, there was a main dining room where Mubarak receives guests. We sat at a horseshoe-shaped table, with our delegation of about ten people on one side, and President Mubarak and his group of about ten on the other.

President Mubarak has been criticized in the West for his level of commitment to democracy and harsh treatment of dissidents. I am also disappointed that there has been little progress—indeed, there has been a regression—in Egyptian-Israeli relations during his time as leader. Despite these things, it's worth considering that Mohammed Atta, one of the ringleaders of the September 11 attacks, was Egyptian, and Egyptians account for the largest national component of al-Qaeda, so President Mubarak has a significant role to play in helping America fight the war on terror. It has been my impression over the years I have known and met with President Mubarak in Cairo and Washington that he shares the goals of a democratic and prosperous Egypt at peace with its northern neighbor, and he seems to be walking a fine line between leading his people and losing them.

As we sat down to breakfast with Mubarak, there were two things on his mind. The first was the conflict between Israelis and Palestinians. Three months earlier, on April 4, President Bush had given what he described as a major policy speech outlining his "road map" to peace in the Middle East. Saying that "we stand ready to help," President Bush announced that he would be sending Secretary of State Colin Powell to the region.

One week prior to our visit, in the Rose Garden with Powell and Secretary of Defense Donald Rumsfeld, President Bush had reiterated this position, while calling for both a new Palestinian state and new Palestinian leaders, "not compromised by terror."[1]

Speaking in English, President Mubarak said to us, "I have been disappointed by the slowness of the President to become engaged in the conflict. Not only is the bloodshed tearing at what is left of the comity between the Israelis and Palestinians, until it is resolved there will be no movement on other regional issues, including a partnership with the U.S. in the war on terrorism. The President's speech has been heard in the street as an unwillingness to become personally or seriously involved in the conflict. It has put me in a difficult position. I understand that the U.S. is an indispensable part of the resolution, but to say that would be politically damaging as the street no longer believes the U.S. is even-handed. So I directed that a statement be issued which was supportive of the President's words, but challenged President Bush to demonstrate by actions his sustained commitment."

President Mubarak continued between bites of scrambled egg. "It would be helpful if the President would send an emissary to the region who has the confidence of the President and the respect of the Arab world. President Carter and his father [George H. W. Bush] would be that type of man. Do not send a State Department official. [The State

Department] has been so marginalized and discredited that its representative would be seen as an affront and an indication of lack of seriousness." Mubarak specifically felt that Colin Powell was not a significant force within the administration, and therefore would have very little pull in getting things accomplished. It was amazing to realize that the petty infighting of the Bush administration could do so much to undermine its Secretary of State overseas, but it had, and Mubarak pointedly did not want Secretary Powell as an envoy to the region.

Mubarak's second concern was Iraq, and here, too, he had some strong words for us. Though he made it clear that he had no love for Saddam Hussein and wouldn't be averse to seeing him removed from power, he said that the overthrow of Saddam's government should be accomplished "by its own people." He continued: "You are making a big mistake if you attack Iraq. I know Saddam well. He is an egomaniac, but no fool. A war will be seen in the streets of Cairo and Damascus as an attack on Islam; there's no way to avoid it. We were a part of the 1991 coalition in the first Persian Gulf War. Egypt will not do so now. You do not understand the consequences of your actions. If you succeed militarily—and you will—and if Iraq were to become a democracy, it would almost surely elect a religious extremist government. You will end up with another ayatollah as the head of the government. And that election could cause a cascading throughout the Middle East. The result of your actions, whatever their intentions, could well be two or three more Irans. Is that what you want?"

It was advice similar to that which he had given President Bush at a private dinner at Camp David one month earlier, advice President Bush seemed to be ignoring.

With his customary grace and hospitality, President Mubarak offered to facilitate our tour on the following day to Luxor. It would be my first time seeing the Valley of the Kings. Besides being the site of extraordinary antiquities, Luxor was a terrorist target. In 1997, a band of gunmen dressed as policemen emerged from the cliffs overlooking the Temple of Hatshepsut, opening fire on the buses and people below. The attack left more than sixty people dead. Coming just two months after nine German tourists and an Egyptian driver were killed when a tour bus was firebombed outside the Egyptian Museum in Cairo, it brought tourism—the country's second-largest source of revenue—to a virtual standstill. Those events galvanized Mubarak to crack down on terrorists in his own country. The Egyptian government responded with a combination of aggressive intelligence, massive incarcerations of suspected terrorists, interrogations that would almost certainly be deemed illegal in America, military trials, and the execution of those found guilty of terrorist acts. The Egyptian approach was unquestionably brutal, but it was also decisive. By the end of the 1990s, Egypt had virtually evicted the terrorists from its soil.

After a blistering 110-degree day in the Egyptian desert, we boarded our Air Force jet for the one-hour-and-forty-five-minute flight to Damascus, Syria.

It was 8 P.M. on July 1 when we walked down the DC-9's steps to a waiting cluster of Syrian and American diplomatic officials. During the formalities, as we walked toward the black Cadillac of the U.S. ambassador, Ted Kattouf, I noticed a Cold War Soviet cargo aircraft parked on the tarmac. On the tail were markings of the Islamic Republic of Iran. I asked one of Ambassador Kattouf's aides, "What would an Iranian cargo aircraft be carrying into Damascus?"

"Probably arms and ammunition, other military equipment for Hezbollah. This is the primary point of delivery."

The next morning, our delegation (minus the wives, who were politely but firmly not invited) went to meet with President Bashar Assad. Our expectations were not high. The United States and Syria had been engaged in a long diplomatic dance with little romance between the partners. Syria felt that the United States had swung from a position of neutrality to become a stooge for the Israelis. Syria's primary international goal was the return of the Golan, a mountainous outcropping to the north and east of the Sea of Galilee. This land had been taken by Israel in the 1967 Six-Day War. Before that war, Syrian artillery would regularly take target practice at the agricultural kibbutzim on the western side of the Galilee. On previous visits to Israel, we had been shown the shelters into which the children were sent during these assaults. Shutting down these random attacks became a priority of the Israeli government. Having exercised control of the Golan for almost four decades, Israel had resisted all Syrian entreaties to return even a square foot. Now that international attention on peace negotiations in the Middle East had shifted to the Israeli-Palestinian conflict, Syria felt abused and irrelevant.

The people at our embassy warned us that Assad would tell us that Syria had challenged terrorism and that he would point out that Syria practiced a more moderate form of Islam than did our friends the Saudis. It was important, too, that though Assad might have progressive tendencies, he was still stuck with many of his father's old-guard advisors.

The presidential palace was located on a hill on the outskirts of Damascus, with a commanding view of the city below. In a city of mud brick, this glass and granite edifice was not only above but separate from the other buildings. I had been there once before, in December 1993. We had met then with President Hafez Assad, the father of Bashar. At this time Assad was an aging man, clearly in declining health. But he maintained his signature characteristic, loquaciousness. The first President Assad was famous for meetings that became marathons, and for making long, serpentine statements in response to questions. It was not unusual for a single inquiry to provoke a forty-minute response. (Assad would have been a good candidate for the U.S. Senate.) Sessions would go on for four or more hours without a break, and one former assistant secretary of state remembers a meeting going nine hours and forty-five minutes with one bathroom break. The first President Bush's Secretary of State, James Baker, said that a meeting with Assad was not so much a diplomatic exchange as a test of one's bladder, and began calling such meetings "bladder diplomacy."[2]

Bashar Assad was never intended to lead Syria—he was not considered particularly politically inclined—and his brother Basil was the one being groomed for leadership. As a result, Bashar went to London to study to become an ophthalmologist, where he married a British woman. When Basil died in a car crash in 1994, Bashar returned home and took his late brother's position as commander of the Syrian army's armored division. When Hafez Assad died in 2000, the Syrian People's Assembly amended the constitution, lowering the president's minimum age from 40 to 34, and the 35-year-old Bashar took office.

We were welcomed at the palace's main entrance and escorted through a 30-foot-high lobby into the president's reception room. Almost a hundred feet away at the far end of the room stood the second President Assad; his foreign minister, Farouk al-Sharaa, a holdover from his father; and the female translator, Bouthaina Shaaban, who was becoming Syria's spokesperson to the world.*

The new president looked like his father—tall, trim, and angular—but the similarities ended there. Bashar has been seen as a turning of the generational and attitudinal page for Syria. Urbane, educated in the West and acculturated to it, and with a seeming openness to technological transformation, he represented modernity for a nation that had experienced little of it.

I had a clear idea of what I wanted to discuss during my time with Bashar: Hezbollah, Lebanon, and Iraq.

After a short opening statement of welcome in which he expressed his vision for a modern Syria, his sympathy for the attacks we suffered on September 11, and the desire that improved relations with the United States be an important part of a modern Syria, President Assad solicited questions. Though he spoke to us through his interpreter, he didn't need to have our questions translated.

As the leader of the delegation, I began with the expected diplomatic niceties. Then, describing the Iranian cargo plane we had seen the night before at the airport, I asked, "Mr. President, Americans are concerned with what appears to have been a pattern of condoning Hezbollah and other terrorists with bases of operation in Syria and the areas of Lebanon under your control. Would you join the global war on terror and discharge these elements from your territory?"

President Assad was annoyed by this frankness but not surprised. It was clear this was not the first time he had been asked some variant of my question. He was prepared.

"We do not agree with the assumption that Syria is harboring terrorists. Many of these groups you dismiss as terrorists are an important part of the civic life of our nation as well as that of Lebanon. Hezbollah provides humanitarian services which frequently the government is unable to perform. It schools children who would otherwise be illiterate, provides medical services to the poor, and in Lebanon it is a recognized po-

---

* In April 2003, I debated Ms. Shaaban at a forum on the future of U.S.–Syria relations hosted by the Washington chapter of the Council on Foreign Relations. She was as adamant then in proclaiming Syria's clean hands as her president had been ten months earlier.

litical party with members in the national parliament. We have no evidence of Hezbollah terrorist activities. In southern Lebanon, Hezbollah has been part of the national resistance against Israeli invasion. That is a legitimate patriotic function, not terrorism. In Syria, there are now no terrorists."

"Mr. President," I replied, "Hezbollah has not only killed many Israelis, it has also killed Jews from Damascus to as far as Buenos Aires. Hezbollah is also responsible for over three hundred American deaths, and we have reason to believe that Saudi Hezbollah was responsible for the 1996 bombing of Khobar Towers in Riyadh, Saudi Arabia. We know that as al-Qaeda's camps are being taken down in Afghanistan, Hezbollah is adding to its training sites."

The President interrupted: "We have no proof that Hezbollah is operating camps for terrorists. Yes, it is training its members in humanitarian and social service skills—teachers, nurses, maybe occasionally to be a policeman—but certainly not terrorism."

Bashar appeared genuinely offended, and I decided at that point to defer to Senators Bayh and DeWine so they could ask their questions, which revolved around the Syrian occupation of Lebanon, an occupation that has been tightening since the mid-1970s and that America would like to see loosened. Senator DeWine also prodded Bashar to discuss a possible linkage between Hezbollah and al-Qaeda, which Bashar denied. This line of questioning set off a rant against Israel, in which the president declared that former national security advisor Sandy Berger and Israeli prime minister Ehud Barak were in cahoots. From there, Bashar moved on to President Bush, who he said had "killed hopes for peace" by telling the Arab world, "You must." It was a question of national dignity, he said, for Arab countries not to be told what to do, and Bush had flouted that.

After this, I returned to the subject of Hezbollah. "Mr. President, my nation has information gathered from persons within your country and in Lebanon as well as our own aerial photographs which have satisfied us that there are camps within your control which are training men and women for terrorist acts. Would you like to see our photographs? Would you allow a representative of the U.S. or an appropriate international agency to visit these sites and independently determine their use?"

"No. I have already seen your pictures. You are confusing civic preparation for terrorism. It would be an affront to our sovereignty to have non-nationals surveying our internal locations. You will have to respectfully accept our representations."

With Assad having put his foot down on the subject of Hezbollah, I turned to the subject of Iraq. "The U.S. and much of the international community are gravely concerned with the failure of your neighbor Iraq to abide by its commitments to the UN in resolutions detailing Iraq's expected deportment in the aftermath of the 1991 Persian Gulf war. We are especially concerned about the lingering suspicions that Iraq has an operational chemical and biological weapons capability and may be close to the same with nuclear. What are your thoughts as to the threat of Iraq?"

The President paused. "Saddam Hussein might be a crazy man but he is not stupid. His people were deeply damaged by the war with Iran before the war with you. Iraq is a battered country. I do not believe it represents a serious threat to anybody. We have a three-hundred-mile border with Iraq and we do not feel threatened. Iraqis have their own way of solving their own problems. They will do it, sometime."

I was struck by the similarities of thought and expression between this young president and the experienced leader in Cairo. Still, I was disappointed by our meeting. The new president seemed to be under the control of the foreign minister, and although more convivial and Westernized than his father, no more willing to engage in a reasoned exchange of ideas.

With social protocols and the exchange of gifts, we departed. I looked at my watch as we left. The meeting had lasted less than two hours.

★

Our next stop was to be Beirut, a prospect exciting to Adele. Her father, Gabriel Khoury, had left Lebanon as a child early in the twentieth century. Throughout the years of conflict, Adele was saddened at what was happening and sorry that she would never see the "Paris of the Mediterranean," as it was when her father left. When we took our first trip to Lebanon in January 1998, shortly after it was permissible for Americans to do so, U.S. airliners and military aircraft were not allowed to land in Beirut, so our delegation drove in from Damascus. At the border, we were joined by Lebanese security. I thought I had been guarded by some world-class protectors before, for instance those who guarded us in Colombia, but nothing like this. We became part of a procession of about a half-dozen military vehicles. The ones before and behind our car carried .50-caliber machine guns on roof-mounted turrets.

The scars of war were evident, from the central city to what had been the posh homes and haunts of the affluent tourists in the town of Jounieh along the Mediterranean. Adele grieved at what had become of her father's homeland.

This trip to Beirut was easier. It is only a thirty-minute flight from Damascus to Beirut. Historically, the divide had been much greater, with Lebanon choosing to serve as a sort of Switzerland of the Middle East, beholden to no nation. But since the "bad times" of the Lebanese civil war, which lasted from 1975 to 1990, and the Israeli invasion and partial occupation, which occurred in 1982 and lasted until 2000, Lebanon had for most purposes been an annex of Syria. Although the number of Syrian troops had declined somewhat since Adele and I first visited four and a half years earlier, Syria's presence and influence remained substantial. No consequential governmental action is taken without first checking with Damascus.

That presence exacerbated a fault line in Lebanon: religious profession. Since the founding of this multicultural nation in 1943, Lebanon has had a religious-profession-based allocation of political power, what is called a confessional political system. Lebanon's "National Covenant," an unwritten agreement negotiated among Lebanese political leaders in 1943, provided for the president to be a Maronite Christian, the prime minister to be a Sunni Muslim, and the speaker of the Chamber of Deputies (renamed the National Assembly in 1979) to be a Shia Muslim. The National Covenant also provided that parliamentary seats and civil service jobs be allocated on the ration of six Christians to five Muslims (including the Druze, a separate religious group often associated with Islam).

To avoid destabilizing an already fractured nation, no census has been taken in Lebanon for more than seventy years. The unspoken reality is that a realignment of political power based on a contemporary enumeration of the people of Lebanon would result in a substantially greater influence for the Islamic population.

This division is also reflected in Lebanese opinion of Syria and

Hezbollah, with the Muslim Lebanese being distinctly more accommodating than the Christian. In fact, Adele had a number of conversations with women in Lebanon who—contrary to President Assad's assertions—pointed to Hezbollah as a problem rather than a solution.

In the summer of 1982, at the request of the Lebanese government, the United States agreed to establish a military presence in Lebanon to serve as a peacekeeping force in the conflict between warring Muslim and Christian factions. Initially, the U.S. forces, along with our French and Italian allies, were able to provide a measure of stability. However, as diplomatic efforts failed to achieve a basis for a lasting settlement, the Muslim factions came to perceive the Marines as enemies, and began a series of attacks on the Marine encampment at the airport. In the early morning of October 23, 1983, a truck laden with compressed-gas-enhanced explosives entered the grounds of the airport. Nothing seemed out of the ordinary until the truck accelerated and headed for the Marines' headquarters building. The resulting explosion and the collapse of the building killed 241 Marines, sailors, and soldiers. After an investigation, Hezbollah was determined to be the culprit. Many observers consider the 1983 bombing of the U.S. Marine barracks the first attack in a terrorist war against America.

★

The following morning, July 3, Evan and Susan Bayh left our trip for July 4 commitments in Indiana, and Mike DeWine and I had our first meeting at the U.S. embassy. This is the third embassy the U.S. has occupied in Beirut since America reestablished a diplomatic presence there in 1952. Following an April 1983 suicide bomb attack, in which forty-nine embassy staff (seventeen of whom were Americans) were killed and thirty-four were injured, the embassy relocated to Awkar, north of the capital. A bombing there, in September 1984, killed twenty-three (two of whom were Americans) and injured fifty-eight. In September 1989, the embassy closed and all American staff were evacuated, due to security threats. In 1990, the embassy was reopened in the same Awkar location, except that the site—a campuslike hilltop compound overlooking the Mediterranean—had been modified into a fortress, with guard towers and both Lebanese and U.S. security personnel.

The issue I was most interested in learning about there was Hezbollah. Although founded and largely supported financially and militarily by Iran and controlled from Damascus, Hezbollah had its most significant operations in Lebanon.

A product of the civil wars and the Israeli invasions, Hezbollah was best known for its aggressive actions against the Israelis while they occupied southern Lebanon and for the shelling and occasional incursions across the border into the upper Galilee.

Our briefers predicted that was about to change. "We have compelling evidence that Hezbollah has made a pact with Palestinian terrorist organizations. Hezbollah has never done this before, but its leadership feels that the climactic moment is at hand in the Palestinian-Israel conflict. They want to be part of that ultimate Islamic victory. Specifically, Hezbollah is working with Palestinians to increase the lethality of the Palestinian attacks. Hamas and Islamic Jihad are still relying on individual suicide bombers. Hezbollah is instructing the Palestinians on the use of car and truck bombs so that rather than destroying a single restaurant and its customers, the devastation can be spread more widely—for example, an office building in Tel Aviv or an apartment in Haifa. Hundreds of deaths. The Mossad [Israeli intelligence] is working this hard."

Our briefer pulled out a map of Lebanon and began to explain that our lack of human assets and of people with the necessary language skills made it nearly impossible to get sound information.

Another Lebanese official whom we had met on our prior trip, and whom Adele and I wanted to see again, was the deputy prime minister, Issam Fares. He had generously offered to host a dinner in honor of the congressional delegation at his mountainside home.

Like Prime Minister Rafiq al-Hariri, the deputy was a very wealthy man, estimated to have a net worth of substantially more than $1 billion. There has been a tradition in the small country of Lebanon, with its population of slightly more than 4 million, that the most economically successful would lead the government. Because Lebanon had served for years as an international center, where the elites of the Arab world had come to shop, vacation, and bank, there is no shortage of wealth.

Though Mr. Fares was the deputy prime minister, under the confessional political structure of Lebanon he was not the prime minister's deputy, but rather the governmental representative of the Greek Orthodox Lebanese.

It was interesting that from each leader of each different religious group, we heard a slightly different recitation of events and view of the world, all colored by a desire not to anger Syria, with its thousands of troops stationed there. However, a couple of points were made by all of Lebanon's leaders: peace with Israel must be achieved, and Geroge W. Bush's lack of leadership had retarded the achievement of that objective. Prime Minister Hariri told us, "There is no leader in the region who can make peace without the United States." Nayla Mouawad, Lebanon's former first lady (her husband was assassinated) and a current member of parliament, told us, "The President's speech was not good. It was a vision, not a plan."

President Emile Lahoud told us that "when peace comes, Syria will leave." This was an especially interesting statement given that when I had first met President Lahoud, he was the chief of staff of the Lebanese army and had been an extremely progressive leader, creating a strong, integrated national army. As president, Lahoud, a Maronite Christian, seemed to have changed; he was now unwilling to challenge Syria on the very issues that once defined him.

President Lahoud also told us that the claims that Iraq had chemical and biological weapons were unimportant because a number of countries in the region had them. He also said that there was no link between Iraq and al-Qaeda, and that if we were to invade Iraq, it would only make things worse. Anything we heard to the contrary was a fiction perpetrated by "Jewish lobbyists and *The Washington Post*." I was not surprised at the comments about Israel. As we had already seen in Cairo and Damascus, the Israeli-Palestinian issue is both an infected sore and a convenient excuse.

On the Fourth of July the delegation returned to the U.S. embassy to help dedicate the memorial that had been erected to the hundreds of Americans and Lebanese in the service of the United States who had been killed in Lebanon over the last two decades.

This was to be the first formal memorial service held at the embassy; Lebanese families of the fallen were in the audience. Their willingness to work with the American embassy in the hopes of building a stronger relationship between the United States and Lebanon had gotten them killed, and to see America honor their loved ones reduced many to tears.

As we remembered the lives lost, I also thought of the lost opportunity that was Lebanon—a multiethnic, multireligious, prosperous nation that could have been an example to the Arab world had instead become impoverished, embracing those who sought to control it, killing those who sought to help it.

★

One of the many ridiculous expressions of the arms-length relationship between neighboring Arab states and Israel is the legal barrier keeping aircraft from flying directly between Israel and most of them. To maintain the pretense of Israel's nonexistence, aircraft must make an intermediate stop in one of the only two Arab states that fully recognizes Israel, the Hashemite Kingdom of Jordan.*

Again, I was particularly disappointed to see Lebanon participating in this silly prohibition, because the Western entrepreneurial spirit of both Lebanon and Israel should make them good candidates for commercial and eventually political collaboration.

On a trip sponsored by the Greater Miami Jewish Federation to Israel in April 1998, Adele and I visited a company called ISCAR, Limited. Built in a well-planned industrial park in the upper Galilee town of Tefen, the ISCAR plant is one of the world's major producers of metal-cutting tools. At the time, they were producing fans for jet aviation engines. It is just a few miles from the southern Lebanese border. At the time, a significant number of the workers there were Lebanese, driving or busing in each day to their well-paid jobs. The founder and CEO of ISCAR, Stef Wertheimer, articulated his philosophy: "Israel is a Mediterranean, not a Middle Eastern, nation. So is Lebanon, and we are destined to be economic partners. The secret to making peace will be economics—we'll be too busy meeting Japanese just-on-time delivery schedules to make war. Everyone can worship their own god as long as they get up at seven A.M. and go to work."

---

* Because Egypt also recognizes Israel, there are direct flights from Cairo.

To me this is the model for long-term peace in the Middle East: when people divided by religion, history, and hatred are able to find in their economic enterprises a shared future of stability and prosperity. As we left that plant I remember thinking, *I bet there are no recruits for Hezbollah among the Lebanese working in this plant.*

Sadly, because the border is now closed, those workers are no longer at the plant. At the time, I noted that places like ISCAR were the exception rather than the rule, and would continue to be so long as the Syrians exercise effective control over Lebanon. Events have proven this fear correct.

What should have been a flight of no more than thirty minutes from Lebanon to Israel took over an hour. Because of the rule against flying directly to Israel, we filed a flight plan for Jordan. This whole charade seemed even more absurd when I realized that planes need not touch the ground in Jordan, but can meet the Muslim test of purity by simply making a low pass over the Amman airport. That is what we did. Our wheels didn't come within 500 feet of the runway, but our approach was enough to absolve us of the sin of flying from Lebanon to Israel, and a few minutes later we landed at Ben Gurion Airport, on the eastern outskirts of Tel Aviv.

While I learned some things about the state of Israel, what I most recall is what I learned about the United States. Our briefer described the architecture of the Israeli intelligence community and how it had been influenced by national history. Prior to the Sinai war in 1956, Israel had followed an amalgam of the American and British models. They had a central organization similar to our Director of Central Intelligence, but with greater authority, and several specialized units, analogous to the signal responsibilities of the National Security Agency. That changed after the Sinai war. There was a public and political outcry that the intelligence agencies had let the country down by not anticipating the war, a failure that denied the civilian and military leadership the opportunity to prepare or preempt. The consequence of this described failure was the creation of a military intelligence capability outside the civilian intelligence community.

The briefer offered the opinion that this bifurcated system gave Israeli decision makers the chance to listen to the intelligence of both the civilian and military agencies and select that which coincided with their view or best validated a preconceived opinion. It was our briefer's assessment that the Israeli government of Prime Minister Ariel Sharon had fallen too much under the influence of the military and that this was undergirding the government's harsh strategy against the Palestinians.

The irony was that the very system that the briefer was describing to us as a way of creating an intelligence failure was exactly what was being constructed in the Pentagon by Secretary of Defense Donald Rumsfeld. In 2002, he created the Pentagon Office of Special Plans. Operating under Rumsfeld's command and directly overseen by Undersecretary of Defense for Policy Douglas Feith, the Office of Special Plans circumvented the standard processes for reviewing intelligence and operated free of the Defense Intelligence Agency, which has supplied operational intelligence information to Secretaries of Defense for over forty years. If you set up competing intelligence collection agencies, the user will simply take information from the agency whose conclusions are closest to what the user wants to hear, especially if one of those agencies is created simply to validate pre-formed opinions. Therefore, it was no surprise that the Office of Special Plans came up with some of the most terrifying—and inaccurate—claims about Iraq's weapons of mass destruction and some of the most wildly optimistic pictures of the reception Americans would be given should we invade.

It had been an extremely valuable tour, which would shape my thinking regarding the impending war in Iraq and what would be required to win the war on terrorism.

15

Discoveries in San Diego

Throughout the summer, the Joint Inquiry accelerated its activities and its preparation for public hearings. It also made two major discoveries.

On August 15, 2002, I was in Tallahassee, Florida, when I received a telephone call from Eleanor Hill. She said she had some urgent information that she could discuss only on a secure line. I suggested she call the Tallahassee office of the FBI to determine whether they had a secure line and, if so, whether I could use it. In less than ten minutes, Eleanor called back to tell me that they did have such a line, and that arrangements had been made for me to use it. I said I would be right over.

The Tallahassee office of the FBI is located in a three-story building just off Tennessee, one of the major streets in Tallahassee, which is named for the home state of territorial Florida's first governor, Andrew Jackson. I was ushered to a small room with cheap paneling, a metal desk, and a telephone with the boxy look of every classified-information-cleared telephone.

These secure phones encrypt the data on one end and unscramble it on the other, so both participants' voices are chopped up with an effect rather like the one produced when you speak on a cell phone that is about to lose battery power.

"What's up, Eleanor?"

"We've had a couple of our best people in San Diego for a few days now. They've been reviewing the files of the FBI field office there and have come on some alarming things. We've confirmed that at least two of the hijackers lived there, one for almost a year. And one of them lived in the home of an FBI asset. The FBI is embarrassed about our finding these files—I can't say now whether they legitimately lost or forgot them or they were trying to hide them—but they are embarrassed."

This was a stunning discovery, and coming five months after we had asked the FBI for all the information they had on the September 11 terrorists, it was a frustrating one. Given how sensitive and explosive this issue could be, we held the information that a terrorist had been living with an FBI asset extremely closely, not even telling the full inquiry staff or members other than the four leaders.

It was a remarkable piece of investigative sleuthing that led to the discovery, one that, in retrospect, the FBI surely would have kept hidden had our staff not made that impossible. Mike Jacobson, a former FBI lawyer and counterintelligence analyst who was working on our inquiry, had been combing through FBI files on the hijackers. In doing so, he came across one informant report that was dated a couple of days after September 11 and that contained a description of Nawaf al-Hazmi leaving San Diego. FBI reports are notoriously poorly written, but Mike felt that something didn't sound right. When he read what the informant was saying about al-Hazmi, it seemed that the individual had reported on al-Hazmi *before* September 11. It looked like contemporaneous reporting—as if one of the FBI's informants actually knew at least one of the hijackers.

Mike gave the informant report to Tom Kelley, a thirty-two-year FBI veteran who had spent his last fifteen years as the Bureau's deputy general counsel and was also serving on our inquiry. Kelley presented the report to the liaison the FBI had assigned to the inquiry, asking what further information the FBI had on the matter. For weeks, despite continued follow-ups, the FBI had produced nothing.

Mike and Tom reported this to Eleanor. The team investigating the

FBI had previously planned a number of visits to several of the field offices, and the San Diego visit was approaching. Eleanor told Tom to call the San Diego field office and have them prepare to make available all of the files and agents dealing with an informant, because our people were going to investigate further. At this point, the idea that there might be an informant who knew one or more of the hijackers was still just a suspicion, but the FBI's reaction indicated that it might be a significant discovery.

Mike and Tom called the San Diego field office early in the week of August 5, and spent the rest of the week preparing their investigation. The day before they were supposed to travel to San Diego, Eleanor got a phone call from FBI headquarters asking whether a number of the FBI brass could meet with her alone regarding "a very sensitive issue."

Eleanor asked for further information, and the caller admitted that the FBI had some concerns about the staff's trip to San Diego that they wanted to discuss with her alone. Knowing full well that it is never a good idea to be the lone person on your side in any meeting lest it devolve into a case of "they said/I said," Eleanor demanded that the Joint Inquiry's deputy director, Rick Cinquegrana, be allowed to join. The caller agreed; within forty-five minutes, a number of FBI representatives, including one of the people who ran the FBI's informant program, showed up at the inquiry's Ford Building conference room.

The FBI representatives proceeded to tell Eleanor and Rick that they were worried about Joint Inquiry staff going to San Diego because the investigators would likely stumble on some information regarding an informant. Eleanor and Rick responded that the informant was going to be a focus of our investigators once they were out there, and would the FBI care to volunteer the information they had on the subject?

At this point, the FBI representatives admitted that, indeed, there was an FBI counterterrorist informant who had had a very close relationship with the two hijackers al-Mihdhar and al-Hazmi.

Eleanor demanded to know why the inquiry hadn't been told about this earlier, to which the FBI responded that we hadn't really asked about it, despite the fact that we had asked for everything they had about the hijackers.

The FBI representatives went on to say that they still felt that our investigators should not go out to San Diego, because they were certain to come across the informant issue, and issues involving informants are highly sensitive.

Eleanor and Rick stood firm, with Eleanor telling them that not only would our people be going to San Diego but also they were to have access to the entire informant file, including information about money that had been paid to the informant, the opportunity to interview the handling agents and the case agents, and anything else they should want. The FBI grudgingly relented on the question of the trip, but did not relent in their general obstructionism.

In San Diego, Mike and Tom discovered that the relationship between the informant and the two terrorists was closer than they had previously thought. The informant has now been identified in press reports as Abdussattar Shaikh, the man in whose house al-Mihdhar and al-Hazmi spent a significant amount of time. Even more amazingly, after al-Mihdhar left the country in June 2000 to recruit the attack's muscle men, al-Hazmi rented a room in Shaikh's house.

The terrorists were living under the nose of an FBI informant, and somehow the connection was never made because the right questions weren't being asked. Mike and Tom also interviewed the agent who had handled the informant, and who had recently retired. The handling agent was furious because, he said, he had read a number of stories in the paper that the CIA had al-Mihdhar and al-Hazmi's names. He (erroneously) thought that the FBI also had their names and knew about their travel to the United States as well, but hadn't told him. This agent believed that had he known the names al-Mihdhar and al-Hazmi, he would have—through focused surveillance and investigation—broken the plot open.[1]

The other person we wanted to talk to was the informant himself. The problem was that the FBI was extremely resistant to our request to interview him, arguing that they had already investigated him and that he was an innocent, with no knowledge of the plans of the men he had befriended. The FBI could not, however, explain a number of inconsistencies in the informant's statements, inconsistencies that our staff—not the FBI—had uncovered in reading the files. Of course, the FBI's investigation of the informant was a self-investigation, so we were skeptical of their conclusion: it might have been colored by self-interest. We kept pressing them to produce the informant. Weeks passed in this way. The

FBI kept arguing that the informant was still a valuable asset who could be rehabilitated. We argued that his name and relationship to the hijackers had by that point been all over the newspapers, and the odds of him being privy to any future information were infinitesimal.

One of our problems was that the informant had been relocated by the FBI "for his own safety." Because only the FBI knew where to find him, it was able to control our access to him.

We decided that the only way to get our questions answered by the informant would be to depose him under oath. We would have to subpoena him to appear before us.

Congressional subpoenas can be served by U.S. marshals, the FBI, and even congressional staff. Because only the FBI knew where the informant could be found, we'd have to ask them to serve the subpoena. On Tuesday, September 26, 2002, several FBI agents came to testify before the Joint Inquiry regarding the Moussaoui case and the Phoenix electronic communication. Afterward, I asked the FBI's then general counsel, Ken Wainstein, to join me in our conference room. He, several other FBI staff who were present, and several of our Joint Inquiry staff gathered in the small conference room situated behind the hearing room. We often used this room to meet with witnesses either before or after their testimony.

We made small talk for a couple of minutes and then the issue of the informant came up. I described our interactions with the FBI so far, and our desire to depose the informant under oath. As I did so, I removed the subpoena from my pocket. The mood in the room suddenly cooled. I turned to Ken Wainstein and asked that the FBI serve the subpoena for us.

He visibly stiffened, locking his hands behind his back, and stammered something like "Let's see if we can find some other way to do this." With the subpoena still in hand, I approached him, holding it inches from his chest. My most enduring memory of that day is Mr. Wainstein's body language. He leaned back from the subpoena as if it were radioactive; his hands remained pinned behind his back. I am certain that had I placed the subpoena in his lapel pocket, his hands still would not have moved. I was about to do just that when Mr. Wainstein said that he'd prefer not to take the subpoena, but would get back to us by the following Monday, and if we hadn't worked something out by then, "the FBI will effect service." Nobody ever got back to us. Never before, in all my time in Congress, had I seen the FBI refuse to serve a subpoena.

When it became clear that the subpoena wouldn't be served, we called a meeting to discuss the issue with Director Mueller in the committee hearing room in the Capitol. Also present were the inquiry investigators who had been most involved in discovering the informant.

Because we had been told by the FBI that our discoveries raised policy questions for the administration and not just for the FBI, we also asked that Attorney General John Ashcroft and DCI George Tenet attend. They both were present (although Ashcroft left halfway through the meeting).

We told them that the FBI's refusal to serve the subpoena and produce a person who could shed serious light on the attacks of September 11 was untenable. FBI Director Mueller made a staunch defense of the informant program, calling it sacrosanct and reminding us that the FBI never allows informants to be identified, or produced.

Eleanor pointed out that that wasn't always true, and named a number of examples of mob union-infiltration cases where informants had been produced.

Mueller pointed out that to disclose the informant's identity would make it infinitely more difficult to recruit informants from the Muslim community.

We argued that the informant would be able to testify in private, not sharing his identity. Besides, we pointed out, a San Diego newspaper and *Newsweek* magazine had already exposed the informant, and thus they were talking about keeping from Congress something the press and public already knew.

They argued that the informant's name hadn't been confirmed officially.

Both Porter Goss and I expressed doubt about the informant's continuing value, but Ashcroft and Mueller were unmoved. They suggested, instead, that we write up some questions; they would deliver them to the informant, who would answer them. So Dana Lesemann, who was also on the FBI team of the Joint Inquiry and had worked at the Office of Intelligence Policy and Review at the Department of Justice, typed up thirty-five pages of interrogatories.

Rather than deliver the questions immediately, the FBI sat on them for weeks, and by the time they reached the informant, we were told, he had secured a lawyer, a well-known former Justice Department attorney. It challenges belief that a man who is so debt-laden that he has to take in boarders would just by chance find a former federal prosecutor who happened to have a strong relationship with the FBI. The circumstances are almost as unbelievable as the "coincidence" that Omar al-Bayoumi happened to walk into a restaurant in Los Angeles to have lunch and befriended the two future hijackers at the next table. It was as if in an effort to protect their informant, the FBI had secured counsel for him.

The interrogatories would not be answered. The informant's lawyer did tell us that if we granted the informant immunity, he would be willing to talk to us; but he would not do so, either voluntarily or under subpoena, unless immunized.

It seemed strange that an individual who claimed to have done nothing wrong, who the FBI was claiming had done nothing wrong, and who the FBI argued continued to be a valuable source of information, would request immunity. Although our committee did have the power to immunize him, we felt that it would be irresponsible to immunize someone who—despite repeated requests to the lawyer—had given us no indication of what he might tell us. What's more, there were a number of inconsistencies in what the informant had said in previous interviews with the FBI, so we had questions about his truthfulness. We needed to know whether the informant was in cahoots with the hijackers; we simply couldn't give blanket immunity to an individual who might have been helping or collaborating with the hijackers.

To this day, the FBI claims that the informant had no knowledge that could have helped prevent the attacks. We have gotten them to concede that the answers the informant provided in response to their questions were at best inconsistent. And they promised that they would investigate further. To my knowledge, they have not.

At the end of the whole FBI experience, one thing was clear: we would not be hearing what the informant had to say.

Besides denying access to the informant, the FBI also, from the day in August when we first uncovered the story, vehemently insisted that we could not, even in the most sanitized manner, tell the American people that an FBI informant had a relationship with two of the hijackers. The

FBI opposed public hearings on the subject and repeatedly deleted any references to this issue from the drafts of the Joint Inquiry's unclassified final report. Not until the summer following the discovery of the informant—nearly a year later—did the FBI finally agree to allow a heavily redacted version of the story to appear in our public report. And that happened only after many rounds of intense negotiations that culminated in discussions with the most senior levels of the Bush administration.

This whole episode invited the question why the FBI was so unwilling to have us talk to their informant, or speak publicly of him. The FBI seemed more concerned with first hiding and then protecting their informant than they were with looking at why they failed to ask the informant the right questions. I've puzzled over this quite a bit, and the most obvious answer is that the informant was a big embarrassment. Was the informant using the FBI? Was the FBI's informant program so shallow that the Bureau didn't discover that its own informant was personally close to these hijackers?

A less obvious and far more damning possibility is that perhaps the informant did know something about the plot that would be even more damaging were it revealed, and that this is what the FBI is trying to conceal.

There was another reason as well, one we wouldn't learn of until November 18, 2002, when a senior member of the FBI's congressional affairs staff sent a candid letter to Congressman Goss and me, explaining why the FBI had been so uncooperative in several instances. In discussing the case of the informant, the letter said, "the Administration would not sanction a staff interview with the source. Nor did the Administration agree to allow the FBI to serve a subpoena or a notice of deposition on the source." We were seeing in writing what we had suspected for some time: the White House was directing the cover-up.

★

Also in San Diego, our investigators made another discovery, one that prompted another secure phone call from Eleanor to me, and one that would come to be one of the most explosive and contentious pieces of information unearthed by the Joint Inquiry.

This call came the day after the first. "You are not going to believe what Mike and Tom found yesterday in San Diego. If you can go to the secure phone line, I'd like to discuss it with you."

Half an hour later, settling into the same government-issue chair I had used the day before, I heard the single most incredible tale of this tragedy.

Eleanor's voice was trembling over the phone. "We've found more in the FBI files in San Diego. . . . There are two money trails to Omar al-Bayoumi."

Eleanor explained that al-Bayoumi's income and his cover came from employment in a subsidiary contractor for the Saudi Aviation Authority, a ghost job from which he received a paycheck but never reported to work. Since 1993, he had worked for a company called Ercan, which in turn contracted with Dallah Avco Aviation, a Saudi government contractor owned by Saleh Kamel, a wealthy Saudi who belongs to what is known as "the Golden Chain," which provides money to Osama bin Laden and al-Qaeda on a regular basis. During his time working for Ercan, he showed up for work only once, a fact that led his supervisor to complain that he should be fired. The supervisor was reportedly told that Ercan's contract would be terminated if they didn't continue al-Bayoumi on the payroll. In fact, it is reported that in 1999, when another attempt was made to end al-Bayoumi's employment, the director general of Saudi Civil Aviation—in a letter marked "extremely urgent"—made clear that the government wanted al-Bayoumi's contract renewed "as quickly as possible."[2] From this "ghost job" al-Bayoumi was getting paid a monthly salary of about $2,800 with allowances of $465 a month.

In March 2000, a month after he had invited al-Hazmi and al-Midhdar to San Diego and got them set up with an apartment and connected with friends at the mosque, al-Bayoumi's monthly allowances from Ercan rose by a factor of eight, from $465 to $3,700. They stayed at that level until December, when al-Hazmi left for Arizona. During that time al-Bayoumi got nearly $30,000 more than he would have normally.

I asked Eleanor if there was any explanation, and her answer agreed exactly with what I was thinking:

"No, but it sure looks as if al-Bayoumi was the conduit for money from Ercan and probably Dallah Avco to al-Hazmi and al-Midhdar."

I then asked about the second money trail Eleanor had mentioned.

She asked whether I remembered al-Bayoumi's friend, Osama Bassnan, and then explained that in April 1998, Bassnan's wife required thyroid surgery. Bassnan pleaded for help on behalf of his wife to the Royal Embassy of the Kingdom of Saudi Arabia in Washington. This is not as strange as it might seem. Besides being the country's largest employer, the oil-rich monarchy curries favor with citizens by giving them direct payments; thus, many Saudis get subsidies of one sort or another without coming under scrutiny. Similarly, the Royal Embassy of the Kingdom of Saudi Arabia will often provide financial assistance for Saudis living in America. As a result of his plea, Bassnan received a check for $15,000. That amount turned out to be insufficient, and Bassnan's wife made a separate request. She appealed to the ambassador's wife, Princess Haifa al-Faisal, was put on the Princess's charity list in January 1999, and began to receive cashier's checks of between $2,000 and $3,000 a month. Apparently an FBI agent had managed to get a copy of one of the checks and found that it was drawn on a Riggs Bank account in the Princess's name. Beginning in 2000, Bassnan's wife began signing her checks over to a woman named Manal Bajadr—the wife of Omar al-Bayoumi. It looked suspiciously like another backdoor way of channeling money to al-Hazmi and al-Mihdhar. This would also justify Bassnan's boast to the FBI that he had done more for the two future hijackers than had al-Bayoumi.

Given that al-Bayoumi is suspected of having used these funds to support al-Hazmi and al-Mihdhar, to follow that stream of income is to trace a line from the Kingdom of Saudi Arabia to the wife of one spy, to the wife of another, and ultimately to the hands of two plotting terrorists.

At the same time, to follow the ebb and flow of the second stream of income, the "allowances" paid to al-Bayoumi from Ercan is to see payments made to a man who does no work—payments made by a contractor of the Saudi government under the threat of losing the contract if they are not made—increasing eightfold during the time he was supporting two future terrorists in San Diego.

What's more, between January 2000 and May 2000, al-Bayoumi had an unusually large number of telephone conversations with Saudi government officials in both Los Angeles and Washington.

It took a minute for all this to sink in. In January 2000, a suspected Saudi spy travels to the Saudi consulate embassy in Los Angeles, where he meets with an official whose activities would later get that official deported. After that meeting, he coincidentally runs into two future terrorists at a Middle Eastern restaurant and offers to help get them set up in San Diego. Once the future terrorists arrive in San Diego, that spy holds a dinner in their honor, introduces them to like-minded individuals, helps them procure official identification, and made the initial payments for their apartment. The spy, Omar al-Bayoumi, describes their meeting as coincidental and his aid as something he would do out of hospitality for any Muslim brother. Except that we had now discovered that al-Bayoumi wasn't just acting out of the goodness of his heart—in the five months that Khalid al-Mihdhar spent in San Diego and the ten months that Nawaf al-Hazmi spent there, al-Bayoumi's income rose in conjunction with his support for them, and that increase came from two sources, a Saudi government contractor and a member of the Saudi royal family. From these two sources, al-Bayoumi was funneled in excess of $40,000 above his usual salary—somewhere between one sixth and one twelfth the estimated total amount needed to fund the September 11 attacks.

A couple of days after this phone call, our investigators found a CIA memo dated August 2, 2002, whose author concluded that there is "incontrovertible evidence that there is support for these terrorists within the Saudi government."[3]

On September 11, America was not attacked by a nation-state, but we had just discovered that the attackers were actively supported by one, and that state was our supposed friend and ally Saudi Arabia.

★

While the FBI was dragging out the informant issue and both the CIA and the FBI were ducking the issue of foreign support, the inquiry moved ahead on other matters, the most important being the public phase of our hearings.

The public portions of the Joint Inquiry were to be held in room 216 of the Hart Senate Office Building, a large, high-ceilinged room designated by the sign outside the door as the Central Hearing Facility.*

* The Hart Senate Office Building is the third of the Senate buildings. When it was completed, in 1981, Senator Pat Moynihan said that its "banality is exceeded only by its expense" and introduced a resolution to re-cover the building in the plastic sheathing that had hidden it during construction.

The first of our public hearings was to be held on September 18, 2002; the question was whom to call as our first witnesses. We felt that since ours was an investigation of the attacks of September 11, the people we most immediately had to answer to were the thousands who lost loved ones on that day. To that end, we decided to hear statements from two individuals nominated by the families as their representatives—Kristen Breitweiser, co-chairperson of the September 11 Advocates, and Steven Push, treasurer of the Families of September 11.

That decision was immediately met with outrage by a number of members of the intelligence community, who thought that the victims of the tragedy would have nothing to offer and would turn our hearings into a circus. One of them, speaking anonymously to *USA Today,* asked, "Who's running this investigation, Oprah?" and complained that having to follow a statement from the families was tantamount to a setup: "The goal is, 'Let's see who we can get to cry on camera.' The next day they will have witnesses from U.S. intelligence come in to explain why all these people are widows and orphans."[4]

We felt, on the contrary, that there would be no more appropriate way to publicly introduce our mission and to remind both the nation and the panel members of the solemnity of our work. We would hear from the victims' representatives, and then we would have the first public staff statement, read aloud by Eleanor Hill.

Guests walking into the room that day saw a raised stage, with twenty high-backed leather chairs arrayed around a half-hexagon table facing the witness and the audience. A step lower and in front of those chairs was another crescent of seventeen chairs, also facing the audience and the witness table. The effect was that of a two-tiered assault, thirty-seven questioners, each facing down the witness.

That first day, the hearing room was packed—and skeptical.

From the internal staff changes, to the delay in the hearing schedule, to the highly publicized NSA leak, we had been pounded by unfavorable media coverage almost from the outset. At the same time, we knew we were doing good work, and the first open hearing would be a chance for us to show it.

At 10:00 A.M., I gaveled the inquiry to order, and commenced our public hearings with an opening statement.

I said that, like all Americans, we now realized that terrorism was no longer something that happened to people over there, on another side of the globe; terrorism could hurt people close to us here at home. I noted that the public hearings were part of our search for the truth—not to point fingers or pin blame, but to identify and correct whatever systemic problems might have prevented our government from detecting and disrupting al-Qaeda's plot. I explained how the hearings would be organized and conducted, and then handed off to the other three leaders to make their opening statements. Our first witness, Kristen Breitweiser, sat at the witness table, ready to begin her statement.

She thanked us for giving her the opportunity to speak for the families; calling their experience "an excruciating and overwhelming twelve months," she asked that we see through her the thousands of children who lost a mother or a father on September 11.

She then spoke of her husband, Ron, who died in the World Trade Center:

My most enduring memory of my husband, Ronald Breitweiser, will be his final words to me, "Sweets, I'm fine, I don't want you to worry, I love you." Ron uttered those words while he was watching men and women jump to their deaths from the top of Tower One. Four minutes later, his Tower was hit by United Flight 175. I never spoke to my husband, Ron, again.

I don't really know what happened to him. I don't know whether he jumped or he choked to death on smoke. I don't know whether he sat curled up in a corner watching the carpet melt in front of him, knowing that his own death was soon to come, or if he was alive long enough to be crushed by the buildings when they collapsed. These are the images that haunt me at night when I put my head to rest on his pillow.

I do know that the dream I had envisioned, that I so desperately needed to believe—that he was immediately turned to ash and floated up to the heavens—was simply not his fate. I know this because his wedding band was recovered from ground zero with a part of his left arm. The wedding band is charred and scratched, but still perfectly round and fully intact. I wear it on my right hand, and it will remain there until I die.

The silence that descended on the room as Mrs. Breitweiser spoke was broken only by muffled sobs. She continued, noting that the carnage and devastation answers the question whether we did enough to prevent the attacks. She concluded by reminding us that we in that room had been targets, also, on September 11. However, "for most of you, there was a relief at the end of that day; a relief that you and your loved ones were in safe hands. You were the lucky ones. In your continuing investigation, please do not forget those of us who did not share in your good fate."

Following the statements by Mrs. Breitweiser and Mr. Push, Eleanor Hill took to the witness table to read the Joint Inquiry's first public staff statement. As that statement was being prepared, the inquiry had tangled with intelligence officials over how much information could be declassified. We wanted to make public as much as possible in order to give the American people as full a picture as we could of the work we were doing, and of our findings. By the night before the first public hearing, we had resolved all of our disputes but two. George Tenet would not allow us to say whether the President had received the August 6 PDB, even though the subject matter of that briefing had been declassified and was included in the public staff statement. It seemed ludicrous to us that the substance of a presidential briefing could be made public but we had to keep secret whether the President actually received it. This ruling by the CIA was clearly intended to protect the President politically, which is simply not an acceptable reason for classification.

The other issue involved the identity of and information about a key al-Qaeda leader who was involved in the September 11 attacks. This remained classified even though the leader's name had been widely reported in the media.

Rather than try to hide or work around these challenges, Eleanor decided to begin the staff statement by simply laying them out as fact, and then going on to say, "The Joint Inqury Staff disagrees with the DCI's position on both issues. We believe the American public has a compelling interest in this information and that public disclosure would not harm national security. However, we do not have independent authority to declassify intelligence information short of a lengthy procedure in the U.S. Congress. We therefore prepared this statement without detailed descriptions of our work in these two areas."

Within two minutes of its first public hearing statement, our inquiry had fired a shot across the bow of the intelligence agencies. We would not be pushovers, we would not be afraid to use public embarrassment as leverage to obtain or declassify information, and the only entity to which we would be beholden was the truth.

Eleanor's statement went on to summarize the work of the Joint Inquiry up to that point, beginning with the scope of our work and the way we went about it, summarizing the evolving terrorist threat and the intelligence community's response. Specifically, she summarized what we knew about bin Laden's intentions, the indications of a possible terrorist attack that appeared in the spring and summer of 2001, citing the twelve—twelve—instances in which we had learned of terrorist plans to use airplanes as weapons.

In twenty-six pages, the staff statement laid out a wealth of information, much of which hadn't been known before and the whole of which had never been assembled in one place. Seeing the information laid out in such a manner made the dots clearly visible and showed how they could have been connected.

The next morning, when I picked up my paper, I didn't see another near obituary for our inquiry. Instead, the lead, by the same writers who had chronicled our woes, now chronicled the discoveries we had made, including that al-Qaeda's desire to use airplanes as terror weapons was more widely known within intelligence circles than the Bush administration had acknowledged, and that bin Laden was extremely interested in carrying out an attack on U.S. soil, contrary to the Bush administration's claim that much of the pre–September 11 intelligence focused on threats overseas. In the days that followed, reports referred to the "litany of missed cues uncovered" and the "sobering portrait of key opportunities missed" our committee was painting.

Our inquiry had made some news, and, more important, earned some respect. We felt good about where things were headed.

★

Although the inquiry was moving along well, the political waters were getting choppier.

It had been a year since the meeting in the White House at which

Senator Lieberman and I argued for our differing visions of a new way of organizing the government to protect against terrorist attack. The President continued to oppose the establishment of a homeland defense coordinator or the creation of a separate department with the mission of protecting the homeland. He asserted that former Pennsylvania governor Tom Ridge, as the President's special assistant, had sufficient authority to defend America. But the American public and the Congress were growing skeptical, especially after Governor Ridge's office announced, with much fanfare, a color-coded alert-level system that quickly created more jokes than comfort.

On June 6, the President announced that he was switching his position, proposing a Cabinet-level Department of Homeland Security to unite essential agencies in fighting the war on terror. Calling this the most extensive reorganization of the federal government since the creation of the Department of Defense in 1947, he asked Congress to pass his plan that year, before the end of the congressional session.

To me, it seemed the President had arrived at a better policy in the most cynical way possible. After months of trying to stop the homeland security train, he had decided to get on board and pretend that he was the conductor.

Having not yet seen the President's proposed bill, I was pleased that he was at last removing his objections, but I still had concerns. A principal reason for my support of a Senate-confirmed director of counterterrorism in the White House, who would coordinate among existing agencies, rather than a massive restructuring, was that we simply didn't know enough at that point to say what would be the most effective homeland security structure.

In less than a year, the country was going from no consideration of a separate department of homeland security, because of the President's steadfast opposition, to the most massive reorganization of the federal government since the 1947 creation of the Department of Defense, the National Security Council, and the CIA.

There had been little time to assess the nature of the myriad vulnerabilities facing this most open of societies, much less to consider which of them should receive primary protection and what would be the best means to do so. In my opinion, the answers to those questions should be the basis for sweeping reform.

To my knowledge, the President had made no attempt to determine what were the best practices in countries that had had long histories of defending themselves against terrorism. For instance, a discussion with Great Britain's domestic intelligence agency, the MI-5 (such as the one I had in August 2001), would have yielded valuable information about how MI-5 served as a terrorism auditor for national critical infrastructure such as transportation, electricity generation and transmission, chemical plants, and other volatile manufacturing and storage facilities. Before locking on to a solution, it would have been wise to assess how others had approached the same problem.

Similarly, if the President had been less resistant to the idea of our committee and an independent commission investigating the failures that led to September 11, we would have been able to present him with recommendations for reform.

The fact that there had been little consultation and less curiosity made me skeptical about the President's true dedication to this idea. The fact that his homeland security proposal had been drafted in secret over the course of seven weeks by four top aides gave me further pause.[5] After all, it is one thing to want to keep a plan secret, another to assiduously avoid outside input.

My second worry about establishing a department was that during the period when disparate entities are being merged, the consolidated entity becomes less effective than the individual components prior to merger. The cultural differences of the previous departments and the energy consumed in consummating their merger take away from the necessity of investing in understanding the enemy and defeating it. Therefore, I thought that enhancing the office within the White House—by giving it statutory status and thus the active involvement of the Congress and the respect of the rest of the executive branch—would have been a preferable interim position.

The President, albeit belatedly, thought otherwise, and now he was trying to push through a very big reform in a very short time. Within the Congress, the lion's share of the responsibility for creating a Department of Homeland Security was given to the government oversight committees in both the House and Senate. The chairman of the Senate Governmental Affairs Committee, Senator Lieberman, handed off sections of the bill to be drafted by committees of jurisdiction. Senator

Shelby and I were given the responsibility to draft the intelligence components.

As the primary foreign intelligence agencies, such as the CIA, are prohibited from gathering information within the United States unless it is in support of an operation outside the United States, we recommended that these agencies not be moved to the new department. It was surprising to me how many senators were clamoring for the CIA's inclusion in the DHS, apparently unaware of that legal restriction on the CIA. However, once they were informed, there was near unanimous agreement that it should be excluded.

As far as the FBI was concerned, we noted that counterterrorism and domestic intelligence gathering were just two of the FBI's many functions, and that it didn't make sense to absorb the entire FBI into this new entity. Besides, we felt that the DHS didn't need an agency to go out and collect information. What we *did* want was a place within the Department of Homeland Security, a "fusion center" where the information gathered by other agencies would be reviewed and analyzed. This led to a debate over whether the "fusion center" would have access to raw data—information collected from the primary source that has not yet been analyzed, consolidated, or otherwise manipulated. Senator Shelby and I agreed that it should.

To clarify the concept of "raw data," if the NSA collects a million phone calls, a computer will narrow the million down to one hundred, and a human being will listen to the hundred to determine if there's anything significant about them. If there is, that person will distill that information into a report. The report is the intelligence; the hundred calls are the raw data. Raw-data access is a subject of considerable sensitivity to the intelligence community, because someone with access to raw data can usually figure out its sources and the methods by which it was obtained. But we thought it couldn't hurt to have some redundancy in the raw-data review process.

The intelligence agencies argued that it could be damaging, that there was already redundancy in their systems and that we would really be risking sources and methods. Ultimately, we agreed that as a general rule, this fusion center would not have access to the raw data but that access could be granted by the President, at the request of DHS.

Our concept of a fusion center became part of the Homeland Security bill. To this day, it is largely an unfulfilled mandate, because the admin-istration has moved many of what we hoped would be fusion-center functions to an organization called TTIC, the Terrorist Threat Integra-tion Center, which is housed at the CIA. TTIC was created at the urg-ing of the leadership of the CIA and the FBI, who were disdainful of the new DHS and concerned that its fusion center might poach their intel-ligence functions. We had hoped the fusion center would be a place in the new DHS that could receive intelligence from both foreign and do-mestic open and clandestine sources, integrate and analyze that infor-mation, and disseminate actionable intelligence to all levels of law enforcement. The decision by the Bush administration to abandon the fusion center may have allowed the President to keep up his relationship with the FBI and the CIA and to keep the peace between them, but it has also had some real adverse consequences. For example, state and local law enforcement agencies continue to be denied access to intelli-gence information that could make them more effective partners in the war on terrorism.

We approached these issues seriously, in the hope of getting a good bill to the President's desk for his signature. However, the longer we worked on the bill, the more it became apparent that many Republicans didn't want a good piece of legislation. They wanted a good fight. While much of the bill was quickly and easily agreed upon, Republicans pressed for two changes that they knew we, as Democrats, would fight. They sought to remove employee protections from people who would work at the Department of Homeland Security, rolling back century-old reforms aimed at keeping civil servants from becoming political pawns. Equally distressing to those of us who cared deeply about the separation of powers was the insistence from administration officials that they be able to move money between the "homeland security" agen-cies without congressional oversight. We didn't see how either of these things had anything to do with anything other than expanding the Bush administration's power, and we fought them. Thus we walked into ex-actly the fight the President had been spoiling for.

16

A "Slam Dunk"?

As the inquiry began its public hearings, the administration seemed to be preparing for a new battle—a war in Iraq. In late August, Vice President Cheney, speaking to the Veterans of Foreign Wars, declared, "Simply stated, there is no doubt that Saddam Hussein now has weapons of mass destruction. There is no doubt he is amassing them to use against our friends, against our allies, and against us." In that speech, he also suggested that "Saddam will acquire nuclear weapons fairly soon."[1]

That speech made headlines, including one in *The New York Times* reading, "Cheney Says Peril of a Nuclear Iraq Justifies Attack."

Dick Cheney wasn't the only one making ominous statements about Iraq's capabilities and intentions. A study conducted by the House of Representatives Committee on Government Reform, requested by Congressman Henry Waxman, found that by October 2002, President Bush,

Vice President Cheney, Secretary Rumsfeld, Secretary Powell, and National Security Advisor Rice had made nearly a hundred misleading or inflated statements about the threat posed by Iraq.

All of these claims were based on intelligence about which I had my suspicions. While the Joint Inquiry was limited to determining the role of U.S. intelligence agencies in the days before September 11 and recommending reform to correct deficiencies, the Senate Intelligence Committee now found itself with contemporary intelligence questions: Did Saddam Hussein pose the threat that many in the administration were claiming he posed? Did the threat justify authorizing war?

On September 5, in order to get an answer to those questions, the Intelligence Committee called George Tenet to testify in closed session. After Tenet had finished his prepared statement, Senator Carl Levin, Senator Dick Durbin, and I asked to see the National Intelligence Estimate on the rationale for invading Iraq and the military and postinvasion occupation expectations.

A National Intelligence Estimate (NIE) is a document prepared by the National Intelligence Council, the intelligence community's center for midterm and longer-term strategic thinking.

The NIE is the most comprehensive analytical document produced by the office of the Director of Central Intelligence. It represents the combined wisdom of the intelligence agencies, with agencies encouraged to include their qualifications, nuances, and dissents in the final recommendation so that the reader can evaluate the credibility of the final estimate. According to the National Intelligence Council, "NIEs are the DCI's most authoritative written judgments concerning national security issues. They contain the coordinated judgments of the Intelligence Community regarding the likely course of future events. The NIC's goal is to provide policymakers with the best, unvarnished, and unbiased information—regardless of whether analytic judgments conform to US policy."

NIEs can be prepared at the request of the executive branch or a congressional oversight committee, or the CIA may also produce them on its own initiative.

During the Cold War, National Intelligence Estimates of Soviet strength were made regularly. That is why it was all the more shocking when our request for the NIE on Iraq was met with blank stares by George Tenet and the other intelligence representatives who were with him.

No NIE had been requested by the White House, and none had been prepared.

I could not believe that the administration was about to take us to war without the best information by which to judge that war's necessity, the tactics we expected to be used against our forces should an invasion become inevitable, the conditions we would face in a postwar occupation, and the steps deemed necessary to maximize the prospect of success and minimize the risk to American lives.

It seemed clear to me that the President and his national security advisors, particularly those who wore suits rather than uniforms, had made up their minds to go to war and didn't want to take the chance that additional facts might show that decision to be flawed, raise questions about the credibility of their claims, or otherwise put their agenda in doubt.

I thought back to my visit to Central Command at MacDill Air Force Base in Tampa, and to General Franks's frustrated claim that we were conducting a manhunt and not fighting a war against terrorism.

Senators Levin, Durbin, and I, on behalf of the Senate Intelligence Committee, directed that an NIE be completed as soon as possible. Given the heated language coming from the administration, we wanted a coolheaded, unbiased assessment of the risks Iraq posed to us, and, should we invade, to our troops.

Director Tenet told us that he could not produce the full NIE we requested because his people were too busy with pressing intelligence functions. He said he would, however, prepare a National Intelligence Estimate (NIE) on Iraq's programs of developing, building, and storing weapons of mass destruction, the programs that were the Bush administration's primary rationale for going to war with Iraq. Frustrated by his dismissive attitude toward something we felt was deeply important, we told him that was not what we thought was needed, but grudgingly allowed that it was the best we were going to get.

About three weeks later, a surprisingly short turnaround time in the world of government bureaucracies, DCI Tenet produced to us a classified NIE roughly ninety pages long. As Director Tenet briefed us on the

NIE, he seemed to be minimizing the dissenting views contained within the report, instead concluding that the Iraqis had a sufficient stockpile of chemical and biological weapons and enough of a restored nuclear capacity to constitute a threat to the United States and to justify the use of military force to eliminate those threats. But what we were looking at was certainly not enough to justify the claim that DCI Tenet would later make to a skeptical George W. Bush, that Iraq's possession of weapons of mass destruction was a "slam dunk."[2]

Senators Levin and Durbin and I were fast becoming a triumvirate of the dubious. We felt that despite the dissenting views expressed in the NIE, it was clearly assembled and analyzed so as to present the strongest case for war. Still, the classified document offered both information and cautions, pointing out which information was thought to be credible and which was less reliable. The NIE also included an assessment of Saddam Hussein's decision making, concluding that Saddam had shown little desire to attack the United States and had few if any contacts with al-Qaeda and no particular interest in assisting Osama bin Laden. Overall, I would not call the report balanced, but in achieving even a modicum of balance it undermined many of the Bush administration's arguments for war with Iraq.

Because we saw the classified NIE as containing information that would be important for the American people to know and because we further felt that much of that information was not of a character that necessitated its classification, we asked Director Tenet to review the report for the purpose of declassifying material whose publication would not entail disclosure of the sources and methods by which the information was gathered. The director agreed to do so, surprisingly quickly.

We made our request for a declassified NIE on October 2. That same day, President Bush declared that "the Iraqi regime is a threat of unique urgency. . . . [I]t has developed weapons of mass death," and that, furthermore, "[t]he regime has the scientists and facilities to build nuclear weapons and is seeking the materials required to do so."[3]

A new, declassified report was provided to us on October 4. This document was twenty-five pages long and was titled, simply, "Iraq's Weapons of Mass Destruction Programs."

Immediately, we were struck by a number of things.

First, the production values of the unclassified version equaled or exceeded those of the classified version—with maps, graphics, photos, and tables. It seems a small point, but the CIA rarely turns around documents of such high production values so rapidly and so well. It appeared to us that the unclassified version must have been in production *before* the presentation of the classified version.*

That suspicion was deepened when we began to read it.

The first sentence of the report read,

Iraq has continued its weapons of mass destruction (WMD) programs in defiance of UN resolutions and restriction. Baghdad has chemical and biological weapons as well as missiles with ranges in excess of UN restrictions; if left unchecked, it probably will have a nuclear weapon during this decade.

The conclusions only got more ominous:

If Baghdad acquires sufficient weapons-grade fissile material from abroad, it could make a nuclear weapon within a year.

All key aspects of R&D, production, and weaponization of Iraq's offensive BW [biological weapons] program are active and most elements are larger and more advanced than they were before the Gulf War.

Iraq maintains a small missile force and several development programs, including for a UAV [unmanned aerial vehicle] that most analysts believe probably is intended to deliver biological warfare agents.

Following the conclusions was a series of exhibits. They included a list of UN Security Council Resolutions and Iraq's (inadequate) response to them, color maps illustrating Iraq's declared nuclear facilities, with each facility denoted by a yellow-and-black radiation warning symbol,

---

* Our suspicion was later proven correct. In the spring of 2002, six months before the Senate Intelligence Committee demanded that an NIE be prepared, the White House asked the CIA for a document that could be used to make the public case for war with Iraq. This was the first declassified document we were shown.

that modern equivalent of the skull and crossbones. Similar maps noted chemical and biological weapons facilities. There were photos of chemical-filled munitions, and satellite images showing sites identified as missile test facilities. Accompanying those images were maps showing what countries could be targeted if Iraq's longest-range missile was fired from any point on Iraq's border. I asked the director how many WMD sites the intelligence community estimated there were in Iraq. Tenet said there were 550 sites where weapons of mass destruction were either produced or stored.

It was, in short, a vivid and terrifying case for war.

The problem was that it did not accurately represent the classified NIE we had received just days earlier. Gone were the assessments of Saddam Hussein's intentions that had made the classified version of the document more balanced. For example, Britain has a more impressive arsenal than Iraq, but we don't consider Britain an imminent threat because it's shown no intention of attacking us. Intent is a huge component of an intelligence assessment, and here it had been selectively removed.

The unclassified version—images from which were now being used in newspapers and on TV—presented a substantially different picture of the risks we would face were we to invade Iraq.

It was as if the unclassified version selectively put forward all the arguments in favor of invading Iraq, while leaving the concerns to the much smaller audience of people with access to the classified version. In fact, what we were looking at wasn't an unclassified version versus a classified version: it was two different messages, directed at two different audiences. I was outraged.

One thing I cannot tolerate is the politicization of intelligence. Intelligence information must exist free from politics. It cannot be sought to validate positions or opinions, nor should it be used with the intent of debunking them. It is what it is—a resource to be used to inform decision makers, nothing more, nothing less. Dictatorships use intelligence to validate opinions. Democracies do not.

I felt that in this case, George Tenet was politicizing intelligence. An hour after the hearing was adjourned, I called Director Tenet on the phone and asked what was going on.

At the time, my relationship with George Tenet was on a downward trajectory. While Tenet is a charming man, his CIA had resisted a number of our committee's efforts to instill in it a sense of urgency in responding to today's new threats. Under his leadership, the CIA had suffered recurring failures. According to David Kay, the former chief U.S. weapons inspector in Iraq, human intelligence at the CIA, already depleted by the Cold War, had been allowed to decay on Tenet's watch to the point that no serious capabilities for clandestine operations—collection of information or covert action—existed. Tenet was reluctant either to accept responsibility or to assume leadership. I was finding this avoidance of accountability frustrating, but I was still willing to give the President the benefit of the doubt for his continuing confidence in Tenet.

Senator Shelby, my Republican counterpart, had a much more difficult relationship with the DCI, one that had deteriorated over policy differences and intelligence failings and was inflamed by personal slights, real and imagined. For example, Capitol folklore holds that Senator Shelby was furious at George Tenet for what he felt was second-class treatment during the 1999 event at which CIA headquarters was renamed the George Bush Center for Intelligence. However, when asked about his difficulties with Tenet, Shelby immediately points to the failure of the intelligence community to realize the extent of India and Pakistan's nuclear programs and North Korea's missile program. Shelby was particularly incensed that Tenet was willing to apologize and say all of the right things, but stopped short of taking responsibility for the changes needed to make sure such failures don't occur in the future.

I was coming around to Shelby's view.

During my time in Washington, I've had the opportunity to know several Directors of Central Intelligence. In its existence, the CIA has had directors who were cowboys, and some who were technocrats. George Tenet was the only one I'd classify as a survivor.

In Washington, jobs that come with great responsibility also carry a great deal of prestige. There is something heady about knowing that when you leave the position, your portrait will hang on the wall, or a bust of you will stand in the lobby. I can only imagine that for the DCI—of whom those things are true—there was also the excitement of being in a position that influenced decisions of war and peace, had the ear of the President on a daily basis, and enjoyed a high profile. There is a risk inherent in such jobs, however, that the person holding the job dedicates himself or herself not to the mission of the job, but to keeping it—

that the desire to continue in office overcomes one's judgment as to the national interest. The love of the job can render someone unable to do it.

The most important quality for an effective DCI is the confidence of the President. The President is the intelligence community's most important client and its leader. George Tenet clearly had the confidence of President Bush. The question is: How did he earn it? I fear he did so by pandering to power, providing the information that would ingratiate him with the President and his inner circle. The best DCIs earn presidential respect by adhering to the admonition "Speak truth to power," that is, by being willing to tell the leader of the nation the truth even if—particularly when—it is not what the President wants to hear.

What a difference it might have made if Director Tenet had told President Bush in September of 2002: "Mr. President, I am, of course, going to give you our best assessment of the situation in Iraq and what our troops will confront if there is to be an invasion and subsequent occupation. But I must tell you the limits of our knowledge. Most of what I will tell you, particularly on Iraq's capability to utilize weapons of mass destruction against our nation and troops, is predicated on historic information. We have no human penetration inside Iraq and, therefore, have no means for independent, current verification. The Defense folks will give you a more robust estimate, but they are relying on the exiles, particularly the Iraqi National Congress and its leader, Ahmad Chalabi. We have no confidence in their assessments. Some of the most vocal exiles haven't been in Iraq in more than twenty years. All the exiles have a shared interest in our returning them to power through the removal of Saddam Hussein. On the other hand, some of the intelligence agencies in which we have the most confidence, particularly the Poles and the Germans, have raised serious doubts that Saddam Hussein has the capabilities that the exiles are attributing to him. Mr. President, we will give you our best, but I want to be certain that you understand the limits of our knowledge and our confidence in that knowledge."

Instead, George Tenet said his intelligence was a "slam dunk."

When Tenet took my call, I lit into him. How could he produce two documents which left such wildly different impressions? Who was telling him to do this?

George immediately chafed at the assumption, and became both hostile and defensive.

I've found that often when you question a policy, defenders of that policy will respond as if you are attacking the people *carrying out* that policy, most of whom are dedicated individuals doing their jobs. For example, when questioned about the wisdom of our war in Iraq, the White House has responded as if the dedication of the soldiers was being questioned. Of course, it was the policy, not the troops, that was the issue.

Tenet responded to my questioning in a similar vein, saying, "Senator, we have an agency of skilled and dedicated intelligence professionals. Some of them have secured this information under very dangerous circumstances and by putting their lives at risk. On behalf of them, I resent your questioning their dedication, even their patriotism."

In the CIA headquarters there is a simple inscription on the wall to your right as you enter. It reads, "In honor of those members of the Central Intelligence Agency who gave their lives in the service of their country." The American and Central Intelligence Agency flags frame the inscription. Carved into the wall below the inscription and between the flags are eighty-three stars. Each star represents a CIA officer lost in the line of duty. Below the stars is a glass-encased book of honor. Forty-eight names of officers are listed, while the names of the remaining thirty-five officers remain secret—even in death.

I have always found that memorial moving, and I resented Tenet's implication that I had anything other than respect for the men and women of the CIA and the risks they face in the gathering of human intelligence. I told Tenet as much.

I wasn't questioning their commitment or professionalism; I was questioning Tenet's presentation—that it was more intended to affect a conclusion than to inform judgment. I told him I wanted more of the original estimate declassified, so that people could draw their own conclusions. He strenuously objected, telling me that I was placing an excessive burden on an already overworked staff and that the agency had gone as far as it could go in scrubbing the NIE. I continued to press him, and, belligerently, he said he'd look into it.

Later, still on October 4, I prepared a formal letter to Director Tenet pointing out specific paragraphs of the classified report that I wished to see declassified, as well as some of the transcript of a closed Intelligence

Committee hearing that we had held on October 2, in which the senior intelligence witness we had testifying also reached conclusions markedly different from those presented in the public NIE. I sent the letter by secure fax to the CIA, and delivered a hard copy with the daily secure courier that runs between the Capitol and the CIA's Langley headquarters.

Three days later, I received a three-page response from the CIA. Unlike the first unclassified version, which was a slick, well-produced booklet, this letter looked as if someone had hastily photocopied it at Kinko's.

Still, while the presentation was less than striking, the information was. From the paragraphs I had identified, the CIA was willing to declassify these words:

> Baghdad for now appears to be drawing a line short of conducting terrorist attacks with conventional or CBW [chemical or biological weapons] against the United States.

> Saddam might decide that the extreme step of assisting Islamist terrorists in conducting a WMD attack against the United States would be his last chance to exact vengeance.

In other words, the now declassified conclusions on Saddam Hussein's intent, conclusions that were conveniently omitted from the October 4 public document, were that (1) Saddam wasn't going to attack us; and (2) he would link up with Islamist terrorists or provide them with weapons of mass destruction only if we attacked him. In short, Saddam Hussein posed no threat to his neighbors or to the United States as long as he was left alone. Only when he was threatened did he become dangerous, and at that point it became possible that he might partner with a non-Iraqi terrorist organization.

The portions of the hearing that we wanted declassified also pointed toward these conclusions.

For example, the CIA declassified this exchange between Senator Levin and a Senior Intelligence Witness (whose name continues to be classified).

Senator Levin: . . . If Saddam didn't feel threatened, did not feel threatened, is it likely that he would initiate an attack using a weapon of mass destruction?

Senior Intelligence Witness: . . . My judgment would be that the probability of him initiating an attack—let me put a time frame on it—in the foreseeable future, given the conditions we understand now, the likelihood I think would be low.

Senator Levin: . . . what about his use of weapons of mass destruction? If we initiate an attack and he thought he was in extremis or otherwise, what's the likelihood in response to our attack that he would use chemical or biological weapons?

Senior Intelligence Witness: Pretty high, in my view.

Director Tenet included a defensive editorial statement in his letter to us: "In the above dialogue, the witness's qualifications—'in the foreseeable future, given the conditions we understand now'—were intended to underscore that the likelihood of Saddam using WMD for blackmail, deterrence, or otherwise grows as his arsenal builds." Of course, we now know that Saddam had no arsenal, much less a "building" one.

Director Tenet's protestations notwithstanding, it seems pretty clear that our witness was telling us that Saddam, having little desire to attack us using WMDs, could be backed into it were we to attack him.

During the classified hearing in which the above exchange took place, Senator Evan Bayh pressed the witness on the relationship (or lack thereof) between Iraq and al-Qaeda.

While the CIA refused to release the transcript of that exchange, it did give us a number of bullet points containing declassified information. For example, these included the statement that "we have solid reporting of senior level contacts between Iraq and al-Qa'ida going back a decade" as well as a number of other statements concerning reciprocal nonaggression and a growing al-Qaeda presence in Iraq. To any student of recent history, these statements would seem odd. Saddam Hussein was not a heroic figure in the Arab world. While his stature had been increased by his ability to survive a war with the United States, many remembered that the war he survived was started by his invasion of Kuwait and threat to Saudi Arabia. His leadership was not about pan-Islamic brotherhood or Muslim fundamentalism. It was about retaining and expanding his own power. Those facts alone argue that Saddam would not want to grant a foothold in Iraq to a group like al-Qaeda, which would be capable of undermining his power at home. Perhaps that is why all of the conclusions linking Iraq to al-Qaeda were undercut by one other point Director Tenet had allowed us to state openly: "Our understanding of the relationship between Iraq and al-Qai'da is evolving and is based on sources of varying reliability. Some of the information we have received comes from detainees, including some of high rank."

We would later learn just how "varying" in "reliability" our sources were. Several were playing the United States to achieve their own goals, and most were just plain wrong. And now the Senate Intelligence Committee, in its July 2004 report on Iraq, has concluded that there was no Iraq–al-Qaeda link.

The three pages Director Tenet had sent us were not nearly all of what we wished to have declassified. Smelling deceit, I wrote Director Tenet again to push for a third round of declassifications. Three days later we were met with a curt no.

The CIA had made public all the information it would allow the American people to see. And Congress would be voting on a resolution authorizing the President to go to war against Iraq within a matter of days.

17

"Blood on Your Hands"

As we were fighting to get the administration to give the American people an honest assessment of Iraq's weapons and intentions, and what we knew and didn't know in reaching that conclusion, the Senate was nearing a vote on authorizing the President to use force against Iraq.

From the day in February when General Franks pulled me aside and told me that his mission in Afghanistan was being compromised by the Bush administration's desire to go to war in Iraq, I had known that the administration would have to make its intentions known publicly at some point, and that at that point, we would be able to have a true debate on the wisdom of fighting a war of choice in Iraq when we had not yet finished a war of necessity in Afghanistan. I was to be very—and visibly—disappointed.

Meanwhile, the administration had begun to further ratchet up the language, with President Bush invoking the specter of a nuclear Iraq attacking America: "America must not ignore the threat gathering against us. Facing clear evidence of peril, we cannot wait for the final proof—the smoking gun—that could come in the form of a mushroom cloud."[1]

While these statements on Iraq were clearly driven by a preset will to go to war and a refusal to allow contrary information to get in the way, what I had learned in my visit to Central Command is that, for reasons of personnel and equipment, the choice between Osama bin Laden or Saddam Hussein was exactly that—a choice. I remembered the briefing where the FBI told me that al-Qaeda had fewer than three hundred operatives worldwide. By dramatically underestimating al-Qaeda's global strength, the FBI could have misled the President as to al-Qaeda's potential presence in the United States.

If the CIA, the NSA, and the immigration service had known that the FBI was briefing the President as to the scale of the al-Qaeda presence in the United States, they might have been in a position to challenge that figure and the assumptions upon which it was based.

I asked both Dick Clarke and Bob Woodward this question: "As President Bush was considering war with Iraq, how did he evaluate the relative threat and consequences of an Iraq war in comparison with other threats in the region, particularly al-Qaeda?"

I got the same answer from both. There was no such comparative analysis. The decision started and ended with the evil of Saddam Hussein.

This was an unforgivable level of intellectual—even commonsense—indifference.

If the President had been more analytical and curious, he would have asked, What should be the standard for prioritizing the threats in this region? Since he never got to that point, he was not required to answer the question. I did, and my answer was: Which of the evils represents the greatest potential to kill Americans? After all, the most fundamental responsibility of the federal government under the Constitution is to provide for the common defense.

To me, there are three criteria in determining which evil we faced had the greatest potential to kill our people: capability, will, and presence in the United States. In every category, al-Qaeda was substantially more ominous than Iraq.

Al-Qaeda had already demonstrated both the capability and will to kill Americans. In the five years before the vote authorizing the President to use force against Iraq, al-Qaeda had taken American lives at two embassies in Africa, on a destroyer in Yemen, and, on September 11 in New York City, at the Pentagon, and in Pennsylvania. As noxious a person as Saddam Hussein might be, he had taken no U.S. lives during that period.

The most striking difference was in the presence of trained terrorists such as al-Hazmi and al-Mihdhar inside the United States. With the exception of the Cold War Soviet Union, which had a massive stockpile of nuclear weapons and was capable of intercontinental delivery, no other country has the will and the means by which to deliver an attack as devastating as was September 11 against the United States from afar. It is the presence of terrorists living among us, waiting for the call to action, that converts capability and will into casualties.

Al-Qaeda has trained between sixty thousand and eighty thousand terrorists at its camps in Afghanistan, and by my estimate several hundred of those camps' graduates were in the United States in the fall of 2002. Hezbollah's presence, by my assessment, was somewhat larger. By comparison, Saddam Hussein was estimated to have no more than fifty governmental or nonofficial agents in the United States, and we knew the identities of most of them.

Based on that comparative analysis, it was clear to me that al-Qaeda represented the greater threat to kill Americans, at home and abroad.

The fact that military and intelligence resources were being diverted from the war against al-Qaeda to prepare for a war against Iraq as early as February 2002 was a recognition that the United States did not have the capability to pursue both conflicts to victory simultaneously. A choice had to be made, and President Bush's choice was Iraq. This choice has exacted enormous costs in American lives, American resources, and respect for America abroad. It has resulted in Osama bin Laden's escape and the regeneration of an almost mortally wounded al-Qaeda into a more decentralized and more violent organization than it was on September 11.

A simple analysis, stripped of ideology, based on sound intelligence, and focused only on the relative threat to America and Americans, would have shown that in terms of capacity, will, and presence, al-Qaeda represented a significantly greater threat to the United States than did Saddam Hussein. President Bush didn't think this was a sufficiently important question to even ask.

★

Although the President predicated his case for war on his claims about Saddam Hussein's weapons of mass destruction, he also argued that there was a direct link between Iraq and the perpetrators of the September 11 attacks.

For example, on October 7, 2002, at a speech in Cincinnati, President Bush implied an Iraq/al-Qaeda connection by saying, "Iraq could decide on any given day to provide a biological or chemical weapon to a terrorist group or individual terrorists" and that "alliance with terrorists could allow the Iraqi regime to attack America without leaving any fingerprints."

These claims were effective. At the time, a poll showed that 70 percent of Americans believed that Saddam Hussein was involved in or directly responsible for the attacks of September 11; rather than disabusing people of the notion, the President tried to solidify it. Instead of using his presidency to teach America about the real terrorist threats we faced, Bush was using it to mislead the country in order to build support for a war against an unrelated threat.[2]

Besides, the fact that President Bush was seeking specific authority for a war in Iraq undermined the validity of the assumption that Iraq was involved in the attacks of September 11. The resolution, adopted a year earlier, that authorized what became the war in Afghanistan gave the President the authority to use all necessary and appropriate force against "those nations, organizations, or persons he determines planned, authorized, committed or aided the terrorist attacks that occurred on Sept. 11 or harbored such organizations or persons. . . ."

If Iraq had been complicit in the attack, the use of force against it would have been covered by the September 2001 congressional authorization, and no further grant of authority would have been required.

Having seen the full extent of the CIA's knowledge, or lack thereof, regarding the Iraq/al-Qaeda connection, and knowing that the buildup to this war had begun long in advance of any public discussion of it, I began working on an amendment to the President's Iraq resolution. My amendment would authorize the President to broaden the scope of the war on terror to terrorist groups that sought to attack America, but were not involved in the attacks of September 11.

In introducing this amendment, I wanted to allow the President to make good on his statement that the war on terror is a war against every terrorist group of global reach.

If Congress was going to give the President the authority to go to war in Iraq, a country that had nothing to do with the attacks of September 11, shouldn't we also give him the authority to wage a true, robust war on the actual sources of terror, by granting the authority to go after the very terrorist groups of global reach he claimed were targets? I thought this would not only be good policy, but could also be a winner on the Senate floor. It would also show that the attention on Iraq was misplaced.

At the time, the State Department had identified thirty-four international terrorist organizations, approximately two thirds of which are headquartered in the Middle East and Central Asia. Of those thirty-four, six had shared characteristics that were of deep concern to me, and should be of deep concern to all Americans. Those six are al-Qaeda, the Abu Nidal organization, Hamas, Palestinian Islamic Jihad, the Palestine Liberation Front, and Hezbollah. Each is supported by a state that possesses weapons of mass destruction, has a long history of hating and killing Americans, and has the ability to strike within the United States.

After the attacks of September 11, the Congress had given the President the authority to go after only one of those groups, al-Qaeda.

I have a long-standing concern about Hezbollah, which Deputy Secretary of State Richard Armitage has referred to as "the A-team of international terrorists" and which I fear could become the next al-Qaeda—or could join with al-Qaeda to form a deadlier alliance both within the United States and abroad.

Hezbollah, whose name, literally translated, means "The Party of God," was formed in 1982 in response to the Israeli invasion of Lebanon.

Based primarily in Lebanon and Syria and financed from Iran, Hezbollah is a radical Shia group that takes its ideological inspiration from the Iranian revolution and the teachings of the Ayatollah Khomeini. Hezbollah formally advocates the establishment of Islamic rule in Lebanon and the liberation of all occupied Arab lands, including Jerusalem. It has expressed as a goal the elimination of Israel.

Hezbollah has been involved, or is suspected of involvement, in a number of deadly attacks on Americans, including the suicide truck bombings of the U.S. embassy in Beirut in 1983, the U.S. Marine barracks there that same year, and the U.S. embassy annex in 1984, and the 1996 attack on the Khobar Towers housing complex in Saudi Arabia. In addition, elements of Hezbollah are responsible for the kidnapping and detention of U.S. and other Western hostages.

Hezbollah receives financial, training, weapons, explosives, diplomatic, and organizational aid from Iran—which, unlike Iraq, happens to be the world's most active state supporter of terrorism and has nuclear weapons or is pursuing them.

More distressingly, Hezbollah has a significant presence within the United States. The President said many times that we could not afford to ignore the gathering threat of Iraq, yet he seemed unconcerned about a threat that had already gathered. I hoped that my amendment would refocus debate on those much more pressing dangers.

I introduced my amendment on October 9, 2002. Given the momentum for a war with Iraq (several prominent Democrats, including the Democratic leader of the House, Dick Gephardt of Missouri, had attended a rally at the White House indicating their support for the President), I had a sense that my amendment would be dismissed, and so I concluded my remarks on a melancholy note.

> I am not optimistic about the prospects for this amendment, but I am deeply concerned, and I am deeply saddened. I am concerned in part because I see us making life-and-death decisions without consideration because we do not have access to what might be critical and, I would suggest, determinative information. I believe the national security interests are being put at risk by this information not being available. I am saddened because I fear the action we are

going to take will increase the risk at home without increasing our capability to respond to that risk.

George F. Will, the syndicated columnist, would later write that my effort made me the only Democrat who had taken on President Bush from the right, calling him out on his timidity in fighting the war on terror—something that many in my party either wouldn't say or didn't see.

After I introduced my amendment, Joe Lieberman, John Warner of Virginia, and John McCain of Arizona got up to respond. In typical senatorial fashion, they all said nice things about my commitment to the issue of terrorism, and generally agreed on the substance of the amendment, adding their words to mine about the threat posed by these groups. Ultimately, they all argued that the Iraq resolution had been carefully negotiated, and that to accept my amendment would be to reopen discussion and thus slow the resolution's passage.

Senator McCain introduced into the Senate Record a letter from the legislative affairs director at the White House, who had written, "The Graham amendment would increase—beyond what was requested by the Administration—the scope of authority provided to the President, and introduce additional elements to the resolution. Modifying the agreement now, as the Graham amendment would, could reopen issues otherwise resolved and slow consideration of this important resolution."

For my part, I didn't care whether consideration was slowed or not, or whether the amendment would force another round of negotiations. I wanted a resolution that actually resolved to do the right thing—to go after the terrorists.

Following Senator McCain's statement, I again took the floor—angry and frustrated at the genial dismissiveness with which my amendment was being treated.

The President in his State of the Union Address on January 29 said our first priority was terrorists—our first priority. And do you know what the first priority of the first priority was? The training camps. Why did he say that? Because . . . if there was one major mistake we made in the 1990s, it was allowing al Qaeda training camps to be a sanctuary where every year thousands and thousands of young people were converted into hardened assassins. . . . [W]hat is going to be our excuse today when similar training camps are in operation in Iran, Syria, and Syrian-controlled areas of Lebanon?

I warned my colleagues about the CIA's honest, still-classified assessment of what would happen were we to invade Iraq:

> I will stand first in line to say he [Saddam] is an evil person. But we, by taking that action, according to our own intelligence reports—and, friends, I encourage you to read the classified intelligence reports, which are much sharper than what is available in declassified form—we are going to be increasing the threat level against the people of the United States.

I urged my colleagues to open their eyes to the larger array of lethal foes who are prepared today to assault us at home. I said that I was as sure as I have ever been of anything in my life that the peril caused by the war in Iraq could be mitigated only if we kept all of the terrorist threats in sight. If the hundreds of hours I had spent delving into raw intelligence data, meeting with foreign leaders, and visiting global hotspots had convinced me of one thing, they had convinced me that any single-minded focus on Saddam Hussein as the threat to America was based on a fundamental misreading of the world.

In frustration at the pending failure of my amendment, and in incredulity that the Senate was about to reject it so as to more quickly approve a resolution enabling the President to use force against a country that had not attacked us, and that I believed was not among the top five threats we faced, I lost my cool:

> If you do not think we ought to give the President authority to use force against groups such as Hezbollah, what do you think we ought to do? Or do you disagree with the premise that we are going to be increasing the threat level inside the United States?
>
> If you disagree with that premise, what is the basis upon which your disagreement is predicated? If you reject that, and believe that the American people are not going to be at additional threat, then, frankly, my friends—to use the term—blood is going to be on your hands.

That got everybody's attention. You could see jaws drop on the Senate floor. A headline in *The Miami Herald* the next day read, "Graham Rips Colleagues Over Iraq." I had undone not only my own reputation for circumspect language but also the civility that had allowed my colleagues to gently try to kill my amendment. But I was unapologetic. To me, the decision we were about to make was one of life and death, and I felt then—as I feel even more strongly now—that to wage a war of choice against Iraq and not to devote our full energies to one of necessity against terror is to choose death. As our second President, John Adams, once wrote: "Great is the guilt of an unnecessary war."

I continued to say that locking on Iraq as the greatest threat we face "is an erroneous reading of the world. There are many evils out there, a number of which are substantially more competent, particularly in their ability to attack Americans here at home, than Iraq is likely to be in the foreseeable future. But . . . we are going to ignore those and we are going to allow them to continue to fester among us. I do not wish to be part of that decision."

I would be voting against a war in Iraq.

My statement got my colleagues' attention, but not their votes. My amendment lost by a vote of 88 to 10.

Early in the morning of Friday, October 11, 2002, the Senate voted 77 to 23 to give the President the authority he wanted.

All I could do in my final words before the vote was to repeat the warning that Winston Churchill offered in 1941: "Never, never, never believe [that] any war will be smooth and easy, or that anyone who embarks on the strange voyage can measure the tides and hurricanes he will encounter. The statesman who yields to war fever must realize that once the signal is given, he is no longer the master of policy but the slave of unforeseeable and uncontrollable events."

18

Stonewall

The President's request for a use-of-force resolution against Iraq left Democrats bitter and divided. As one of very few members of my party to vote to authorize the use of force for the first President Bush during the first Gulf War, I had no intention of supporting this Gulf War.*

Meanwhile, Republicans, led by President Bush, who had gone from threatening a veto of a Department of Homeland Security on numerous occasions to championing the department's creation, were using the issue to bludgeon Democrats. For example, in Georgia, Max Cleland, a first-term senator, a Bronze and Silver Star winner who lost three limbs to a grenade explosion in Vietnam, had his patriotism impugned in one

---

* In January 1991, Senate Majority Leader George Mitchell invited me to go on a trip to Saudi Arabia, Jordan, and Israel. The unstated purpose was to convince me and a number of other senators to vote against President George H. W. Bush's request to use force to remove a nation that had invaded its neighbor. The irony was that almost every senator that George Mitchell invited to go on this trip, seeing the threat Saddam Hussein posed to the region at the time, ended up voting for the war.

television ad, which showed Senator Cleland and Osama bin Laden side by side, visual brothers in arms. Tim Johnson in South Dakota, Paul Wellstone in Minnesota, and Jean Carnahan in Missouri were being subjected to similar attacks, and they were having an effect.

Sensing that they might do well in November's elections, some of the Senate Republicans on the Joint Inquiry who had been resistant to the idea of a joint inquiry from the outset started to slow-walk the committee's deliberations in an attempt to run out the clock.

For example, after we had, for weeks, followed a routine of reading staff statements before hearing from witnesses, some senators wanted the full Joint Inquiry to approve the staff reports before they could be publicly released.

This procedural change was a tried-and-true delaying tactic, one that would virtually ensure that our report would not be complete before the end of the 107th Congress. I had seen tactics like this before. For example, after the attack on the U.S.S. *Cole* on October 12, 2000, the Senate Intelligence Committee had proceeded to look into the attack and create a congressional analog to the military "after incident report." Because of some relatively minor but deeply held differences of opinion between two of the nineteen members of the committee as to how much weight should be given to the conclusions of a particular analyst in the Defense Intelligence Agency, the report took many months to be approved. And *that* was a classified document that would not be seen by the public. Such was the power of a strong-willed member of our committee. If we were to require preclearance for every staff report, the inquiry would never be able to complete its work by the end to the 107th Congress and the termination of our charter. Porter and I recognized that to succumb to this request for a change of the rules was tantamount to terminating the inquiry. We refused.*

The administration intensified its foot-dragging as well. Much of the information we were dealing with was classified. In my view, the U.S. government has a huge overclassification problem: too much information is classified that need not be. A major part of the problem is timid-

---

* Senators Jon Kyl of Arizona and Pat Roberts of Kansas would later file an addendum to the final report, writing, "While the Report should be a useful historical document on which to base further inquiries, we cannot vouch for its contents." They added: "The record should also reflect some of the difference in opinion among Members on how the report was prepared."

ity, and covering one's posterior. No one at an agency has ever been sanctioned for classifying too much; a few have for classifying too little. A secondary problem is the propensity of those doing the classifying to put loyalty to their respective organization above the national interest.

In the course of our inquiry, we dealt with a number of documents that could have and should have been made public. They did not risk our sources and methods, but they could help inform the American people. To get these documents declassified required making a declassification request of the CIA, which has people who, along with appropriate staff at other affected agencies, consider just this type of request. For mundane declassification requests, these were the people our inquiry staff dealt with. However, to overrule an unsatisfactory determination at that level, or for requests that might be politically sensitive, we dealt with DCI Tenet, who often would defer to the White House. If the White House requested that something be declassified, it was as good as done. Otherwise, every request we made triggered a bureaucratic skirmish. That is why White House cooperation was so important; short of slow and virtually unprecedented congressional action, its assent was the only way for us to get any information declassified.

As we reached October, White House officials were regularly delaying the declassification of documents until it was too late for us to use them effectively in a public hearing. This was a gentler form of the shameful way in which this White House has used the selective leak or declassification of sensitive material to achieve political goals. Two instances have been particularly egregious. The first is the reckless disclosure that Ambassador Joseph Wilson's wife worked for the CIA, a disclosure made after Ambassador Wilson publicly questioned the Bush administration's claims about Iraq's efforts to procure nuclear material from Africa. The disclosure not only put Ambassador Wilson's wife at risk, but also sent a chilling message to those involved in the dangerous work of gathering clandestine intelligence and those who might consider doing so. The second was Attorney General Ashcroft's conveniently quick declassification of a document with the intent of damaging the credibility of former Deputy Attorney General Jamie Gorelick, a Democratic member of the independent commission investigating the attacks of September 11, by implying falsely that she was the original author of the legal standard that created a wall between criminal and intelligence information. In fact, this standard was long-standing and had been reaffirmed by Attorney General Ashcroft himself.

The White House stonewalling took other forms as well. For example, it resisted allowing certain witnesses, particularly FBI field agents, to testify. We were able to overcome that resistance only through repeated and often contentious meetings, and by our stated intention, met with surprise and dismay by the agencies, that we would use a screen to shield from public view any witnesses whose identities they did not wish us to reveal. Ultimately, we did end up securing most of the witnesses from whom we wanted to hear, and occasionally we did use the screen to shield their identities.

It was increasingly clear that the administration's initial promises of cooperation had been discarded. There was one notable exception to this trend, and that was General Michael Hayden, director of the NSA. He was consistently helpful and was genuinely interested in improving his agency's performance. This was refreshing, though not surprising. Throughout our investigation, we found, as had Dick Clarke, that the NSA was the agency within the intelligence community that provided the most credible intelligence.

In virtually every other area, though, the more we learned, the less curious the administration seemed about what had happened on September 11. The more we pressed for information, the more resistant the White House became to giving it. In my view, this behavior bore all the hallmarks of a cover-up. We had discovered an FBI asset who had a close relationship with two of the terrorists; a terrorist support network that, at least at one point, went through the Saudi embassy; and a funding network that went through the Saudi royal family. And the more discoveries we made, the more the administration's obstructionism intensified. I still believe there is more to be learned.

Our final public hearing was held on October 17, 2002. We all felt a sense of satisfaction that this phase of the investigation was done, and done well. We had worked hard to fulfill our obligation to the families of the victims, to the intelligence community, and to the nation, often against stiff resistance. We knew, however, that the job was not over, and there were no celebrations—or at least not any to which I was invited.

I hadn't anticipated that leading the Joint Inquiry would be so draining. Porter Goss and I joked about the toll on our health taken by one year of daily battles and frustrations. But much of the work was complete, and we were proud that, despite all the obstacles and intransigence we had faced, we had learned a great deal about what had gone wrong and were on our way to preparing significant recommendations about how to make it right.

Meanwhile, everything was bogging down as the elections approached. The White House continued its efforts to grind our investigation to a halt. The Homeland Security bill became mired in debate; despite several efforts at compromise, none was reached by mid-October, when, after the Iraq resolution vote, the Senate effectively ended its legislative business until after the November elections—elections that saw Max Cleland and Jean Carnahan defeated and Tim Johnson of South Dakota squeak to victory by a mere 524 votes. Paul Wellstone, who died tragically in a plane crash, was replaced on the ballot by Walter Mondale, who lost as well.

The following two months were devoted to completing the inquiry's final report. This was no small task given that, in all, the staff of the Joint Inquiry had reviewed almost 500,000 pages of relevant documents from the intelligence agencies and other sources, of which about 100,000 pages were selected for incorporation into the Joint Inquiry's records. Staff members conducted approximately 300 interviews, and had participated in briefings and panel discussions that involved almost 600 people from the intelligence agencies, other U.S. government organizations, state and local entities, representatives of foreign governments, and private individuals. We had held thirteen closed sessions and nine public hearings. We had dueled with just about every intelligence agency, and had been stymied in some requests and successful in others.

Now, to summarize.

We made both findings of fact and findings of systemic, persistent conditions. They included such discoveries as the fact that during the spring and summer of 2001, the intelligence community noticed a significant increase in information indicating that bin Laden and al-Qaeda intended to strike against U.S. interests in the very near future. Furthermore, at the same time a modest but steady stream of intelligence reporting indicated the possibility of terrorist attacks within the United States. We found that it was the general view of the intelligence community that the threatened attacks would most likely occur against U.S. interests abroad, despite the indications of bin Laden's desire to attack within the United States.

We also found that from at least 1994, U.S. intelligence agencies received information indicating that terrorists were contemplating the use of aircraft as weapons, and that this information did not lead to any specific intelligence assessment of this form of threat or any government reaction to it.

Our final factual conclusion was that although relevant information regarding the attacks, significant in retrospect, was available to the intelligence community before September 11, 2001, intelligence agencies too often failed to focus on that information and consider or appreciate its collective significance in terms of a probable terrorist attack.

Neither did the intelligence community demonstrate enough initiative in coming to grips with the new transnational threats. Though the stream of information being collected was vast, some significant data were overlooked, and others were not recognized as potentially significant at the time and therefore not disseminated. Other pieces of information required additional action on the part of foreign governments before a direct connection to the hijackers could have been established. For example, during 1999, the National Security Agency intercepted a number of communications connecting individuals to terrorism who, after September 11, were identified as participants in the plot. Other examples were the contact that two of the hijackers had with an active FBI informant, the ignored Phoenix electronic communication, and the Moussaoui investigation.

Though some of our factual findings were and continue to be explosive—the Phoenix electronic communication, the Moussaoui debacle, the fact that two of the hijackers had regular and repeated contacts with an FBI informant, and the direct Saudi support to the hijackers—we believed that our systemic findings would be more helpful in trying to prevent future attacks.

For example, we found that prior to September 11, U.S. intelligence agencies were neither well organized nor well equipped (nor did they adapt) to meet the challenge posed by global terrorists focused on targets within the United States. Serious gaps existed between the collection coverage provided by the U.S. foreign and U.S. domestic intelligence capabilities. U.S. foreign intelligence agencies paid inadequate attention to the potential for a domestic attack. The CIA's failure to watch-list suspected terrorists reflected a lack of emphasis on a process designed to protect the U.S. homeland. At home, the counterterrorism effort suffered from the lack of an effective domestic intelligence capability. The FBI was unable to identify and monitor the extent of activity by al-Qaeda and other international terrorist groups operating in the United States. Taken together, these problems exacerbated America's vulnerability to an increasingly dangerous and immediate international terrorist threat inside the United States.

We also found that before September 11, 2001, neither the U.S. government as a whole nor the intelligence community in particular had a comprehensive counterterrorist strategy for combating the threat posed by bin Laden. Furthermore, the director of Central Intelligence was either unwilling or unable to marshal the full range of intelligence agency resources necessary to combat the growing threat to the United States.

Additionally, we found:

★ Between the end of the Cold War and September 11, 2001, overall intelligence community funding fell or remained even, while funding for counterterrorism efforts increased substantially. Despite those increases, the accumulation of additional intelligence priorities had the effect of increasing reliance on supplemental appropriations (funds made available on a periodic and not necessarily recurring basis) for counterterrorism funding. The uncertainty of funding made it difficult for intelligence agencies to effectively plan the allocation of resources against this emerging threat.

★ Technology has not been fully utilized in support of our counterterrorism efforts. Persistent problems include a lack of collaboration among agencies, a reluctance to develop and implement new technical capabilities aggressively, and, in particular, the FBI's reliance on outdated and insufficient technical systems and the lack of a central counterterrorism database.

★ Prior to September 11, the intelligence community's understanding of al-Qaeda was hampered by insufficient analytic focus and quality, especially in strategic analysis. Analysis and analysts were not always used effectively because of a perception in some parts of the intelligence community that they were less important to

agency counterterrorism missions than were operations personnel. As a result of this stigma, the quality of counterterrorism
analysis was inconsistent, and many analysts were inexperienced,
unqualified, and undertrained, and left without access to critical
information. This led to a dearth of creative, aggressive analysis
and an inability to understand the collective significance of individual pieces of intelligence. These analytic deficiencies seriously
undercut the ability of policy makers to understand the full nature
of the threat and to make fully informed decisions.

★ Before September 11, the intelligence community was not prepared for the challenge of translating the quantities of foreign-
language counterterrorism intelligence it collected. Translations
were backlogged, and language specialists and language-qualified
field officers were in short supply.

★ The U.S. government does not bring together in one place all
terrorism-related information from all sources. While the CIA's
Counterterrorist Center does manage overseas operations and has
access to most intelligence agencies' information, it does not collect terrorism-related information from all sources, domestic and
foreign. Intelligence agencies did not adequately share relevant
counterterrorism information. This breakdown in communications was the result of a number of factors, including differences
in the agencies' missions, perceived legal strictures (as the Moussaoui case demonstrated), and cultures. Information was not sufficiently shared, not only among intelligence agencies but also
within individual agencies, and between intelligence and law enforcement agencies.

★ Before September 11, 2001, the intelligence community did not
effectively develop and use human sources to penetrate al-Qaeda.
The lack of reliable and knowledgeable human sources significantly limited our intelligence agencies' ability to acquire intelligence that could be acted upon before the attacks. This lack of
U.S.-recruited counterterrorism sources was both a cause and a
result of excessive reliance on foreign liaison services.

★ Difficulties with FBI applications for Foreign Intelligence Surveillance Act (FISA) surveillance and the FISA process—especially
during the summer of 2001, when the intelligence community

was bracing for an imminent al-Qaeda attack—led to a diminished coverage of a suspected al-Qaeda operative in the United States. The effect of these difficulties was compounded by the perception among FBI personnel at headquarters and the field offices that the FISA process was long and difficult.

★ Senior U.S. military officials were reluctant to use U.S. military assets to conduct offensive counterterrorism efforts in Afghanistan, or to support or participate in CIA operations directed against al-Qaeda before September 11. This reluctance was produced at least in part by the military's view that the intelligence community was unable to provide the intelligence needed to support military operations.

★ The intelligence community depended heavily on foreign intelligence and law enforcement services for the collection of counterterrorism intelligence and the conduct of other counterterrorism activities. The results were mixed in terms of productive intelligence, reflecting the huge differences in the ability and willingness of the various foreign services to target the bin Laden and al-Qaeda networks.

★ Perhaps most explosively, we found that the activities of the September 11 hijackers in the United States appear to have been financed, in large part, from abroad. More broadly, before September 11, there was not only no coordinated government-wide strategy to track terrorist funding and close down financial support networks, there was an actual reluctance to do so.

Some of our findings are still classified, but it is safe to say that these systemic problems we found hindered the intelligence community's counterterrorism efforts, and that, if not addressed, these weaknesses will continue to undercut our counterterrorist efforts. Not nearly all of these problems have been solved, and every day that they go unsolved is a day we are losing the battle against terrorism.

★

On December 10, the Joint Inquiry met once more, in closed session, to approve the final report. It was presented and adopted by voice vote.

After the inquiry had adjourned for the last time, Porter, Nancy, Dick, and I met in the conference room. I expressed my appreciation for the enormous amount of time and energy each had given to the effort, often under serious external pressure. Porter worked himself to exhaustion. In addition to helping lead the inquiry, Nancy was also leading the Democratic caucus in the House of Representatives, the first woman ever to do so. And Dick had calmed the waters when partisan considerations could have swamped us. Without our unity, this unique congressional effort never would have been successful, and one of the most gratifying aspects of the inquiry for me had been the friendships that were formed or reinforced while we served through this adventure.

With the end of the Congress, our charter expired and our funds expended, the staff of the inquiry disbanded. Eleanor and Rick stayed on to fight one final battle: getting the report declassified.

The experience of cochairing an inquiry into one of America's most searing tragedies was having an effect on me. The more I delved into the reasons for this failure of intelligence, the more concerned for America's safety I became. Throughout my career, I have prided myself on being calm and levelheaded, no matter the circumstance. My staff still jokes with me about the time during my governorship when I was on a trade mission to Brazil and the plane had a mechanical failure. Before I grabbed the oxygen mask that had fallen from the ceiling, I pulled out my notebook and recorded: "2:39 p.m.—pilot announces hydraulic failure, must make emergency landing."

I tend not to be a particularly anxious person, and I usually operate within a relatively narrow emotional spectrum. Perhaps that's because I'm a bit of a fatalist. But now my advancing age, or my eleven grandchildren, have changed things. The more I learned about the threats we're ignoring, the more I saw the Bush administration leading us into a war of choice, the more aware I became that there are hundreds of people living in America who would like nothing more than to kill Americans, the angrier I got.

I got angry that my colleagues weren't as focused on the threats as they should be.

I got angry that we were already losing the sense of urgency and common purpose that was so palpable after September 11.

And I got angry that we had a President who wasn't doing anything about it.

My late sister-in-law, Katharine Graham, who knew every President from Calvin Coolidge to George W. Bush, told me that the indispensable characteristic in running for and serving as President was passion. The candidate and occupant of the Oval Office had to feel, deep in his soul, that what he was doing was more than an act of personal gratification or ego. Rather, he had to be driven by a calling, a fundamental sense that his ideas would create a better America, and that his service was necessary to move toward that better America. Without that calling, a campaign would be a painful, grueling slog. Without that passion, the White House would be a lonely place. However, with that passion, the campaign would be not so much a job as an incredible journey, which, if things went well, would lead to the White House. If the campaign didn't go well, at least every day presented the opportunity to make an argument to the American people about the issues that matter most deeply to the candidate, and the satisfaction of being in the arena, striving to make a difference.

In December of 2002 I was sixty-six years old and had held elective office for thirty-six years. For eight years I was the governor of one of the largest and most complex states in the nation, and I like to think I was an effective one. For sixteen years I had been immersed in national politics and had educated myself on the challenges that our nation faces in the world. Five times I had been elected statewide in Florida, a large, diverse, and conservative state, and my margins of victory had generally been nearly two to one.

On several occasions I had contemplated running for President and felt that I was at least as prepared to serve as the other potential candidates. But I lacked the element of passion. Now I had it.

The inquiry into the events of September 11, an experience with a President who spoke frequently, if ineloquently, of his patriotism but in practice disrespected the capability of the American people to be given the truth and to use that truth responsibly, had lit a fire within me.

Although he spoke often of trusting people to make decisions, President Bush was the ultimate nanny-state President, making far-reaching decisions to protect the American people from themselves.

I did not discuss my growing passion. Not with Adele or our daughters, not with my brother, not with any political confidants or members of my staff. I didn't want to take any action or utter any remark that would politicize and potentially derail the important work of the Joint Inquiry.

On December 20, 2002, Representatives Porter Goss and Nancy Pelosi, Senator Richard Shelby, and I filed the final report of the Joint Inquiry with the Speaker of the House and the President Pro Tempore of the Senate, and I started giving further thought to my future.

19

Final Battles

Every citizen of Athens, on a periodic basis, was required to assume a job that served the public interest. It might be as menial as collecting garbage or as exalted as commanding the Athenian navy. No job was considered too little or too large for a citizen of Athens to perform. For the Athenian legislators, these experiences with ordinary citizens became a connection for the most powerful to the lives of all the people of Athens.

During my first run for governor of Florida, in an attempt to connect with the people I hoped to represent, I adopted a modern-day equivalent of the Athenian method: over the course of the campaign, I would spend 100 days alongside average Floridians, not as a photo op, but actually working hard at the jobs they did.

On June 28, 1977, on my lunch break from a workday as a sidewall installer at the Vindale Mobile Home plant in Tallahassee, I announced my candidacy for governor of Florida.

In the years since, I have completed close to four hundred such work-days, spent as everything from teacher to preacher, busboy to bellhop, roofer to another person who cares greatly about the craftsmanship of people's roofs—Santa Claus. If there is an issue I want to learn more about, from Medicare reform to infrastructure improvement, I will work at several jobs that put me in direct contact with that subject and the people who work at it every day. In preparation for the Joint Inquiry, I worked as a security officer at an airport, a seaport, and a nuclear power plant. I also worked as a Coast Guard flight officer, a watch officer for an intelligence center, and an agent with a FBI counterterrorism task force.

Three days after the Joint Inquiry's report had been filed, I took my final workday for 2002 and my 385th since I had worked as a twelfth-grade civics teacher in 1974.

I was working as a disc jockey and morning news personality at WRHB, Radio Carnivale, the principal Haitian radio station in Miami. My boss was the "every hour on the half hour" news anchor, Ed Lozama. Each segment, he would call me over for an interview. (Radio Carnivale doesn't get a lot of politicians dropping by.) In each interview, Ed would ask me in his lilting Creole-tinged English, "Are you going to run for President? Would you consider running for President?" They were seductive questions. For the first four hours of the workday I held Ed off, replying that I felt there were a number of things the current administration was not doing well. Shortly after noon, in what has to be the most unscripted declaration of presidential candidacy on record, I said, "I'm thinking about it."

Even giving that equivocal answer made me feel good. It sounded right. It felt right.

Of course, one of the things that made my workdays so successful politically is that TV cameras and local reporters would often check in to see what I was doing. That offhand (and truthful) comment brought a herd of cameras and print journalists to the cramped radio offices in the middle of Miami's Little Haiti. Ed Lozama seemed to have broken a big story.

The following day, *The Miami Herald*'s lead story, complete with a color picture of me in radio headphones, was on the almost-announcement.

"Florida Sen. Bob Graham, calling the 'nation scandalously ill-prepared' for another terrorist attack and expressing concern about the Bush administration's handling of the economy and potential war with Iraq, said Monday he is 'seriously considering' a bid for the White House."

One lesson I had learned during my first race for governor was the importance of an early start. In this presidential campaign, I would be the next-to-last candidate to declare. This denied me the time to establish a national fund-raising base and to dominate the field on the issue I felt passionate about, and on which I differed from almost every other "Washington" candidate—the distraction of the war in Iraq from the war on terrorism. I was motivated by a passionate belief that President Bush had taken the country in a dangerously wrong direction and that I had the best chance of removing him from the driver's seat.

Before I began my campaign, Adele urged that I get my health checked, especially given that I had suffered a health scare when my heart fell out of rhythm on our trip to the Middle East and I was appearing increasingly fatigued. It turned out that I was suffering from coronary artery disease, that my aortic valve was not closing properly, and that I would need surgery. At the moment when I needed to be getting a campaign started, I'd be laid up from my operation. Once I recovered, I hit the trail. Although events in Iraq were making my prediction of the previous October look more and more prescient, I was unable to break through the hammerlock Howard Dean had on the antiwar issue. As I campaigned, I began feeling more and more energetic, but I still looked like someone who had had open-heart surgery in the last six months. And our treasury dwindled to close to zero.

In early October, I considered the situation with Adele, my brother Bill, and the new leadership of the campaign. We concluded that the opportunity to win the Democratic nomination was close to nil. The choices were to revert to a Dennis Kucinich–style threadbare campaign and hope for magic in the bottle, or to withdraw. On October 6, 2003, I chose the second course. I made my announcement during an interview with my friend of many years from his Miami radio days, Larry King.

I said that I was proud of what we had been able to accomplish during the campaign, gratified at the number of people across the country

who believed in me, supported me, and were committed to seeing America take a new direction, but that I had made the judgment that I was not going to be elected President of the United States.

A month later, I announced that I would not be seeking reelection to the Senate.

★

The final battle to be fought on behalf of the Joint Inquiry was the creation of a public report to supplement the classified report we had filed on December 20. As it stood, the only nonclassified portions of the report were the cover page, the table of contents, the list of findings and conclusions (without the accompanying narrative), and the recommendations. We felt strongly that the public should be able to see the body of our report—after all, it was their safety at stake, and their money that had funded our efforts. Moreover, in an administration as secretive as this one, I felt it would be appropriate to try to set a different precedent, under which, without disclosing information vital to national security, we could trust the people to look at our work and draw their own conclusions.

The day we filed the classified report, Staff Director Eleanor Hill and Deputy Staff Director Rick Cinquegrana drove out to Langley to hand-deliver a copy of it to the CIA with the request that the Agency look it over and see what information remained classified and would need to be redacted. In March, over three months after they had received the 800-page-plus report, the CIA had completed only 200 pages. And after the CIA was finished, the report would still have to go to the FBI and to the White House for approval.

Finally, in late spring, the CIA presented its version of the unclassified report. Huge swaths of text were blacked out. Some of the very pieces of information that the CIA had declassified for the public staff statements of the Joint Inquiry were now reclassified. Some information that was never classified to begin with was now classified, the argument being that although the individual pieces of information were unclassified, assembling them as we had created a "mosaic" that now had to be classified. The CIA thought its work was done. Eleanor and Rick, however, disagreed. They went through every section the CIA wanted out,

and checked the information there against open-source documents— newspapers, government reports and websites, and public statements from officials. With pages and pages of open-source material that made a mockery of the CIA's attempts at classification, Eleanor and Rick went back for another round.

Ultimately, they convened a meeting with classification representatives of the CIA, the FBI, and the NSA, and went through the report page by page, arguing over what could be released. The agencies found the process infuriating. Why hadn't we simply worked with them to create an unclassified version of the report from scratch? The reason, of course, was that had we done that, we would have ended up with the most wishy-washy and uninformative document imaginable. We all agreed that were we to have any impact, we would have to start from the classified version and move backward.

As Eleanor, Rick, and the agencies worked through the classification issues, the parts of the report that were to remain classified—the redactions—appeared simply as black lines between the text that was suitable for release. The White House assumed that when we released the report, we would simply delete the black lines and rewrite the report so that the redactions would be invisible and the public would have no idea where they had occurred. Under the White House's plan, the reader of the declassified version would have no way of appreciating how much material, or what sort of material, was being withheld. We considered reformatting tantamount to additional classification, and we refused to accept it. Progress was stalled for almost a month by this controversy. Finally and reluctantly, the White House retreated, and while the public had its vision shrouded, at least Americans were able to see where that was taking place.

Finally, on July 24, 2003, more than seven months after the initial submission, the report was released.

Significant portions of virtually every section of the report had been censored. I agreed that several of the censored areas were redacted for the right national security reasons. However, there was one area that did not need to be kept secret, and it was the one area where the White House simply refused to relent. This was, not surprisingly, the section of the report that related to the Saudi government and the assistance that government gave to some and possibly all of the September 11 terrorists.

This section had been redacted in its entirety, all twenty-seven pages. Senator Shelby and I, after rereading those twenty-seven pages, independently concluded that 95 percent of that material was safe for public consumption, and that these pages were being kept secret for reasons other than national security.

I felt that since the terrorists weren't deterred by the prospect of death, the one way to prevent future attacks was to find, stop, and destroy the systems that supported them in the United States. Eliminating the support systems that facilitated their evil in the United States was a critical line of domestic defense, and yet the part of the report that would give the American people the clearest window into that system and who was responsible for it was censored. It was ironic to me that a President who had initially thought that Iraq must have been the perpetrator of September 11, because only a nation-state could have carried out such a sophisticated and violent attack and avoid detection for twenty-one months, had now concluded that a nation-state that *had* aided the terrorists should not be held publicly to account. Again, it was as if the President's loyalty lay more with Saudi Arabia than with America's safety.

I had been able to get a look at the report as it was to be released, and I photographed the twenty-seven redacted pages. That day, during the second of two press conferences with the families of the victims, I displayed the twenty-seven pages, each a nearly text-free sea of blank spaces, an easel-sized poster for each page. I hoped that at least the knowledge that so much information was being kept from the American public would galvanize people to exert pressure on the White House to be candid about not only what was classified, but why it was classified. My efforts had no influence on the White House.

CONCLUSION

The Realities of Today

Thursday, March 11, 2004, dawned like any other weekday in Madrid, Spain. People went about their business, heading to work. Local news was focused on the elections to be held just three days later.

And then, shortly before 8:00 A.M., at the main Atocha commuter station in the heart of the city, an explosion cut a train in two, mangling the cars and sending pieces of metal flying through the air. Dozens of people were burned to death where they sat. The survivors crawled out of the train and into the street.

In rapid succession, a series of explosions ripped through the nearby Santa Eugenia and El Pozo stations. Rescuers combed through the bloody wreckage, trying to separate the dead from the living. When the smoke cleared, the scope of the attack could be seen. In all, ten bombs destroyed four commuter trains, killing 191 people.

It was a coordinated attack. And though the Spanish authorities initially blamed the Basque separatist group ETA, a van was found near

Madrid with detonators and a tape of Koran verses. A group claiming
links to al-Qaeda later came forward to take responsibility.

The next day, the front page of the largest daily newspaper, *El Pais*,
ran the headline "11-M"—"11 Marzo." The implication was clear: this
attack was Spain's September 11.

The bombing in Spain served as brutal evidence of al-Qaeda's regeneration. What is important to note is that there didn't have to be a resurgence at all. While America was waging war in Afghanistan, we had
al-Qaeda on the run. During the seven months between September 11,
2001, and April 11, 2002, al-Qaeda did not manage one successful terrorist attack. Not one. Between the time of my discussion with General
Tommy Franks in February 2002 about our resources being drawn
away from Afghanistan and the beginning of the public buildup to the
war in Iraq in August 2002, al-Qaeda pulled off just two small terrorist
attacks, one in Tunisia and one in Pakistan. Remembering what General Franks told me at Central Command, that means that in the time
that America was fully committed to the war on terror, and not de-
voting resources, energy, or focus to Iraq, al-Qaeda was rendered harm-
less.

Then, once America turned to Iraq, al-Qaeda was able to regroup,
refocus, and begin carrying out attacks again. From September 2002
until the train bombings in Spain in 2004, al-Qaeda carried out twelve
attacks that took, in all, more than 600 lives. The deadliest was the
bombing of a Bali nightclub that killed 202 people. Overall, the number
of al-Qaeda attacks more than doubled in the last three months of 2002
from all of 2001, and then doubled again over the course of 2003.

On March 1, 2003, when George Bush stood on the deck of the U.S.S.
Abraham Lincoln and declared that "the battle of Iraq is one victory in
a war on terror that began on September the 11th, 2001," he was not
just wrong, he was 180 degrees wrong. At best, the war in Iraq distracted from the war on terror. At worst, it set us back significantly. John
Adams once said, "Facts are stubborn things." The facts behind al-
Qaeda's resurgence tell the story. We let them off the hook. That is the
fact.

The level of direct al-Qaeda involvement in the Spain attacks remains, as of this writing, an open question. My guess is that what the
attacks in Spain represented was the new and different form that al-

Qaeda will take in the future—one in which attacks are al-Qaeda affiliated, sanctioned, or operationally supported, but not necessarily executed at the formal direction of Osama bin Laden.

This is a change born of necessity. American military action in Afghanistan cost al-Qaeda its Taliban sanctuary and at best an estimated one out of five of its combatants, and forced it to retreat from its base in Kandahar to the mountains and caves of the Afghanistan-Pakistan border. Osama bin Laden had no choice but to confront his lessened capabilities.

I am reminded of a briefing I received in Bogotá in the spring of 2001. The subject was the transition that had occurred in the terrorist group known as the Revolutionary Armed Forces of Colombia, or FARC. Growing out of a rural force with political grievances, the FARC evolved into an economic guerrilla group, affluent from the dollars paid by the drug cartels for its security services. With the success of the Colombian and U.S. "decapitation strategy" in disrupting the drug cartels in Medellín and Cali, the FARC changed to adapt to a changing landscape. Instead of simply providing security to others, it became an entrepreneur, taking control of critical and lucrative components of the now fractured drug-trafficking enterprise. The briefer described the new FARC as a "necklace" or "bead" organization. Each of the approximately forty individual units or "beads" was assigned a mission, such as flying coca paste from Bolivia to Colombia. The beads had significant autonomy, but were linked to the center based on the profitability of their mission. The center provided significant support such as strategic leadership, intelligence, and the redistribution of funds where the individual unit was unable to generate sufficient funds to support its undertaking.

We're seeing something similar with al-Qaeda. I've often compared al-Qaeda to a blob of mercury. If you bring your fist down on it, it bursts into dozens of other tiny blobs of mercury. In Afghanistan, we did an excellent job of bringing our fist down on al-Qaeda. However, just when we should have been taking the next step, eradicating the smaller units into which we had broken al-Qaeda, President Bush decided to move on to another task, war with Iraq. As President Mubarak had predicted in our breakfast a year and a half earlier, "A war will be seen in the streets of Cairo and Damascus as an attack on Islam; there's no way to avoid it." The war had become a giant recruiting poster for radicalized Islamists.

The distraction also gave al-Qaeda and its newly acquired partners in terrorism throughout the world the time and breathing room to regroup, and fresh combatants and suicide bombers to recruit. One of the results was the carnage of March 11 in Madrid.

The Spanish attacks had another result, as well.

Spain's opposition Socialist party had been attacking the center-right prime minister, José María Aznar, for his support of America in Iraq, an overwhelmingly unpopular decision. The Socialist leader, José Luis Rodríguez Zapatero, had made the centerpiece of his campaign a promise that were he elected, he would withdraw the 1,300 Spanish troops stationed in Iraq.

Many Spanish voters suspected that al-Qaeda plotted the attacks to punish Prime Minister Aznar for supporting the war in Iraq, and that feeling, along with the anger and grief over his handling of the Madrid attacks, swept his party out of office three days later. It was a stunning upset. Just twenty-four hours after he was sworn in, Mr. Zapatero ordered Spain's defense minister, José Bono, to "do what is necessary" to bring the Spanish troops home as soon as possible.

America's "coalition of the willing" shrank by one, and Spain, whose troops we may or may not have needed for our operations in Iraq but whom we most certainly need as an ally in the war on terror, now has an anti-U.S. government in place.

The loss of Spain's troops, however, was one of the more minor setbacks we faced in Iraq, where the situation has been deteriorating since American forces arrived in Baghdad and President Bush declared our mission accomplished.

As of this writing, in midsummer of 2004, we have lost more than 900 of our brave young men and women in Iraq, and thousands more have been grievously wounded. More than half of those casualties have occurred since President Bush declared an end to major combat operations. As a point of comparison, the combined number of postconflict American combat casualties in our engagements in Germany, Japan, Haiti, Bosnia, and Kosovo was zero.[1] That is the importance of planning for what happens after a war.

In the case of Iraq, it is not that there was no planning—in fact, no fewer than five government agencies warned that there would be significant armed resistance to a U.S.-led occupation—it is that the reports went ignored or unread. When then Army chief of staff General Eric K. Shinseki told Congress that several hundred thousand occupation troops would be needed, Deputy Defense Secretary Paul Wolfowitz rejected his estimate as "wildly off the mark."[2] Because his candid assessment flew in the face of administration claims, Secretary Rumsfeld announced Shinseki's replacement fourteen months before the scheduled end of the Army chief of staff's term, making him a lame duck. This was both an unprecedented bureaucratic maneuver and a disgraceful treatment of a distinguished combat veteran.

Ahmad Chalabi, the Iraqi exile and darling of the neoconservative establishment who was once the choice of leading Defense Department civilians to run Iraq after the American occupation, and to whose organization America paid $33 million, has turned on the Bush administration. He is now reported to have told Iran that the United States had broken the secret communications code of Iran's Ministry of Intelligence; if this is so, he is assumed to have compromised all the information his Pentagon allies shared with him and has cut off a vital source of information about a nation that, unlike Iraq, is actively moving forward with a nuclear program.[3] This is a grave setback in the war on terror and in the critical project of avoiding the proliferation of nuclear weapons.

According to polls, more Iraqis believe that Americans should leave their country than think they should stay. Nearly half said that the invasion and occupation had done more harm than good, and only 7 percent of Iraqis regard Americans as liberators.[4]

Speaking before the Senate Foreign Relations Committee in May 2004, Marine General (ret.) Joseph Hoar, a former commander of U.S. forces in the Middle East, said, "I believe we are absolutely on the brink of failure. . . . We are looking into the abyss."

Larry Diamond, a former advisor to the U.S. occupation authority in Baghdad, warned: "If the current situation persists, we will continue fighting one form of Iraqi insurgency after another—with too little legitimacy, too little will and too few resources. . . . There is only one word for a situation in which you cannot win and you cannot withdraw: Quagmire."[5]

When you look back at the Bush administration's march to war in Iraq, you can distill the many rationales for the invasion into three main points.

The first, and most significant, was that Saddam Hussein had weapons of mass destruction and was dangerously close to achieving a nuclear weapon.

The second argument was that Iraq was linked to al-Qaeda, and thus a war in Iraq would be part of the war on terror.

Third, that this would be a humanitarian war of liberation, and that as bringers of democracy we would be welcomed with sweets and roses.

On the argument that Iraq had weapons of mass destruction, Secretary of Defense Rumsfeld even went so far as to declare that we knew where the weapons were, a claim that may have been based on the CIA's report that it had identified 550 sites where weapons of mass destruction were either being produced or stored. It now appears that Saddam Hussein's WMD capabilities were vastly overstated, and that America allowed itself to be misled by informants whose information had been dismissed by other countries. No weapons of mass destruction have been found. At a March 2004 black-tie dinner I attended in Washington, President Bush gave a humorous speech in which he showed slides of himself looking around various parts of the White House. The joke, as he narrated, was "Nope, no WMDs there." It was one of the more offensive things I have witnessed. Having recently attended the funeral of an American soldier killed in Iraq, who had left behind a young wife and two preschool-age children, I found nothing funny about a deceitful justification for a war.

The second justification was that Iraq was linked to al-Qaeda. As the parts of the NIE I was able to get declassified show, this claim was not only incorrect, it was the exact opposite of the truth. Our intelligence officials found no credible link between Saddam Hussein and al-Qaeda. What they found was that Saddam Hussein would form a bond with al-Qaeda only if we attacked him. Once the war began, CIA analysts expressed concern that the "chaos after war would turn Iraq into a laboratory for terrorists." Time has proven that prediction correct. Rather than stamping out terrorism, our campaign in Iraq is now a terrorist recruitment tool, further fueling the rage that can help turn people into terrorists, allowing Islamic extremists to point to America as waging a war against Islam, and providing hundreds of thousands of American targets. Because of the terrorist groundswell he has created in Iraq, President Bush now calls Iraq a "central front" in the war on terrorism.[6] The problem is that it isn't a central front, it is an unnecessary front, one that is taking time and attention from fronts such as those identified to me by General Franks where the real war on terrorism needs to be fought.

The third argument—that we would be a humanitarian force of liberation that would foster a democratic Iraq—is a moral argument, and its power always depended on our occupying the moral high ground. That is why the revelations of mistreatment of prisoners at Abu Ghraib prison were so terribly damaging. They undercut the rationale for our occupation. You can tell the Iraqi people that America has the fastest-growing freely worshipping Muslim population in the world, and that from Bosnia to Kuwait, America has waged war on behalf of Muslims, but one picture is worth more than any of those words.

I do not claim to know what the answer is in Iraq. All I know is that I wish I had been able to do more to keep us from having to ask the question.

As the prison abuse scandal simmered, a piece of news passed by with little note, a piece of news that actually involved terrorists and weapons of mass destruction. In early 2001, it appears, North Korea secretly provided Libya with nearly two tons of uranium that, if enriched, could have been used to produce a nuclear weapon. Libya turned the uranium over to the United States in 2004 as part of its agreement to give up its nuclear program, but the question remains: to what other nations or entities has North Korea sold nuclear material?[7] Only effective intelligence will be able to tell us.

★

After the attacks of September 11, Omar al-Bayoumi, the man who was al-Mihdhar and al-Hazmi's first friend in San Diego, was detained in the United Kingdom at the FBI's request and charged with visa fraud.[8] At the time of his arrest, he had in his possession the number of a contact at the Saudi embassy in London. The British asked the United States whether we had any questions for al-Bayoumi. Receiving no guidance from the FBI, and because visa fraud is not an extraditable offense, the British released al-Bayoumi after a couple of days, and he returned to Saudi Arabia.

Osama Bassnan, al-Bayoumi's friend and one of the terrorists' supporters in San Diego, was deported to Saudi Arabia on November 17,
2002.

In late July 2003, the Saudi interior minister, Prince Nayef bin Abdulaziz, vowed not to extradite Omar al-Bayoumi, saying, "We have never
handed over a Saudi to a state or a foreign side, and we will never do it."
At the same time, al-Bayoumi told a Saudi newspaper, "I stopped being
a suspect for over a year now. Do you imagine that if any of what has
been rumored in the media about me is true, would the FBI or Scotland
Yard have set me free?"[9]

If al-Bayoumi was truly no longer a suspect, the FBI had informed
him of that fact eight months before it informed the American public.
On March 24, 2004, a small Associated Press story appeared under the
headline "FBI Concludes 2 Saudis Not Intel Agents."

In part, it read:

Dispelling a theory raised by congressional investigators, the FBI
has concluded that two Saudi men questioned about the Sept. 11 hijackers were not intelligence agents for their country or aiding the
terrorist plot, officials said.

After conducting additional interviews and reviewing documents, FBI agents recently closed down their investigation into
Omar al-Bayoumi and Osama Bas[s]nan, two friends who raised
suspicions because one briefly lent money to two of the 19 hijackers
while the other received money from the Saudi royal family.

The FBI concluded at most the two Saudi men occasionally provided information to their kingdom or helped Saudi visitors settle
into the United States, but did so in compliance with Muslim cus-
tom of being kind to strangers [rather] than out of some relationship with Saudi Intelligence, the officials said.

Knowing that the money was not loaned, but given, and that it
may have been in the ballpark of $40,000; knowing that before his
"chance" encounter with al-Mihdhar and al-Hazmi, al-Bayoumi had
told at least one person he was going to "pick up a friend"; and knowing
that al-Bayoumi first met with a suspected terrorist at the Saudi consulate before his "chance" meeting at a restaurant more than two hours

from his home, I could scarcely believe the conclusion the FBI was drawing.

Now add to those facts the additional evidence we found: that al-Bayoumi had made an unusually large number of phone calls to Saudi government officials during the time the two terrorists were in San Diego, and that the CIA had referred to al-Bayoumi and Bassnan, in contemporary reports, as "spies" or "agents," and declared that there was "incontrovertible evidence" that there was support for them within the Saudi government. The FBI's inability to see a connection between Saudi Arabia, al-Bayoumi, Bassnan, al-Mihdhar, and al-Hazmi baffles me.

As soon as I saw the AP story, I had my national security advisor, Bob Filippone, call the FBI and ask whether it was true. The FBI told Bob that it wasn't. They weren't sure, they said, how this information had gotten out, but the investigation was ongoing and they hadn't cleared anyone yet. In fact, they noted that there had been no change in the status of the investigation since I received my last formal briefing as Intelligence Committee chairman—a briefing on this issue—in January 2003.

Although I wasn't satisfied with the investigation's speed, I was glad that it was at least still going on, and I gave the matter no further thought. A month later I turned on *Meet the Press* to see Tim Russert interviewing Prince Bandar of Saudi Arabia. Turning to the issue of terrorism funding, Russert asked about a *Newsweek* report that a federal investigation into the bank accounts of the Saudi embassy had found more than $27 million in "suspicious" transactions. In responding, Prince Bandar said, "Here is the problem. When a story like this, that has a prince, a princess, money, terrorism, it is exotic . . . But one thing that is done in this country that really disappoints me, and I could say something stronger, is when somebody puts a story like that like *Newsweek* did, it's a big story. When the two people that started all of this, Mr. Bassnan and Bayoumi, a month ago the FBI came and said, 'After two years of investigation, there is no connections. There is no foul play.' Guess what? How many times did you make a special program about it or *Newsweek* have an announcement? They didn't."

My ears perked up. Here was Prince Bandar citing the same AP story that the FBI had disavowed as his defense against claims of terrorism funding. Frustrated that Bandar was using this faulty information in a promotional way, I called Robert Mueller and asked him what the FBI was doing to get the perception corrected. He told me that what his office had told Bob was still true—the investigation was ongoing.

Shortly thereafter, Bob got another call from the FBI, telling him that the FBI had looked further and that the AP story clearing Bayoumi and Bassnan was indeed correct—that the two men had been cleared of being Saudi spies and of having any witting involvement in the September 11 plot. The FBI caller said that this conclusion was reached after agents interviewed both al-Bayoumi and Bassnan in Saudi Arabia (an interview, we later learned, that was supervised by Saudi government officials).

Coincidentally, I'd be seeing Mueller at a dinner that week, so rather than phone him again I confronted him at the dinner.

Director Mueller told me that he was unaware of the change in the investigation, but would get back to me, which he did a couple of days later. Now he confirmed that the news report was correct, and that the case on Omar al-Bayoumi and Osama Bassnan had been closed, something that al-Bayoumi himself seemed to have known eight months earlier. If that was so, I told him, I wanted to meet with the agents who reached this conclusion. Director Mueller's response was immediate. "No. If we do this for you, we have to do it for every senator."

Increasingly frustrated, I told him, "I devoted a year of my life to investigating these guys. You've reached a conclusion that runs counter to a core finding of our investigation. I want the agents to explain to me how they came to that result."

Mueller told me he understood, but it was just a matter of policy. I asked him whether it was a matter of policy that his people could speak to the Associated Press but not to a senator. Director Mueller told me he'd get back to me.

When he did, he said that the decision about giving me access to the agents was a policy matter that would have to be handled by the Justice Department; if I wanted the policy changed, I would have to do so through the Attorney General. That day, I placed a call to Attorney General Ashcroft, who told me he'd get back to me.

While awaiting his response, I cowrote a letter with Senator Arlen Specter of Pennsylvania, a former Republican chairman of the Senate Intelligence Committee, who shares my interest in and suspicion about America's relationship with Saudi Arabia. We wrote, in part: "We are concerned that this report [the AP story] is being used as a response to al-

legations of foreign government involvement in the September 11 attacks. If it is now clear that a foreign government was not directly involved, then that government deserves broad public recognition of its
non-involvement. Inversely, if it appears that a foreign government may
have been involved in the attacks, then the citizens of the Unted States
have the right to know more details of that involvement."

We concluded by asking for a briefing with the appropriate agents.

The FBI set the meeting for the following Thursday, a date when
Senator Specter could attend. Within a few hours of the meeting time,
the FBI canceled and rescheduled for Friday morning, a time when Senator Specter had a previous commitment in Pennsylvania. I met with
two FBI representatives who had little knowledge of the contradictory
findings of the Joint Inquiry and the FBI. Because it was immediately
obvious that the meeting was not going to be productive, the FBI representative promised to reschedule it for the follwing week with agents
who were familiar with the facts of the case.

The next Tuesday, the chief of congressional affairs for the FBI called
to say that in spite of the commitments that had been made four days
earlier, there would be no meeting that week or any other week. I called
the Attorney General and told him what had happened, and said I was
very distressed that the FBI had sent a representative who clearly knew
little about the case, promised to send an informed person the following
week, and then reneged. Ashcroft said he would call back.

As of this writing, we have not heard back. Given Attorney General
Ashcroft's position on Justice Department openness and the FBI's attitude throughout the Joint Inquiry, I'm not optimistic about the chances
of finding out more about something it seems that neither the FBI nor
the Bush administration wants the American people to find out about.

As our inquiry was completing its work, we found that the FBI had
also cleared Anwar Aulaqi, the cleric whom the two hijackers met in
San Diego and who moved with them to Virginia. In 2002, Aulaqi left
for Yemen; he returned briefly in the fall of 2002 to "liquidate his assets"
and is reported to have left again. His whereabouts are unknown.[10]

In late 2003, Mohdar Abdullah, who at Omar al-Bayoumi's urging
was one of the first people to befriend al-Hazmi and al-Mihdhar in San
Diego and who is thought to have helped them obtain identification and
arrange for flying lessons, was arrested for lying to a U.S. immigration

officer. He also admitted to being a friend of Hani Hanjour. None of those allegations was addressed when he pleaded guilty to the immigration charge. After serving a six-month sentence, he was deported.[11]

Kenneth Williams, who wrote the hauntingly prescient Phoenix electronic communication, is back in the Phoenix FBI office, continuing his work.

The agent who was handling the informant in San Diego has retired from the FBI, in part out of his frustrated conviction that had he only been given a little more information, he would have broken open the September 11 plot.

As for that informant, the FBI was last keeping him at an undisclosed location "for his protection." It is unclear whether he is still in the United States.

After the release of the public report of the Joint Inquiry and my complaint about the twenty-seven pages that had been kept completely classified, Prince Bandar fumed that the pages were probably kept classified because what they contained could not be substantiated. "Saudi Arabia has nothing to hide," he maintained. He went on to announce that the Saudi foreign minister, Prince Saud Faisal, was flying to Washington to meet with President Bush to discuss the matter.[12]

On July 28, 2003, citing Prince Bandar's stated desire to have the pages declassified, I wrote a letter to President Bush again asking him to do so. Before Prince Saud arrived, the President stated that he would not be declassifying the offending pages.

It seemed to me that George W. Bush and Prince Bandar were performing a sort of good cop–bad cop routine, in which Prince Bandar got to claim innocence on behalf of Saudi Arabia, while George W. Bush protected him by being the bad cop who wouldn't release troubling information. Having spent a significant amount of time with those twenty-seven pages, I can say unequivocally that the information they contain raises serious questions about Saudi Arabia's governmental support for at least some of the terrorists. The ponderous and nonproductive FBI investigation raises serious questions as to who was directing the Bureau's actions. The Bush administration's response raises even more serious questions about the politicized use of the classification process to hide from the American people information that involves their security.

I still want to know whether other hijackers had received support similar to that accorded to al-Hazmi and al-Mihdhar in San Diego. What would cause these two of the nineteen to receive special treatment? On what intelligence would we believe the al-Qaeda and Saudi support systems were dismantled after September 11? And does the infrastructure remain in place to assist future terrorists inside the United States?

I asked the FBI to undertake the review of the Riggs Bank records to determine if there was a money trail to other terrorists. I suggested the FBI look at other Saudi firms with ties to al-Qaeda's "Golden Chain." I wondered if the FBI had a plan to monitor suspect Saudi interests in the United States. To my knowledge, none of these investigations have been completed. And we still know nothing about "the brothers"—the mysterious addressees of the note found in the bag that Nawaf al-Hazmi and Khalid al-Mihdhar left at the local mosque before embarking on their fatal flight. Nor do we know anything else about what I believe to be a state-sponsored terrorist support network that still exists, largely undamaged, within the United States.

★

On July 14, 2003, I was asked about the increasingly harsh words I was using about George W. Bush in my campaign for the Democratic presidential nomination. Specifically, I was asked: if President Bush were held to the same standards as President Clinton had been, would he be impeached?

I've been in politics long enough to know a dangerous question when I hear one, so I tried to answer diplomatically. I said that impeachment was not a realistic outcome, that impeachment proceedings are conducted by the House of Representatives, and in a Republican-controlled House it wasn't likely those proceedings would ever be started. I added that the decision to remove a leader from office (what most people think about when they think about impeachment) is made by the U.S. Senate, and so my answer to the question of impeachment was that the American people had the opportunity to compress both stages of the process by voting to remove George W. Bush from office on the first Tuesday in November 2004.

I should have moved on to the next question, but instead continued,

"If the standard of impeachment that the Republicans set for Bill Clinton, that a personal, consensual relationship was the basis for impeachment, would not a President who knowingly deceived the American people about something as important as going to war meet the standard of impeachment?"

The result was the same as if I had said, simply, yes. Of course the answer was yes. It ignited a small firestorm. I had introduced the idea of impeachment into the presidential debate, and my comments were being represented as a call for George W. Bush's impeachment.

Lost in the brouhaha is the fact that I have no shortage of reasons to believe the American people have been ill served by President Bush, ranging from the economy to the environment. Because the scope of this book is limited to the issues of intelligence and terrorism, I would like to lay out the eleven reasons that I found in my work as chairman of the Senate Intelligence Committee and cochair of the Joint Inquiry into Intelligence Community Activities before and after the Terrorist Attacks of September 11, 2001.

* After he was briefed in August 2001, that al-Qaeda was making preparations consistent with hijackings, the President did not take executive action to alert the Federal Aviation Administration, the Department of Defense, or other agencies that might have used this information to harden commercial aviation against an attack.
* Throughout 2002, the President directed the FBI to restrain and obfuscate the investigation of the foreign government support that some and possibly all of the September 11 hijackers received.
* In spite of the specific congressional authority the President had sought and received to conduct war on al-Qaeda and the Afghanistan government, early in 2002 the President directed that intelligence and military resources necessary to win the war against the Afghanistan-based terrorists be relocated to commence the preparation for an as yet unauthorized war against Iraq.
* The President declared, "Our war on terror begins with al-Qaeda, but it does not end there. It will not end until every terrorist group has been found, stopped, and defeated." However, the

President failed to seek or obtain authority to use force against terrorist networks of "global reach," specifically Hezbollah, Hamas, and Islamic Jihad, nor has he developed a plan to find, halt, and defeat these international terrorists.

★ Although the President knew that Syria was providing sanctuary for a number of terrorist organizations—including Hezbollah, which is responsible for more than 300 American deaths—he was late and lax in exerting economic or political influence on the government of Syria.

★ Even as he represented Baghdad as the next front in the war on terror, the President, as commander-in-chief, failed to prepare adequately for the war in Iraq and its consequences. As a result, the capabilities of al-Qaeda and other international terrorists have been strengthened.

★ In the fall of 2002, the President allowed intelligence agencies under his control to present erroneous, misleading, and incomplete information to the Congress, our allies, and the American people in support of the war in Iraq.

★ The President further adulterated that intelligence by selective use and presentation of the evidence to justify a preemptive war to the American people and the Congress, and to the world community at the United Nations.

★ The President failed to prepare the Congress and the American people to judge what was the greater threat—international terrorist networks or Saddam Hussein—by refusing to release the information he had in his possession as to the relative number of international terrorists and Iraqi operatives present in the United States.

★ Through delayed, halfhearted, and political use of the proposal to create and expeditiously activate a Department of Homeland Security, the President has failed to protect our country.

★ The President has engaged in a cover-up, withholding from the American people the evidence that supplies the basis of several of the above charges. He has done so by misclassifying information as national security data. While the information may be embarrassing or politically damaging, its revelation would not damage national security.

Any *one* of these things would warrant a leader's removal from office. Taken together, they are a searing indictment of a President who, despite lofty words to the contrary, has not been a leader, has not been honest, and has not made America safer. America needs a President who will bring to the White House a sense of urgency about the still undone reforms needed in our intelligence agencies, and the steps we must take to make our country safer.

While George W. Bush's political future remains to be determined, I have made a decision about my future. By the end of the 108th Congress in January 2005, I will have held elective public office for thirty-eight years. Every day has been a learning experience; every chance to serve has been a blessing.

In the fall of 2005, I'm going to become a fellow at Harvard's Kennedy School of Government, where I hope to teach a unit on intelligence issues from the perspective of the users of intelligence.

I will also be working to establish, at one or more universities in Florida, a center which will be dedicated to three things. The first is the creation of an ROTC-like program to bring more young people into intelligence work. The second will be a leadership training and mentoring effort for young people who are interested in politics. And the third will be to provide a training and networking forum for legislators, particularly those in Latin American parliaments, which are assuming their critical role in a democratic society.

Adele and I have owned a town house on Capitol Hill since 1988 (we bought it from Senator John Kerry), but we have never truly taken the time to explore the city and the areas around it. We recently decided not to sell the house just yet, in the hopes that maybe we can spend some time as tourists. We've also decided to take a couple of months to do something we have talked about for many years: return to some of the places we visited either as tourists or in an official capacity and spend time learning about and enjoying them. Our first destination will be Spain.

I also intend to take a lot more time and simply be "Doodle"—the name my eleven grandchildren have bestowed on me. (Adele is Deedle.)

★

My work with American intelligence has alerted me to the new threats we face. As a nation we have moved beyond the day when we could follow our national cultural inclinations and submerge our consideration of intelligence matters. America cannot be ignorant of the threats we face and the gap between those threats and our capability to understand and avert them. I intend to remain engaged in America's intelligence community and active in working to reform it to meet today's challenges.

If our national experience in the first four years of this new century has taught us anything, it is that, now more than ever, intelligence matters, to us all.

APPENDIX

Lessons Learned

There has been no shortage of significant American intelligence failures in the last twenty years. The failures to predict the Soviet Union's fall, India and Pakistan's nuclear tests, and North Korea's long-range missile capabilities come most immediately to mind.

The events surrounding the tragedy of September 11 and the deepening quagmire of the war in Iraq add five more serious policy and intelligence failures to that ignominious list. They are the failure to capture or kill Osama bin Laden before he initiated the September 11 plot; the failure to interdict the plotters before they struck; the failure to use the insights gained from investigations into September 11 as catalysts for intelligence reform; the failure to acquire and present accurate information about the presence of weapons of mass destruction in Iraq; and the failure to acquire or use intelligence to develop a strategic plan for the occupation of Iraq. These failures have resulted in the loss of nearly 4,000 American lives, hundreds of billions of dollars in public and private costs, vastly diminished international credibility, and a heightened vulnerability to future terrorist strikes.

If September 11 awakened us to the need for reform, the war in Iraq is a report card on how we're doing. With some exceptions, there is no indication that our intelligence agencies, this administration, or the Congress has used these tragic failures as the impetus for initiating the reforms that will reduce the chance of us falling victim to another devastating attack. At a time when intelligence matters more to the American people than ever before, the sad truth is that those who are responsible for its direction are not prepared to provide the leadership necessary to institute the intelligence reforms America's security demands.

Why has there been this passivity? For starters, to talk about the needed reforms is to admit that there is a problem. President Bush has steadfastly declined to make this obvious admission. From the President through the national security apparatus and the Congress, there has been a failure to appreciate the importance of credible intelligence. When the enemy is no longer the predictable Soviet Union, but rather a swarm of secretive and loosely connected terrorists, intelligence is no longer only a force multiplier or a support to the military—it is an essential component of an integrated security network.

Another reason for the lethargic response is the lack of significant public pressure for reform. Reform requires a constituency. In the military, there is no shortage of constituencies for reform. Millions of Americans served in the military or have a family member who did. Millions more actively feel that they have a stake in decisions the military makes. There are ample organizations representing currently serving military and veterans. The military is spread over posts, stations, and bases in virtually every corner of America. The press, general and specialized, reports on what the military is doing. All of this creates a public awareness—a capability to contribute to the debate on military matters.

The same is not true of the intelligence community. The extended intelligence "family" is significantly smaller than that of the military. By its essence, intelligence is shrouded in secrecy, remote, little discussed, and, except as featured in Tom Clancy novels and James Bond movies, out of the minds of Americans. This shroud of secrecy is made even more impenetrable as information that is potentially politically embarrassing is declared to be sensitive to national security, such as the role of the Saudis in the September 11 attacks, and withheld from Americans. The public can't respond to things it isn't told, or seek reforms to problems it is kept from seeing.

There needs to be a realization in this country that in the coming years, the American people will be deeply affected by the quality of the intelligence used to send them or their loved ones to war, enact a trade treaty that will affect their jobs, or stop a terrorist attack against their community.

I hope that this book will contribute to the rising understanding of the need for reform and the political support necessary to make it happen.

The question, then, is, what shape should those reforms take? One of the legislative successes I discussed earlier was the Goldwater-Nichols Act, a 1986 law that reformed the U.S. military by forcing greater cooperation among the services by establishing joint commands. There is another lesson to be learned from the passage of that law. When Senators Barry Goldwater and Sam Nunn were developing their ideas in the Senate, they discussed the reforms they sought to achieve. Many in the military found these changes threatening, and argued—vociferously and successfully—against them. For several years, the status quo was winning. However, when Goldwater and Nunn began talking about the problems rather than the reforms, the opposition retreated. They used as examples the then-recent military mistakes in the hostage rescue mission in Iran and the invasion of Grenada to build their case. When the American people and members of Congress understood the extent of the problems in the military and how those problems affected the capability of the United States to accomplish a national security mission, the status quo crumbled. The problems were too obvious, the weaknesses of the status quo too exposed, to resist change.

In that same vein, I'd like to present what I believe are five of the major problems and challenges for American intelligence. By doing so, I hope to illustrate the imperative need for reform and explain what direction it should take.

One, we have failed to adapt to a changing adversary and global environment.

American intelligence is a survivor. Most species that have been so slow to evolve in response to changes in their environment would have vanished long ago.

Though the need for effective intelligence had been known from America's earliest war for independence, American intelligence as we know it today is really a child of the Cold War. The Soviet Union was an ally during World War II, and a full partner in planning for the postwar world. Two years after the war, it was emerging as America's most serious foe. To better understand this adversary, President Truman recommended, and the Congress created, the Central Intelligence Agency.

For the first two decades after its creation, the CIA (and the other components of the new American intelligence community) were culturally beholden to their World War II military role model, the Office of Special Services (OSS). The OSS was the most extensive and assertive clandestine effort in the nation's history to that date. Its primary orientation was to what we now describe as covert action: parachuting combatants behind enemy lines, inserting agents into enemy operational headquarters, and the like. This orientation to covert action dominated the adolescent CIA. It was not until the 1961 Bay of Pigs invasion failed, in large part due to flawed strategic and operational intelligence on Fidel Castro and the Soviets, that President John F. Kennedy and the leadership of the CIA began to rethink the Agency's role for the Cold War in which they were engaged rather than the World War through which they had lived.

That early history of failure to adapt to a new enemy, and to appreciate the new information requirements of decision makers and the United States position in the world, was repeated in the aftermath of the two most jarring geopolitical events in the history of the CIA, the November 9, 1989, fall of the Berlin Wall, and the collapse of the Soviet Union itself two years later.

The intelligence community had been stamped with the image of the Soviets. Our countries were based on different ideologies, but our national security apparatuses were analogous. As a result, we were two behemoths staring at our reflections in the mirror.

The two superpowers had institutional methodologies of transparency to limit the potential for unintended actions and reactions. The red "hotline" telephones between the Kremlin and the White House symbolized the maturity of the relationship.

Almost all of these similarities between our Cold War adversary and us have been impediments to reform in the post–Cold War era. Just as it was difficult forty years earlier to transition from the practices of the OSS against the Germans and Japanese, today's intelligence community has found it even more difficult to shift from the Cold War to the war on terror.

Our new enemy is distinctly different from us. It is a non-nation-state; the conflict is asymmetrical in the extreme. Our enemy is motivated by a religious belief that denies the legitimacy of governments which intrude on the direct relationship they believe should exist between Allah and man. These are people, as General Ahmed explained in our September 11 breakfast, living for paradise after death, so how can the loss of one's life be a deterrent to violent actions here on earth?

We are almost deaf to the numerous, frequently arcane, languages that our new adversaries speak, so we are unable to understand them at the most basic level. As a people and as a nation the United States has had limited experience with their cultures.

In the Joint Inquiry's report, we optimistically stated that "the cataclysmic events of September 11, 2001 provide an unique and compelling mandate for strong leadership and constructive change throughout the Intelligence Community."

The progress since September 11 has not been encouraging. The intelligence community has been slow to accept the concept that a non-nation-state can challenge the United States of America. We have taken only the first steps necessary to understand the terrorists. Satellites will not give us the information we need to understand the capabilities and intentions of Osama bin Laden, yet the allocation of intelligence resources continues to be dominated by the maintenance of the Cold War satellite architecture and the development of a new generation of satellite technology. The recruitment and training of human intelligence has accelerated but is inadequate to the need. A sense of urgency is required to dramatically increase the number of men and women in the intelligence agencies with command of the languages and cultures of the Middle East, Central Asia, and China.

In none of our intelligence agencies is this failure to transition to the new demands more evident than in America's domestic intelligence agency, the FBI. The FBI is first and foremost a law enforcement agency. In that important responsibility, the priorities and professional rewards center on investigating a crime that has already occurred, arresting the culprit, providing the court admissible evidence to secure a conviction, and sending the criminal to jail.

That is not the orientation of an intelligence agency. There the objective is to understand the threat before the act has occurred so that the plot can be interdicted. The standard for action is reasonable suspicion. The FBI's difficulty in remaking itself as an effective post–Cold War domestic intelligence agency was illustrated during a hearing of the Joint Inquiry: I asked an FBI supervisor of a counterterrorism unit how many terrorists there were in a major American city. His answer was fewer than ten. That seemed like a very small number given the reported terrorist activities in that city. I asked why he believed the number was so small. He replied, "It is the number of open files, the number of active criminal investigations we have under way related to terrorism, so we assume that is the number of terrorists."

By failing to make the transition to the new world we inhabit in this new millennium, U.S. intelligence is making itself less and less capable of providing the security which our citizens need and deserve. So what should we do?

The United States can begin by learning a lesson from the foe. After September 11 and the war in Afghanistan, al-Qaeda both regrouped and decentralized, establishing alliances with terrorist groups in more than 60 countries.

This may seem counterintuitive, but for us to deal with this decentralization, we must first centralize. Since their inception, the agencies that make up our foreign intelligence community have focused on assignments like the collection of signals or visual images. While each agency focuses on its own responsibilities, the larger realities—like the changed nature of the enemy—go unattended. They are nobody's business.

That is why the Joint Inquiry recommended that the United States centralize greater control over the foreign intelligence agencies through the creation of the position of Director of National Intelligence, to "make the entire US intelligence community operate as a coherent whole."

Currently, the CIA director also serves as the overall director of Central Intelligence. That practice should be ended. The analogy would be if the secretary of the Army also served as the secretary of the Department of Defense. Each of these jobs has a different perspective and focus. The reality is that having a dual-hatted intelligence leader has contributed to scandalously inadequate direction of the intelligence community.

Once the agencies are drawn into a coherent whole, I would recommend that they, like the combined military commands of Goldwater-Nichols, be reorganized around specific missions, such as terrorism, the global proliferation of weapons of mass destruction, or the region encircling the Caspian Sea.*

This new architecture would itself be subject to constant change as old threats decline or go away and new ones replace them. Such a structure would require constant attention to these questions: Who is our enemy today? Who is he likely to be tomorrow? What do we need to know in order to successfully confront this enemy?

A second reform designed to keep the intelligence community focused on both today and tomorrow is to increase the linkages between the community and other sources of information and analysis. There have been successful attempts to reach out to some academic programs and private-sector think tanks. These initiatives should be expanded and integrated as a permanent component of the intelligence agencies rather than an occasional effort.

The intelligence community also needs to reach out to consumers of intelligence. In a commercial venture, the needs and desires of the customer drive the success of the provider; the intelligence community could be structured likewise. What a difference it might have made if before September 11 a unit of the FBI had been tasked to understand the status and processes of America's most vulnerable systems—airlines, seaports, power and industrial plants—to assess their vulnerabilities and determine whether current intelligence suggests a need for changes in their traditional means of operation.

Specifically in relation to the FBI, the Joint Inquiry recommended a

---

* I would exclude from this architecture the foreign intelligence agencies that are focused on tactical support of a specific armed service or the Coast Guard. When one of these agencies is needed to serve a national intelligence mission, the Director of National Intelligence should be empowered to task it appropriately.

three-step process of reform. (That recommendation appears in full on page 261.)

Recognizing that for the foreseeable future the FBI will be America's domestic intelligence agency, a series of immediate enhancements was recommended. To the credit of Director Bob Mueller, most of these internal reforms are under way.

For the longer term, Americans must decide how much domestic security they will accept and the inevitable intrusion that it will cause on our individual civil liberties. The debate on that balance has yet to begin.

Finally, once its mission is defined, we need to determine whether the reformed FBI is capable of meeting it—or does America need a security agency independent of law enforcement, such as the United Kingdom's MI-5?

The second failure is that repeatedly, the intelligence community has not provided "big picture" strategic intelligence.

The late Pat Moynihan would recite to any who would listen his troubled observation that while the U.S. intelligence services had provided us with information on how many telephones there were in the Kremlin and how many sailors manned the latest class of Soviet ship, they had not been able to figure out that the Soviet Union was on the verge of collapse. Up until the end, U.S. intelligence estimated that the Soviets had an economy capable of supporting a military competitive with ours, and that the Soviets were continuing to invest in cutting-edge research that matched our scientific, military, and space advances. Little of that turned out to be true, and the Soviet Union would soon cease to exist.

Consider the consequences of a failure to focus on the world threat through a telescope, rather than a microscope. In the summer of 2001, intelligence reported to U.S. decision makers that, yes, al-Qaeda was an increasing threat to U.S. interests, but outside the United States, not in our homeland. As a result, we continued to spend hundreds of millions of dollars to fortify our embassies abroad, but did virtually nothing to increase the safety of our domestic commercial aviation.

Consider further the fact that, as the planning for the war in Iraq was intensifying in the winter and spring of 2003, Secretary of Defense Donald Rumsfeld and Deputy Secretary of Defense Paul Wolfowitz reached two conclusions. These conclusions were validated by false and anti-quated intelligence, vouched for by the Rumsfeld-established intelligence agencies within the Department of Defense. These agencies claimed that U.S. troops would be warmly received as liberators, as were the American troops in Paris in 1944, and that the Iraqis would turn on the faucet to the nation's oil riches and pay for the occupation and re-building of their nation. Of course, neither of those projections came true. Iraq is looking more like Vietnam in 1972, and the costs in both human and financial terms are being borne heavily by the United States. For a community with the word "intelligence" in its name, this is a dismal and deeply disturbing series of strategic failures.

Senator Moynihan had a solution: he wanted to abolish the American intelligence agencies. I respectfully disagree. Should we throw up our hands in despair, which I imagine is what many American did after reading the Senate Intelligence Committee's July 2004 report about the extent of the intelligence failures leading up to the war in Iraq? We can't. Despite the seriousness of the failures, the threats are more serious still. The possibility that a nuclear device may fall into the hands of terrorists alone warrants a robust, and reformed, intelligence effort.

For starters, the President should have the new Director of National Intelligence expand the number and orientation of voices that con-tribute to the intelligence process. The Bush administration has been ac-cused, correctly, of practicing incestuous amplification. People with the same point of view are invited to the table. They reach a conclusion. Their views are then vetted by people who hold the same beliefs. As a re-sult, the original conclusion is endorsed and amplified.

After the attacks of September 11, the intelligence community was accused of failing to connect the dots. Incestuous amplification is un-likely either to connect the dots or to expand the number of dots that are visible.

Two places to start a counterattack on incestuous amplification are the State Department and openly available sources of information. The State Department has been the orphan of this administration. The re-mark by Hosni Mubarak that America's State Department had been so "marginalized and discredited that its representative would be seen as an affront and an indication of a lack of seriousness" reflects a judgment not limited to Cairo.

This is a shame, given that the State Department has gotten it right more times than any other security agency. From the beginning, Secretary of State Colin Powell was skeptical of the stories coming out of Africa and Damascus about Saddam Hussein's restoration of his nuclear capabilities. Using information from our own sources as well as European allies, the State Department made our best assessment of conditions in a postwar Iraq. This is as it should be. For more than two centuries, our country has invested in a Foreign Service to be able to provide exactly that insight. It needs to be respected, not ignored and marginalized, as it has been for the past several years.

Internally, the intelligence community needs to be more amenable to the use of intelligence collected from open sources. The percentage of open-source information that will contribute to a wise ultimate judgment is increasing.* The intelligence community continues to venerate the clandestine information it generates. In many foreign posts, for example, the duty of reading the newspapers and assessing the significance of events reported openly in the host country is assigned to the newest, least experienced intelligence or Foreign Service officer. But there are post–September 11 indicators that press and television reports in the Middle East should have raised concerns that a tragedy was in the making.

In recognition of the value of open-source information and to facilitate analytical integration, the Joint Inquiry recommended that "Congress and the Administration should ensure the full development within the Department of Homeland Security of an effective all-source terrorism information fusion center that will dramatically improve the focus and quality of counterterrorism analysis and facilitate the timely dissemination of relevant intelligence information, both within and beyond the boundaries of the Intelligence Community."

This idea was signed into law as a counterterrorism "fusion center" within the Department of Homeland Security, but has languished since. Instead, the President has shifted virtually all of its functions to a less effective center set up at the CIA called the Terrorist Threat Integration Center, or TTIC. The goal of the fusion center was not only to perform analysis that would fill the gap between foreign and domestic intelligence and between open and clandestinely acquired intelligence, but

---

* It is estimated that 90 percent of our total usable information comes from open sources.

also to share information with state and local law enforcement and to assess vulnerabilities. Instead, TTIC is an FBI/CIA creation that is performing none of those vital tasks. In fact, its existence seems largely to be an effort to keep power away from the Department of Homeland Security. Not only is TTIC not performing the full array of tasks we had intended for the fusion center, it has already embarrassed itself by failing to accurately perform the one task it does see as its responsibility, monitoring terrorist activity. In April 2004, TTIC's analysis formed the basis of a State Department report that the number of terrorist acts carried out in 2003 had dropped to a thirty-year low—a seemingly politically motivated conclusion based on a selective use of the statistics. Secretary of State Powell later called this report a "big mistake."[1]

The third failure is the failure to establish intelligence community–wide priorities and then deploy behind them.

In December 1998, George Tenet, who was then the Director of Central Intelligence, announced that terrorism was the intelligence community's primary target, and that America was "at war with al-Qaeda." Within the CIA and the other intelligence agencies, few heard the call and even fewer acted. Richard Clarke told me that in 1996, he began asking the CIA, "How much money does it cost to be al-Qaeda? Where do they get their money from? Narcotics? Saudis? Donations from mosques? Where do they keep it, and how do they move it around?" Clarke told me that he didn't ask for exact numbers; he was simply trying to get a sense of the order of magnitude. He was never able to get an answer—nor have I received one to this day. If the CIA, the FBI, and the Treasury Department had truly heeded George Tenet's 1998 declaration, we would have those answers.

This failure is exacerbated by this administration's politicization of intelligence. One of my lowest days in the U.S. Senate was June 27, 2002, when I was told that the Senate the night before had amended the defense authorization bill by a voice vote to create a new position in the Pentagon, undersecretary of defense for military intelligence. There had been no hearings on the concept in the Armed Services or Intelligence Committee. The proposal was waved through with the explanation that it would bring enhanced efficiencies in the Defense Department, and furthermore, this was something Secretary Rumsfeld wanted.

I knew immediately this was a bad idea. So did my colleague Porter Goss, who had been caught similarly unawares in the House. We worked to have the provision deleted in the conference committee, but failed. This new office is now on the organizational chart of the Department of Defense and the intelligence community.

Setting up an office in the Pentagon to make intelligence "more efficient" was a thinly veiled ploy to expand the already significant military role in intelligence and further dilute the central authority of the Director of Central Intelligence. What I didn't realize then was that the new office would become a means by which the Secretary of Defense, the Vice President, and finally the President himself would be given yet another alternative set of intelligence information and analysis from which they could draw whichever view of the truth most coincided with their predetermined judgments. Rather than speaking truth to power, giving the decision makers its unvarnished professional judgment, this new office has allowed the leadership of this administration to assign it to collect exactly the intelligence the White House sought. Paul Wolfowitz basically admitted as much when he described "a phenomenon in intelligence work, that people who are pursuing a certain hypothesis will see certain facts that others won't, and not see other facts that others will. . . . The lens through which you're looking for facts affects what you look for."[2]

Rather than set up intelligence systems to validate convenient political notions, we need a system that pursues mutually agreed-upon priorities. To that end, the Joint Inquiry recommended, "The President should take action to ensure that clear, consistent, and current priorities are established and enforced throughout the Intelligence Community. Once established, these priorities should be reviewed and updated on a regular basis to ensure that the allocation of Intelligence Community resources reflects and effectively addresses the continually evolving threats."

The restructuring of intelligence agencies suggested above can significantly contribute to a more coherent set of intelligence initiatives; but, without leadership and commitment from the President, no progress will be made.

Fourth, the intelligence community has not implemented the policies necessary to recruit human intelligence staff, to train them, diversify them, reward or sanction them, or maintain their skills.

The collection of intelligence through human sources (HUMINT) declined during the Cold War because the work was difficult and dangerous and other means of intelligence gathering were so effective. Today, what is left of our human intelligence corps is heavily oriented and acculturated toward the countries of the former Soviet bloc. We have people who speak Russian and other Eastern European languages and who understand the history and cultures of that region of the world. The United States' human intelligence at the end of the Cold War has been described as very deep in its knowledge of the Russian target, almost ignorant about everything else.

In the places where we most need human intelligence, for example the Middle East, we are woefully deficient. For example, there was no U.S. human intelligence in Iraq prior to the war.

The typical work of an intelligence operative is to penetrate the target and learn his capabilities or intentions. Unlike James Bond, this is rarely done through direct action. More frequently it is attempted by gaining the confidence of someone who is close to the target, recruiting him or her to gather information, and establishing a means by which information can be communicated to the case officer. Done directly or indirectly, this is hard, risky work. It certainly helps if our operative can communicate and connect with the organizations or individuals we hope to penetrate or recruit.

When you don't have that affinity—something I saw in Haiti, something Senator Shelby saw in India and Pakistan—the ability to get good information is hugely diminished.

The intelligence community's current recruitment and training regimes, which rely heavily on university career days, have been inadequate to overcome this handicap. Of particular concern to me is the difficulty a first-generation American of Arabic ancestry will have in receiving a security clearance. These are precisely the young Americans who are most likely to have absorbed colloquial Arabic, Farsi, or Pashtun at home, and who may have the interpersonal skills that will increase their value as case agents. Of course, they are likely to have something else: a family. An intelligence security background check includes interviews with family members, and if those family members live in Syria, for example, it may be difficult or impossible to get a clearance. If one of the family members—even a distant one—has been in the service of that foreign government, the college graduate is likely to be rejected, even though he or she is a patriotic American. By failing to find ways to overcome this bias, we are denying ourselves the benefit of one of our greatest assets, our diversity.

Another frequently cited reason for the difficulty in recruiting intelligence officers is the mid-1950s culture of the intelligence community. While most other aspects of our society have become accustomed to frequent turnover in careers (the average American can anticipate working at seven or more distinctly different jobs or places of employment over his or her work life) intelligence agencies seek to employ people who are prepared to make a lifetime commitment.

The effect of these constraints is that we are confronting terrorists with a band of men and women who, although eager to perform the challenging intellectual work of an analyst or the dangerous undertakings of an operative, often lack the necessary skills to be as effective as we need them to be.

In my opinion, we need to rethink our system of intelligence recruitment, training, and performance evaluation.

The intelligence community, and especially the CIA, recruited its initial leadership from the same place as had the OSS, the law firms and banking houses of Wall Street. This reflected a "best and the brightest" attitude toward the aptitudes required to be an intelligence officer. A residue of that attitude remains.

Our Joint Inquiry recommended a series of reforms to bring the human talent in intelligence work into line with the current challenges. Those included a focus on bringing mid-career professionals into the intelligence community, allowing for more time-limited service for college graduates, finding ways to bring in more native speakers of various languages, and other efforts at diversification. George Tenet deserves credit for the fact that some of that work is under way.

I mentioned that one effort I hope to be involved in after I leave office is developing an intelligence equivalent of the Reserve Officer Training Corps at a number of colleges and universities. Such a recruitment and training program would provide financial aid in exchange for a commitment to service within the intelligence community. This could, in my opinion, be a useful response to the need for proficiency in some of the world's more difficult languages, such as Farsi, Arabic, and Chinese, which require many years of conventional language instruction and a period of study abroad in a region where the language is spoken. Having these students under supervision would also facilitate the clearance of first-generation Americans into the intelligence service. It would have, as do the military ROTCs, the further benefit of facilitating "jointness" once these young adults enter their respective intelligence agencies, because many of them will know one another from this shared preparatory experience and will be more at ease in soliciting and sharing information and analysis.

The fifth failure is the failure to realize that many of the most important decisions made by the intelligence community that were previously described as tactical have now become strategic. Unfortunately, the level and perspective of those tasking the gathering of that intelligence have not changed, often with terrible consequences.

One of the reasons that congressional oversight of the intelligence community actually exists is because in 1960, in the days before a planned summit between President Eisenhower and Soviet leader Nikita Khrushchev, the Soviet Union downed an American U-2 spy plane. The tension surrounding the plane's downing aborted the summit and enraged Senator Mike Mansfield. "Not a single member of the Cabinet nor the President exercised any direct control whatsoever over the ill-fated U-2 flight at the critical moment at which it was launched," he declared. He continued that the flight "owe[d] its origin more to bureaucratic inertia, lack of coordination and control and insensitivity to its potential cost than it [did] to any conscious decision of politically responsible leadership."[3] In short, a tactical blunder had set back a strategic goal.

Today especially, tactical intelligence-gathering operations need to appreciate the strategic implications of their acts.

During the Cold War it was common practice of the United States to wiretap almost all foreign leaders when they visited. The same thing happened to us. On my first trip behind the Iron Curtain, I was told to anticipate that all of my bags would be searched when I left them unattended and instructed never to leave anything in the hotel room that I was not prepared to have examined by the KGB.

In the United States during that time, the wiretap or search was accomplished through a FISA warrant, which theoretically could be secured only after the approval of the Attorney General and the Secretary of State. However, the practice was so common that in fact mid-level bureaucrats in the Department of Justice and the Department of State were delegated this responsibility with minimal oversight. The purpose was to monitor foreign leaders in case they might have or disclose intentions that were of interest to the United States. We knew the surveillance was happening; they knew it was happening. It was part of the Cold War game, whose rules were understood if not liked.

Five years after the end of the Cold War, President Bill Clinton invited all the heads of state in the Americas, with the exception of Fidel Castro, to attend a Summit of the Americas in Coral Gables, Florida. A FISA warrant was issued for all but one of the attendees. The meeting was hailed as highly successful. Economic and trade issues were at the top of the agenda. As a Floridian with a long commitment to improved relations within the Western Hemisphere, I was proud that my state had been chosen to host the meeting.

A month later, a U.S. television network aired the story that the hotel rooms of the heads of state had been wiretapped. This caused a firestorm. Several of the leaders said that they thought the Cold War rules had been abrogated and that as invited guests of the President of the United States they were offended that their privacy had been invaded and their honor disparaged. U.S. ambassadors to hemispheric nations were caught unawares as they had not been informed of the wiretaps until they heard about them in the news. Much of the goodwill the summit was intended to engender had been squandered.

I was incensed. As the newest member of the Senate Intelligence Committee, I did not know enough about the FISA process to evaluate what had gone wrong. So I asked for a briefing from the people at Justice and State who approved the FBI's requests for FISA warrants.

"What was the purpose of the warrants? What were we trying to find out?"

The answer: "Would any of the delegations put the subject of Cuba on the table? The U.S. government didn't want to have that conversation. And the President's staff wanted him to know of any other issues which a Latin leader thought would be worthy of considering so the President would not be surprised." My temperature jumped by several degrees.

"You mean to say that to get that level of information we have severely damaged our reputation and influence with our neighbors and guests? If our embassies aren't able to find out what their host country's position is on Cuba or what's likely to be on their agenda, and do so without wiretapping the president, what use are they?"

My briefers shrugged. I asked how far up the chain of command in their departments the decision to seek authority to wiretap had gone. "Did Attorney General Janet Reno and Secretary of State Warren Christopher sign off?" They pointed at themselves. "We've always been responsible before."

This was not an isolated incident. In other, still clasified situations, decisions as to the collection of sensitive information were made at the tactical level, without a more strategic view as to the implications.

With the advice of the FBI, the CIA, and other involved intelligence agencies, the President and his national security leadership and the ultimate FISA request decision makers, the Attorney General and the Secretary of State, must take a personal role in evaluating the possible impact of these operations on the strategic interests of the United States.

★

The Congress has a role in each of these areas. As political generalists, the members of the intelligence committees should be expected to press for information about the relevance of proposed actions to current threats. I wish I had done more in challenging the CIA's stale intelligence on weapons of mass destruction in Iraq. The committees need to be more strategic. It isn't feasible for members of Congress, as laypersons, to be experts on individual operations. It is critical that we, as representatives of the American people, ask the probing questions about the level of confidence, the reliability of sources, and the currency of the information we are receiving. At the same time, the committees should also be advocates for the intelligence community and work to ensure that they have the resources they need to counter terrorism, rebuild our human and clandestine capabilities, and meet the other national priorities discussed herein.

I also feel that the congressional committees themselves need to be reformed. Understanding the intelligence community and its activities is not an intuitive gift. Most members of Congress come to the intelligence committees with no previous experience with intelligence, one of the most complex activities of the federal government. One of the most important contributions to improving congressional oversight of intelligence would be a training program for members on the role of users of intelligence.

Also, the practice of placing an eight-year term limit on members of the Senate Intelligence Committee has resulted in the removal of members just at the time they had sufficiently mastered the technical and human matters of intelligence and were best able to apply seasoned judgment. The term limits, which in the Senate are unique to the Intelligence Committee, were intended to prevent the members from forming too close an association with the agencies being overseen, and thus losing their objectivity. At this time, I would risk that possibility to get the certainty of more informed congressional engagement.

★

The Joint Inquiry evolved nineteen more specific recommendations, which can be found reprinted starting on page 255.

I found working on the recommendations one of the most satisfying experiences of my time on the Senate Select Committee on Intelligence. That's because most of the time spent overseeing intelligence is devoted to problems or failures: a CIA agent turns out to be a Soviet spy; an innocent aircraft and its crew are shot down because of misidentification as a drug trafficker; the entire computer system of the NSA has crashed. In paying attention to these "rearview mirror" issues, we don't often attend to what is ahead of us—the foggy front windshield of emerging threats and required responses. Virtually all the committee's time from September 11, 2001, to the end of my term, in January 2003, was devoted to the tragedy. One of our few forward-looking efforts was the attempt to get better intelligence before the war in Iraq. We had hardly finished that work when the war began and the intelligence failures associated with it ensued. Back to the rearview mirror.

Looking backward is worthwhile only if what we learn produces the foundation for reform, if we can use what we've learned to reduce the chances that we have to live through a similar tragedy in the future. America lost more than 3,000 of our people on September 11. We lost our sense of invulnerability.

Reform is needed, because our safety and our future are too important to be left to chance. Luck may spare us, but it will never protect us.

From innocence to wisdom, from surprise to security, from horror to hope, from the fears of the past to the challenges of the future—this is the journey we must all take, because only then will we be able to gain something from all that we have lost.

RECOMMENDATIONS

OF THE JOINT INQUIRY INTO INTELLIGENCE
COMMUNITY ACTIVITIES BEFORE AND AFTER
THE TERRORIST ATTACKS OF SEPTEMBER 11, 2001

December 10, 2002

Since the National Security Act's establishment of the Director of Central Intelligence and the Central Intelligence Agency in 1947, numerous independent commissions, experts, and legislative initiatives have examined the growth and performance of the U.S. Intelligence Community. While those efforts generated numerous proposals for reform over the years, some of the most significant proposals have not been implemented, particularly in the areas of organization and structure. These Committees believe that the cataclysmic events of September 11, 2001 provide a unique and compelling mandate for strong leadership and constructive change throughout the Intelligence Community. With that in mind, and based on the work of this Joint Inquiry, the Committees recommend the following:

1. Congress should amend the National Security Act of 1947 to create and sufficiently staff a statutory Director of National Intelligence

who shall be the President's principal advisor on intelligence and shall have the full range of management, budgetary and personnel responsibilities needed to make the entire U.S. Intelligence Community operate as a coherent whole. These responsibilities should include:

* establishment and enforcement of consistent priorities for the collection, analysis, and dissemination of intelligence throughout the Intelligence Community;
* setting of policy and the ability to move personnel between elements of the Intelligence Community;
* review, approval, modification, and primary management and oversight of the execution of Intelligence Community budgets;
* review, approval, modification, and primary management and oversight of the execution of Intelligence Community personnel and resource allocations;
* review, approval, modification, and primary management and oversight of the execution of Intelligence Community research and development efforts;
* review, approval, and coordination of relationships between the Intelligence Community agencies and foreign intelligence and law enforcement services; and
* exercise of statutory authority to insure that Intelligence Community agencies and components fully comply with Community-wide policy, management, spending, and administrative guidance and priorities.

The Director of National Intelligence should be a Cabinet level position, appointed by the President and subject to Senate confirmation. Congress and the President should also work to insure that the Director of National Intelligence effectively exercises these authorities.

To insure focused and consistent Intelligence Community leadership, Congress should require that no person may simultaneously serve as both the Director of National Intelligence and the Director of the Central Intelligence Agency, or as the director of any other specific intelligence agency.

2. Current efforts by the National Security Council to examine and revamp existing intelligence priorities should be expedited, given the immediate need for clear guidance in intelligence and counter-terrorism efforts. The President should take action to ensure that clear, consistent, and current priorities are established and enforced throughout the Intelligence Community. Once established, these priorities should be reviewed and updated on at least an annual basis to ensure that the allocation of Intelligence Community resources reflects and effectively addresses the continually evolving threat environment. Finally, the establishment of Intelligence Community priorities, and the justification for such priorities, should be reported to both the House and Senate Intelligence Committees on an annual basis.

3. The National Security Council, in conjunction with the Director of National Intelligence, and in consultation with the Secretary of the Department of Homeland Security, the Secretary of State and Secretary of Defense, should prepare, for the President's approval, a U.S. government–wide strategy for combating terrorism, both at home and abroad, including the growing terrorism threat posed by the proliferation of weapons of mass destruction and associated technologies. This strategy should identify and fully engage those foreign policy, economic, military, intelligence, and law enforcement elements that are critical to a comprehensive blueprint for success in the war against terrorism.

As part of that effort, the Director of National Intelligence shall develop the Intelligence Community component of the strategy, identifying specific programs and budgets and including plans to address the threats posed by Usama Bin Ladin and al Qa'ida, Hezbollah, Hamas, and other significant terrorist groups. Consistent with applicable law, the strategy should effectively employ and integrate all capabilities available to the Intelligence Community against those threats and should encompass specific efforts to:

★ develop human sources to penetrate terrorist organizations and networks both overseas and within the United States;

⋆ fully utilize existing and future technologies to better exploit terrorist communications; to improve and expand the use of data mining and other cutting edge analytical tools; and to develop a multi-level security capability to facilitate the timely and complete sharing of relevant intelligence information both within the Intelligence Community and with other appropriate federal, state, and local authorities;

⋆ enhance the depth and quality of domestic intelligence collection and analysis by, for example, modernizing current intelligence reporting formats through the use of existing information technology to emphasize the existence and the significance of links between new and previously acquired information;

⋆ maximize the effective use of covert action in counterterrorist efforts;

⋆ develop programs to deal with financial support for international terrorism; and

⋆ facilitate the ability of CIA paramilitary units and military special operations forces to conduct joint operations against terrorist targets.

4. The position of National Intelligence Officer for Terrorism should be created on the National Intelligence Council and a highly qualified individual appointed to prepare intelligence estimates on terrorism for the use of Congress and policymakers in the Executive Branch and to assist the Intelligence Community in developing a program for strategic analysis and assessments.

5. Congress and the Administration should ensure the full development within the Department of Homeland Security of an effective all-source terrorism information fusion center that will dramatically improve the focus and quality of counterterrorism analysis and facilitate the timely dissemination of relevant intelligence information, both within and beyond the boundaries of the Intelligence Community. Congress and the Administration should ensure that this fusion center has all the authority and the resources needed to:

⋆ have full and timely access to all counterterrorism-related intelligence information, including "raw" supporting data as needed;

★ have the ability to participate fully in the existing requirements process for tasking the Intelligence Community to gather information on foreign individuals, entities and threats;

★ integrate such information in order to identify and assess the nature and scope of terrorist threats to the United States in light of actual and potential vulnerabilities;

★ implement and fully utilize data mining and other advanced analytical tools, consistent with applicable law;

★ retain a permanent staff of experienced and highly skilled analysts, supplemented on a regular basis by personnel on "joint tours" from the various Intelligence Community agencies;

★ institute a reporting mechanism that enables analysts at all the intelligence and law enforcement agencies to post lead information for use by analysts at other agencies without waiting for dissemination of a formal report;

★ maintain excellence and creativity in staff analytic skills through regular use of analysis and language training programs; and

★ establish and sustain effective channels for the exchange of counter-terrorism-related information with federal agencies outside the Intelligence Community as well as with state and local authorities.

6. Given the FBI's history of repeated shortcomings within its current responsibility for domestic intelligence, and in the face of grave and immediate threats to our homeland, the FBI should strengthen and improve its domestic capability as fully and expeditiously as possible by immediately instituting measures to:

★ strengthen counterterrorism as a national FBI program by clearly designating national counterterrorism priorities and enforcing field office adherence to those priorities;

★ establish and sustain independent career tracks within the FBI that recognize and provide incentives for demonstrated skills and performance of counterterrorism agents and analysts;

★ significantly improve strategic analytical capabilities by assuring the qualification, training, and independence of analysts, coupled with sufficient access to necessary information and resources;

★ establish a strong reports officer cadre at FBI Headquarters and field offices to facilitate timely dissemination of intelligence from agents to analysts within the FBI and other agencies within the Intelligence Community;

★ implement training for agents in the effective use of analysts and analysis in their work;

★ expand and sustain the recruitment of agents and analysts with the linguistic skills needed in counterterrorism efforts;

★ increase substantially efforts to penetrate terrorist organizations operating in the United States through all available means of collection;

★ improve the national security law training of FBI personnel;

★ implement mechanisms to maximize the exchange of counter-terrorism-related information between the FBI and other federal, state and local agencies; and

★ finally solve the FBI's persistent and incapacitating information technology problems.

7. Congress and the Administration should carefully consider how best to structure and manage U.S. domestic intelligence responsibilities. Congress should review the scope of domestic intelligence authorities to determine their adequacy in pursuing counterterrorism at home and ensuring the protection of privacy and other rights guaranteed under the Constitution. This review should include, for example, such questions as whether the range of persons subject to searches and surveillances authorized under the Foreign Intelligence Surveillance Act (FISA) should be expanded.

Based on their oversight responsibilities, the Intelligence and Judiciary Committees of the Congress, as appropriate, should consider promptly, in consultation with the Administration, whether the FBI should continue to perform the domestic intelligence functions of the United States Government or whether legislation is necessary to remedy this problem, including the possibility of creating a new agency to perform those functions.

Congress should require that the new Director of National Intelligence, the Attorney General, and the Secretary of the Department of

Homeland Security report to the President and the Congress on a date certain concerning:

★ the FBI's progress since September 11, 2001 in implementing the reforms required to conduct an effective domestic intelligence program, including the measures recommended above;
★ the experience of other democratic nations in organizing the conduct of domestic intelligence;
★ the specific manner in which a new domestic intelligence service could be established in the United States, recognizing the need to enhance national security while fully protecting civil liberties; and
★ their recommendations on how to best fulfill the nation's need for an effective domestic intelligence capability, including necessary legislation.

8. The Attorney General and the Director of the FBI should take action necessary to ensure that:

★ the Office of Intelligence Policy and Review and other Department of Justice components provide in-depth training to the FBI and other members of the Intelligence Community regarding the use of the Foreign Intelligence Surveillance Act (FISA) to address terrorist threats to the United States;
★ the FBI disseminates results of searches and surveillances authorized under FISA to appropriate personnel within the FBI and the Intelligence Community on a timely basis so they may be used for analysis and operations that address terrorist threats to the United States; and
★ the FBI develops and implements a plan to use authorities provided by FISA to assess the threat of international terrorist groups within the United States fully, including the extent to which such groups are funded or otherwise supported by foreign governments.

9. The House and Senate Intelligence and Judiciary Committees should continue to examine the Foreign Intelligence Surveillance Act and its implementation thoroughly, particularly with respect to changes made as a result of the USA PATRIOT Act and the subse-

quent decision of the United States Foreign Intelligence Court of Review, to determine whether its provisions adequately address present and emerging terrorist threats to the United States. Legislation should be proposed by those Committees to remedy any deficiencies identified as a result of that review.

10. The Director of the National Security Agency should present to the Director of National Intelligence and the Secretary of Defense by June 30, 2003, and report to the House and Senate Intelligence Committees, a detailed plan that:

★ describes solutions for the technological challenges for signals intelligence;
★ requires a review, on a quarterly basis, of the goals, products to be delivered, funding levels and schedules for every technology development program;
★ ensures strict accounting for program expenditures;
★ within their jurisdiction as established by current law, makes NSA a full collaborating partner with the Central Intelligence Agency and the Federal Bureau of Investigation in the war on terrorism, including fully integrating the collection and analytic capabilities of NSA, CIA, and the FBI; and
★ makes recommendations for legislation needed to facilitate these goals.

In evaluating the plan, the Committees should also consider issues pertaining to whether civilians should be appointed to the position of Director of the National Security Agency and whether the term of service for the position should be longer than it has been in the recent past.

11. Recognizing that the Intelligence Community's employees remain its greatest resource, the Director of National Intelligence should require that measures be implemented to greatly enhance the recruitment and development of a workforce with the intelligence skills and expertise needed for success in counterterrorist efforts, including:

★ the agencies of the Intelligence Community should act promptly to expand and improve counterterrorism training programs within the Community, insuring coverage of such critical areas as information sharing among law enforcement and intelligence personnel; language capabilities; the use of the Foreign Intelligence Surveillance Act; and watchlisting;

★ the Intelligence Community should build on the provisions of the Intelligence Authorization Act for Fiscal Year 2003 regarding the development of language capabilities, including the Act's requirement for a report on the feasibility of establishing a Civilian Linguist Reserve Corps, and implement expeditiously measures to identify and recruit linguists outside the Community whose abilities are relevant to the needs of counterterrorism;

★ the existing Intelligence Community Reserve Corps should be expanded to ensure the use of relevant personnel and expertise from outside the Community as special needs arise;

★ Congress should consider enacting legislation, modeled on the Goldwater-Nichols Act of 1986, to instill the concept of "jointness" throughout the Intelligence Community. By emphasizing such things as joint education, a joint career specialty, increased authority for regional commanders, and joint exercises, that Act greatly enhanced the joint warfighting capabilities of the individual military services. Legislation to instill similar concepts throughout the Intelligence Community could help improve management of Community resources and priorities and insure a far more effective "team" effort by all the intelligence agencies. The Director of National Intelligence should require more extensive use of "joint tours" for intelligence and appropriate law enforcement personnel to broaden their experience and help bridge existing organizational and cultural divides through service in other agencies. These joint tours should include not only service at Intelligence Community agencies, but also service in those agencies that are users or consumers of intelligence products. Serious incentives for joint service should be established throughout the Intelligence Community and personnel should be rewarded for joint service with career advancement credit at individual agencies. The Director of National Intelligence should also require Intelligence Community agencies to participate in joint exercises;

★ Congress should expand and improve existing educational grant programs focused on intelligence-related fields, similar to military scholarship programs and others that provide financial assistance in return for a commitment to serve in the Intelligence Community; and

★ the Intelligence Community should enhance recruitment of a more ethnically and culturally diverse workforce and devise a strategy to capitalize upon the unique cultural and linguistic capabilities of first-generation Americans, a strategy designed to utilize their skills to the greatest practical effect while recognizing the potential counterintelligence challenges such hiring decisions might pose.

12. Steps should be taken to increase and ensure the greatest return on this nation's substantial investment in intelligence, including:

★ the President should submit budget recommendations, and Congress should enact budget authority, for sustained, long-term investment in counterterrorism capabilities that avoid dependence on repeated stop-gap supplemental appropriations;

★ in making such budget recommendations, the President should provide for the consideration of a separate classified Intelligence Community budget;

★ long-term counterterrorism investment should be accompanied by sufficient flexibility, subject to congressional oversight, to enable the Intelligence Community to rapidly respond to altered or unanticipated needs;

★ the Director of National Intelligence should insure that Intelligence Community budgeting practices and procedures are revised to better identify the levels and nature of counterterrorism funding within the Community;

★ counterterrorism funding should be allocated in accordance with the program requirements of the national counterterrorism strategy; and

★ due consideration should be given to directing an outside agency or entity to conduct a thorough and rigorous cost-benefit analysis of the resources spent on intelligence.

13. The State Department, in consultation with the Department of Justice, should review and report to the President and the Congress by

June 30, 2003 on the extent to which revisions in bilateral and multi-lateral agreements, including extradition and mutual assistance treaties, would strengthen U.S. counterterrorism efforts. The review should address the degree to which current categories of extraditable offenses should be expanded to cover offenses, such as visa and immigration fraud, which may be particularly useful against terrorists and those who support them.

14. Recognizing the importance of intelligence in this nation's struggle against terrorism, Congress should maintain vigorous, informed, and constructive oversight of the Intelligence Community. To best achieve that goal, the National Commission on Terrorist Attacks Upon the United States should study and make recommendations concerning how Congress may improve its oversight of the Intelligence Community, including consideration of such areas as:

* changes in the budgetary process;
* changes in the rules regarding membership on the oversight committees;
* whether oversight responsibility should be vested in a joint House-Senate Committee or, as currently exists, in separate Committees in each house;
* the extent to which classification decisions impair congressional oversight; and
* how Congressional oversight can best contribute to the continuing need of the Intelligence Community to evolve and adapt to changes in the subject matter of intelligence and the needs of policy makers.

15. The President should review and consider amendments to the Executive Orders, policies and procedures that govern the national security classification of intelligence information, in an effort to expand access to relevant information for federal agencies outside the Intelligence Community, for state and local authorities, which are critical to the fight against terrorism, and for the American public. In addition, the President and the heads of federal agencies should ensure that the policies and procedures to protect against the unauthorized

disclosure of classified intelligence information are well understood, fully implemented and vigorously enforced.

Congress should also review the statutes, policies and procedures that govern the national security classification of intelligence information and its protection from unauthorized disclosure. Among other matters, Congress should consider the degree to which excessive classification has been used in the past and the extent to which the emerging threat environment has greatly increased the need for real-time sharing of sensitive information. The Director of National Intelligence, in consultation with the Secretary of Defense, the Secretary of State, the Secretary of Homeland Security, and the Attorney General, should review and report to the House and Senate Intelligence Committees on proposals for a new and more realistic approach to the processes and structures that have governed the designation of sensitive and classified information. The report should include proposals to protect against the use of the classification process as a shield to protect agency self-interest.

16. Assured standards of accountability are critical to developing the personal responsibility, urgency, and diligence which our counter-terrorism responsibility requires. Given the absence of any substantial efforts within the Intelligence Community to impose accountability in relation to the events of September 11, 2001, the Director of Central Intelligence and the heads of Intelligence Community agencies should require that measures designed to ensure accountability are implemented throughout the Community.

To underscore the need for accountability:

★ The Director of Central Intelligence should report to the House and Senate Intelligence Committees no later than June 30, 2003 as to the steps taken to implement a system of accountability throughout the Intelligence Community, to include processes for identifying poor performance and affixing responsibility for it, and for recognizing and rewarding excellence in performance;

★ as part of the confirmation process for Intelligence Community officials, Congress should require from those officials an affirmative commitment to the implementation and use of strong accountability mechanisms throughout the Intelligence Community; and

★ the Inspectors General at the Central Intelligence Agency, the Department of Defense, the Department of Justice, and the Department of State should review the factual findings and the record of this Inquiry and conduct investigations and reviews as necessary to determine whether and to what extent personnel at all levels should be held accountable for any omission, commission, or failure to meet professional standards in regard to the identification, prevention, or disruption of terrorist attacks, including the events of September 11, 2001. These reviews should also address those individuals who performed in a stellar or exceptional manner, and the degree to which the quality of their performance was rewarded or otherwise impacted their careers. Based on those investigations and reviews, agency heads should take appropriate disciplinary and other action and the President and the House and Senate Intelligence Committees should be advised of such action.

17. The Administration should review and report to the House and Senate Intelligence Committees by June 30, 2003 regarding what progress has been made in reducing the inappropriate and obsolete barriers among intelligence and law enforcement agencies engaged in counterterrorism, what remains to be done to reduce those barriers, and what legislative actions may be advisable in that regard. In particular, this report should address what steps are being taken to insure that perceptions within the Intelligence Community about the scope and limits of current law and policy with respect to restrictions on collection and information sharing are, in fact, accurate and well-founded.

18. Congress and the Administration should ensure the full development of a national watchlist center that will be responsible for coordinating and integrating all terrorist-related watchlist systems; promoting awareness and use of the center by all relevant government agencies

and elements of the private sector; and ensuring a consistent and comprehensive flow of terrorist names into the center from all relevant points of collection.

19. The Intelligence Community, and particularly the FBI and the CIA, should aggressively address the possibility that foreign governments are providing support to or are involved in terrorist activity targeting the United States and U.S. interests. State-sponsored terrorism substantially increases the likelihood of successful and more lethal attacks within the United States. This issue must be addressed from a national standpoint and should not be limited in focus by the geographical and factual boundaries of individual cases. The FBI and CIA should aggressively and thoroughly pursue related matters developed through this Joint Inquiry that have been referred to them for further investigation by these Committees.

The Intelligence Community should fully inform the House and Senate Intelligence Committees of significant developments in these efforts, through regular reports and additional communications as necessary, and the Committees should, in turn, exercise vigorous and continuing oversight of the Community's work in this critically important area.

ACKNOWLEDGMENTS

This book would not have become a reality without the help of my family, friends old and new, and the dedicated staff and public servants with whom it has been my honor to work.

Nothing I have done would be possible without my wife and best friend, Adele. She has simply been my everything—encouraging me to take on new challenges, nursing me through illness, and tolerating me throughout countless hours I spent sequestered in my office.

I am also inspired by my four daughters Gwen, Cissy, Suzanne, and Kendall. I should also note that in addition to his insights, Suzanne's husband, Tom Gibson, also gave this book its title.

Of course, this book is really for my eleven grandchildren. I only hope that the ideas and lessons contained within it will make the world they will inherit safer.

I am also indebted to a gifted friend and collaborator, Jeff Nussbaum. It was a joy and an honor to share this process with him.

David McCullough is a good friend and my daughter Cissy's father-in-law. I benefited greatly from his advice as I began thinking about this project. Perhaps the best thing he gave me was the phone number of a truly gifted researcher, Mike Hill. Mike's knowledge of history and his ability to find the most obscure of facts and integrate them into a larger narrative is a thing to behold, and I was lucky to have him on this project.

I also want to thank Librarian of Congress Jim Billington for putting me in touch with Dick Best. Dick Best, along with Senate historians Dick Baker and Don Ritchie, were invaluable in the research process. For months, I peppered them with queries on everything from dates and places to the history of major policies. Like clockwork, they came back to me with every question answered.

Another person whose assistance was vital in taking this book from an idea in my head to a project worthy of a publisher was Bob Barnett. I am deeply grateful for his advice and counsel, and I am indebted to Senator Hillary Clinton for putting us in touch. If Bob made the idea a reality, Jonathan Karp at Random House was the one who made it into a book. Jonathan is a gifted editor, and I've come to see why he is so widely regarded as a rising star in the world of publishing. Also at Random House, Jonathan Jao's editorial input was extremely helpful, Steve Messina's production editing help was essential, and Jolanta Benal's copyediting was masterly.

I've noted a number of times in the book the importance of a good staff, and I happen to think that I have one of the best.

I especially want to thank Sharon Liggett, my deputy chief of staff. More than any other person, Sharon manages my professional life. Without her help, I never would have been able to do my day job while also writing this book. Beyond her overstuffed official portfolio, Sharon has also found time to serve as my informal IT advisor, and has been a patient and dedicated tutor as I've slowly tried to bring my computer skills up to speed.

Bob Filippone, my national security advisor, has been nothing less than my alter ego when it comes to intelligence matters. His ideas and insight have been as valuable to my public service as they were to this book.

Paul Anderson, my communications director, is a gifted writer and editor, and I consider myself lucky to have had his input and advice throughout the process.

Buddy Menn, my chief of staff, is both a good friend and a trusted advisor, and I am grateful for his many contributions to this project and to my political career.

Also on my staff, I'd like to thank Mary Chiles, Lisa Kanarek, John Provenzano, and Conrad Stroman.

In the Senate family, I want to thank the decent and dedicated Al Cumming, who served as the staff director during my time on the Intelligence Committee. He and Steve Cash were vital to the Senate Intelligence Committee and were exceedingly gracious and helpful with this book.

I also want to thank the dedicated staff of the Joint Inquiry, and in this I need to single out Eleanor Hill, who brought our inquiry back from the dead (at least that's what it had been declared by *The Washington Post*), and turned it into an effort that opened a remarkable window onto the events of September 11 and the need for major reforms in our intelligence community. Eleanor was a consistent source of wisdom in her time with the Joint Inquiry and has remained a good friend and trusted advisor ever since.

Also from the staff of the Joint Inquiry, Tom Kelley and Dana Lesemann were particularly helpful in reviewing drafts and helping me reconstruct the events of that time. I am also appreciative of Rick Cinquegrana, John Keefe, and Britt Snider.

In addition to these individuals, I want to thank the dozens of colleagues and former staffers who served our work so well and were willing to sit for interviews so that I could glean both their memories and their ideas. There are some whom I am not at liberty to name, so a simple "You know who you are" will have to suffice. Those whom I can name and would like to recognize are: Senator Evan Bayh, Senator Mike DeWine, Senator Jon Kyl, Senator Carl Levin, Senator Barbara Mikulski, Senator Dick Shelby, Congressman Porter Goss, Congresswoman Jane Harman, Colonel Ted Pusey, Richard Clarke, Ken Johnson, Robin Gibson, Buddy Shorstein, and L. Garry Smith, Jr.

Also generous with their knowledge were the current chairman and ranking members of the Intelligence Committee, Senators Pat Roberts and Jay Rockefeller; the former ranking member on the House Intelligence Committee, Nancy Pelosi; as well as Graham Allison, Howard Berman, Ash Carter, John Eisold, Mary Graham, Alene Grossman, Lee Hamilton, Michael Hayden, Ken Jenne, Stan Moskowitz, Tim Roemer, Jeff Smith, and Bob Woodward.

I am also deeply indebted to Senator George Mitchell, who appointed me to the Senate Intelligence Committee in 1993, and to Senator Jim Jeffords, whose act of conscience in switching his party affiliation from Republican to Independent made me that committee's chairman.

I am grateful for the trust and support of the families of the victims of September 11. It was their advocacy that gave our investigation life, and their strength that inspired our work.

Finally, I want to thank the people of Florida, who have elected me to serve them for thirty-eight years. Without the opportunity they have given me to serve, I would not have been able to share the incredible experiences I have had. I will be forever grateful to them for putting their trust in me.

Early in the process, Jeff Nussbaum told me that a book is one of the greatest gifts you can give the people and country you love. The truth is that the work that all of these people contributed to this project was the real gift. I only hope that you find this book worthy of their efforts, and mine.

NOTES

Part I: Before

Chapter 1: A Meeting in Malaysia

1. Karl Vick, "Assault on a U.S. Embassy: A Plot Both Wide and Deep," *The Washington Post,* November 23, 1998.
2. Leslie Lopez, "An Experiment Gone Radically Wrong: The Path of Suspected Terrorist Yazid Sufaat," *The Wall Street Journal,* January 19, 2003.
3. Michael Isikoff and Daniel Klaidman, "The Hijackers We Let Escape," *Newsweek,* June 2, 2002.
4. Maria Rissa, "Uncovering Southeast Asia's Jihad Network," CNN, February 26, 2004.
5. "Q&A: Moussaoui Trial," BBC News, July 15, 2003.

Chapter 2: Arrival in America

1. Michael Isikoff and Daniel Klaidman, "Failure to Communicate," *Newsweek,* August 4, 2003.
2. Kelly Thornton, "Ex–San Diegan Suspected as Terrorists' Advance Man," *San Diego Union-Tribune,* October 25, 2001.

3. www.cia.gov/cia/information/info.html

4. Evan Thomas, *The Very Best Men* (New York: Simon & Schuster, 1996), p. 9.

5. I.C.B. Dear, ed., *The Oxford Companion to World War II* (New York: Oxford University Press, 1995), pp. 832–33.

6. Ibid., p. 834.

Chapter 3: Settled in San Diego

1. Kelly Thornton, "Chance to Foil 9/11 Plot Lost Here, Report Finds," *San Diego Union Tribune,* July 25, 2003.

2. Loch K. Johnson, *A Season of Inquiry: Congress and Intelligence* (Chicago: Dorsey Press, 1988).

3. Ronald Kessler, *Inside the CIA* (New York: Pocket Books, 1992), p. 81.

Chapter 4: Beginning Training

1. Kelly Thornton, "Hijackers Left Trail of Clues Across Country," *San Diego Tribune,* September 30, 2001.

2. Amy Goldstein and William Booth, "Hijackers Found Welcome Mat on West Coast," *The Washington Post,* December 29, 2001.

3. Robert P. King and Sanjay Bhatt, "Suspects Recalled as 'Dumb and Dumber' but They Eluded FBI Agents During 2-Week-Plus Search," *Palm Beach Post,* October 16, 2001.

4. Peter L. Bergen, *Holy War, Inc.* (London: Weidenfeld & Nicolson, 2001), p. 56.

5. Roland Jacquard, *In the Name of Osama Bin Laden* (Durham, N.C.: Duke University Press, 2002), p. 11.

6. "*Frontline:* Hunting bin Laden: Who Is Osama bin Laden and What Does He Want?," www.pbs.org/wgbh/pages/frontline/shows/binladen/who/, September 13, 2001.

7. Mary Anne Weaver, "The Real Bin Laden," *The New Yorker,* January 24, 2000.

8. "Al Qaeda Financing Documents Turn Up in Bosnia Raid," Associated Press, February 19, 2003.

9. "*Frontline:* Hunting bin Laden: Who Is Osama bin Laden and What Does He Want?"

10. Weaver, "The Real Bin Laden."

11. www.guardian.co.uk/alqaida/page/0,12643,852377,00.html

12. Robert D. Kaplan, "The Lawless Frontier," *The Atlantic Monthly,* September 2000.

13. "*Frontline:* Hunting bin Laden: Who Is Osama bin Laden and What Does He Want?"

14. Ibid.

Chapter 5: A Gathering Storm

1. Evan Thomas, *The Very Best Men* (New York: Simon & Schuster, 1995), p. 23.

2. www.govexec.com/dailyfed/1202/122002h2.htm

Chapter 6: Hanjour Joins al-Hazmi

1. Jim Yardley and Jo Thomas, "Traces of Terror: The FBI," *The New York Times,* June 19, 2002.

2. Ibid.

3. William Wan, "Agent Uneasy in 9/11 Spotlight; His FBI Memo from Phoenix Is Now Famous," *Atlanta Journal-Constitution,* June 1, 2002.

4. Dana Priest and Richard Leiby, "Phoenix FBI Agent Accused of Naming Terrorism Informant; Operative Had Ties to Palestinians," *The Washington Post,* May 24, 2002.

5. Yardley and Thomas, "Traces of Terror: The FBI."

6. William Wan, "Agent Uneasy in 9/11 Spotlight; His FBI Memo from Phoenix Is Now Famous," *Atlanta Journal-Constitution,* June 1, 2002.

7. Jim Yardley, "The Conspiracy Charge; E-mail Sent to Flight School Gave Terror Suspect's 'Goal,' " *The New York Times,* February 8, 2002.

8. Dan Eggen, "9/11 Panel Points to Missed Chances, Publicizing Threat May have Halted 'Jumpy' Hijackers," *The Washington Post,* April 17, 2004.

Chapter 7: Teaming Up

1. David Usborne, "CIA Had Name and Number of 11 September Hijacker in 1999," *The Independent* (London), February 25, 2004.

2. James Risen and Eric Lichtblau, "CIA Given Data Long Before Sept. 11; German Tipped U.S. on Future Hijacker," *International Herald Tribune,* February 26, 2004.

Chapter 9: Final Preparations

1. "Ashcroft Flying High," CBSNews.com, July 26, 2001.

2. Walter Pincus and Dana Priest, "NSA Intercepts on Eve of 9/11 Sent a Warning; Messages Translated After Attacks," *The Washington Post,* June 20, 2002.

3. Frank Davies, "How the '20th Hijacker' Was Halted," *The Miami Herald,* January 27, 2004.

4. Christopher Cooper et al., "A Careful Sequence of Mundane Dealings Sows a Day of Bloody Terror for Hijackers," *The Wall Street Journal,* October 16, 2001.

5. Greg B. Smith, "Hijacker in City September 10 Used Navigational Tool to Pinpoint WTC Site," New York *Daily News,* May 22, 2002.

6. Philip Shenon and David Johnston, "A Nation Challenged: The Investigation; Call by bin Laden Before Attacks Is Reported," *The New York Times,* October 2, 2001.

7. "Bush: Memo Had No 'Actionable Intelligence,' " CNN.com, April 12, 2004.

Chapter 10: Zero Hour

1. Sarah Downey and Michael Hirsh, "A Safe Haven?," *Newsweek,* September 30, 2002.

2. Bob Woodward, "In Hijacker's Bags, a Call to Planning, Prayer, and Death," *The Washington Post,* September 28, 2001.

Part II: After

Chapter 11: The Aftermath

1. Dan Morgan, "Powell Says He Was 'Committed' to Iraq War; Responding to Book, Secretary Cites His Close Involvement in Planning of Attack," *The Washington Post,* April 20, 2004.

2. Jean Heller, "TIA Now Verifies Flight of Saudis," *St. Petersburg Times,* June 9, 2004.

3. Orrin Hatch, *Square Peg: Confessions of a Citizen Senator* (New York: Basic Books, 2002).

4. Mary Leonard, "Bush Says Memo Lacked Hard Details; No Actionable Intelligence in 2001 Briefing," *The Boston Globe,* April 12, 2004.

5. Frank Davies, "Florida Congressman Wields Influence on War Issues; Sanibel's Goss Gained Knowledge as a CIA Agent," *The Miami Herald,* April 28, 1999.

6. Mark Bowden, "The Kabul-ki Dance," *The Atlantic Monthly,* November 2002.

7. Evan Thomas and Martha Brant, "Tommy Franks," *Newsweek,* May 19, 2003.

Chapter 12: A Meeting at MacDill

1. "National Security Advisor Speaks at Conference," www.whitehouse.gov/news/releases/2002/02/20020201-6.html, February 1, 2002.

2. Evan Thomas, "Bulking Up for Baghdad," *Newsweek,* December 30, 2002.

Chapter 13: The Inquiry Begins

1. Joby Warrick, "Russia's Poorly Guarded Past—Security Lacking at Facilities Used for Soviet Bioweapons Research," *The Washington Post,* June 17, 2002.

2. Terry McDermott, "The Plot: How Terrorists Hatched a Simple Plan to Use Planes as Weapons," *Los Angeles Times,* September 1, 2002.

3. Ibid.

4. Walter Pincus and Dana Priest, "NSA Intercepts on Eve of 9/11 Sent a Warning; Messages Translated After Attacks," *The Washington Post,* June 20, 2002.

5. Lydia Adetunji, "Congressmen Attacked for Leaking Terror Messages," *The Financial Times,* June 21, 2002.

Chapter 14: Into the Middle East

1. Karen DeYoung, "President Outlines Vision for Mideast; Palestinian Statehood Depends on Arafat's Removal, Bush Says," *The Washington Post,* June 25, 2002.

2. Lee Michael Katz, "President Likely to Get an Earful from Long-Winded Assad," *USA Today,* October 27, 1994.

Chapter 15: Discoveries in San Diego

1. Interview with Eleanor Hill, April 2, 2004.

2. Glenn R. Simpson, "Riyadh Paid Man Tied to Hijackers," *The Wall Street Journal,* August 8, 2003.

3. Dana Priest, "White House, CIA Kept Key Portions of Report Classified," *The Washington Post,* July 25, 2003.

4. Kathy Keily and John Diamond, "Intelligence Officials Fear Panel's Emotional Indictment," *USA Today,* August 15, 2002.

5. Dana Milbank, "Plan Was Formed in Utmost Secrecy; Final Proposal Came from 4 Top Bush Aides; Most Others Out of Loop," *The Washington Post,* June 7, 2002.

Chapter 16: A "Slam Dunk"?

1. "Vice President Speaks at VFW 103rd National Convention," www.whitehouse.gov/news/releases/2002/08/20020826.html, August 26, 2002.

2. Bob Woodward, *Plan of Attack* (New York: Simon & Schuster, 2004), p. 249.
3. "President, House Leadership Agree on Iraqi Resolution," www.whitehouse.gov/news/releases/2002/10/20021002-7.html, October 2, 2002.

Chapter 17: "Blood on Your Hands"

1. "President Bush Outlines Iraqi Threat," www.whitehouse.gov/news/releases/2002/10/20021007-8.html, October 7, 2002.
2. Dana Milbank and Claudia Deane, "Hussein Link to 9/11 Lingers in Many Minds," *The Washington Post,* September 6, 2003.

Conclusion: The Realities of Today

1. Daniel Benjamin, "Condi's Phony History—Sorry, Dr. Rice, Postwar Germany Was Nothing Like Iraq," *Slate,* August 29, 2003.
2. Walter Pincus, "Spy Agencies Warned of Iraq Resistance," *The Washington Post,* September 9, 2003.
3. James Risen and David Johnson, "Chalabi Reportedly Told Iran That U.S. Had Code," *The New York Times,* June 2, 2004.
4. Jim Lobe, "U.S., Iraqi Views of Occupation Converging," IPS—Inter Press Service, April 29, 2004.
5. Doyle McManus, "Iraq Setbacks Change Mood in Washington," *Los Angeles Times,* May 23, 2004.
6. Pincus, "Spy Agencies Warned of Iraq Resistance."
7. David E. Sanger and William J. Broad, "Evidence Is Cited Linking Koreans to Libya Uranium," *The New York Times,* May 23, 2004.
8. Jerry Seper, "Princess's Cash Went to al Qaeda 'Advance Man,'" *The Washington Times,* November 26, 2002.
9. Faiza Saleh Ambah, "Saudi Says U.S. Cleared Him of 9/11 Ties," Associated Press, July 30, 2003.
10. Massimo Calabresi, Timothy J. Burger, and Elaine Shannon, "Why Did the Imam Befriend Hijackers?," *Time,* August 11, 2003.
11. "Saudi Man Held on Immigration Charges," Associated Press, May 28, 2004.
12. Glenn Kessler and Dana Priest, "Saudis and Bush Meet Over 9/11 Allegations," *The Washington Post,* July 29, 2003.

Appendix: Lessons Learned

1. Dan Eggen, "Powell Calls Report 'a Big Mistake,'" *The Washington Post,* June 14, 2004.
2. Eric Schmitt and Thom Shanker, "A CIA Rival; Pentagon Sets Up Intelligence Unit," *The New York Times,* October 24, 2002.
3. Francis R. Valeo, *Mike Mansfield, Majority Leader: A Different Kind of Senate, 1961–1976* (Armonk, New York: M. E. Sharpe, 1999); Don Oberdorfer, *Senator Mansfield: The Extraordinary Life of a Great American Statesman and Diplomat* (Washington, D.C.: Smithsonian Books, 2003).

INDEX

280

INDEX

Air France, 82
Airman Flight School, 49, 54–55
Algeria, 82
al-Itihaad al-Islamiya, 30
al-Kifah, 40
Allen, George, 63
Al-Madina Al-Munawara mosque, 11, 19
al-Muhajiroun, 43
al-Qaeda, xv, 8, 29, 83, 173, 194, 203, 205
  on Afghan-Pakistan border, 87–88
  al-Hazmi and, 6–7
  al-Kifah and, 40
  al-Mihdhar and, 6–7
  anthrax-tainted letters and, 134
  in Camp X-Ray, 123
  Chechen rebels and, 55, 57
  Director of National Intelligence and, 257
  Egyptians in, 145
  FBI investigation of, 38–39, 191
  formation of, 27, 28
  funding of, 84, 167, 225, 229
  growth of, 30
  Hamburg cell of, 132–33
  hunted in Afghanistan, 121, 126
  Iraq and, 188–89, 191–94, 222
  Iraq War and, 125–26, 180, 188–89, 190, 218–19, 230–31
  Madrid attack and, 218
  membership in, 38, 191
  Moussaoui and, 55–56
  Pakistani intelligence on, x–xi
  pre–September 11 preparations of, 230
  in President's Daily Brief, 81
  recruitment process of, 133
  regeneration of, 192, 218–19, 240
  Rice on, 123
  as September 11 suspects, 99
  Taliban and, 31
  as target of war on terror, 108, 230, 245
  in "use of force" resolution, 105
  U.S. presence of, 84, 192
  U.S. underestimation of, 205–7, 242
  in Yemen safe houses, 5
American Revolution, 13
Anderson, Paul, 95–96
Armitage, Richard, 194
Army, U.S., 14
  Intelligence, 15

Ashcroft, John, 72, 226, 227
  Gorelick and, 201–2
  at Joint Inquiry meeting, 164
  USA Patriot Act and, 110, 112
Assad, Bashar, 147–51, 153
Assad, Basil, 148
Assad, Hafez, 148
Association of Flight Attendants, 83n
Athens:
  in Peloponnesian War, 126–27
  public service in, 211
Atta, Mohammed, xviii
  al-Qahtani and, 77
  arrival in U.S., 33
  aviation training of, 33, 61
  call to Khalid Shaikh Mohammed by, 78
  contents of bag of, 91–92
  as Egyptian, 144
  in Hamburg al-Qaeda cell, 133
  September 11 activities of, 91–92
  surveillance flight of, 77
  traffic tickets of, 36–37
  World Trade Center visit of, 78
Attas, Hussein al-, 51, 53
Aulaqi, Anwar, 19–20, 227
aviation training:
  of al-Hazmi, 26, 41, 61, 66, 113–14, 227
  of al-Mihdhar, 26, 32, 114, 227
  of al-Shehhi, 33, 61
  of Atta, 33, 61
  and bin Laden, 44
  of Hanjour, 41, 44, 61, 66, 137
  of Jarrah, 33–34, 61
  of Moussaoui, 49–51, 77
  of Soubra, 43, 44
  of terrorists, 39, 43, 44–45
Aznar, José María, 220

Bajadr, Mamal, 12, 168
Baker, James, 148
Bali, terrorist attack in, 218
"Ballad of the King's Jest, The" (Kipling), 89
Bandar, Prince of Saudi Arabia:
  on classified pages of Joint Report, 228
  on *Meet the Press,* 225
  in September 13 meeting with Bush, 105–7

ABOUT THE AUTHORS

BOB GRAHAM, a former two-term governor of Florida, is now in his third term in the United States Senate. While recognized for his leadership on issues ranging from health care to environmental preservation, Senator Graham is best known for his ten years of service on the Senate Select Committee on Intelligence—including eighteen months as chairman in 2001–2002, during which he co-chaired the House-Senate Joint Inquiry into the intelligence community's failures prior to 9/11. Following the release of a declassified version of the Joint Inquiry's final report in July 2003, Senator Graham advocated reform of the intelligence community and sponsored legislation to bring about needed changes. In 2002, Graham was one of the most visible critics of President Bush's decision to wage preemptive war with Iraq before the conclusion of the war against al-Qaeda in Afghanistan, and he has called for more aggressive diplomacy with other countries that harbor terrorist networks, such as Syria. Graham has labored alongside airport security screeners, nuclear-plant security officers, FBI and customs agents, and military personnel on some of his four hundred "workdays" in order to gain insight from the front lines of the homeland security effort.

JEFF NUSSBAUM has worked as a speechwriter for Vice President Al Gore and Senate Democratic leader Tom Daschle. He is the co-author, with Democratic strategist James Carville, of *Had Enough? A Handbook for Fighting Back*. A graduate of Brown University, he lives in Washington, D.C.

ABOUT THE TYPE

This book was set in Granjon, a modern recutting of a typeface produced under the direction of George W. Jones, who based Granjon's design upon the letter forms of Claude Garamond (1480–1561). The name was given to the typeface as a tribute to the typographic designer Robert Granjon.

penchant
polemic
complicit(y)
élan
flitted
contravening
repudiated
strictures
cursory
brooding
chided
scion
fortuitous
interdict